Practical English Grammar

An active-learning approach to *learning*, *practising* and *revising* grammar
with key to all the exercises

Rachael Roberts

Viva Books Private Limited
New Delhi • Mumbai • Chennai • Kolkata • Bangalore • Hyderabad
4737/23 Ansari Road, Daryaganj, New Delhi 110002

~~Ref: Practical English Grammar~~

First Published 2004
Reprinted 2006, 2007

VIVA BOOKS PRIVATE LIMITED

- 4737/23 Ansari Road, Daryaganj, New Delhi 110 002
  E-mail: vivadelhi@vivagroupindia.net, Tel. 42242200
- Plot No. 76, Service Industries, Shirvane, Sector 1, Nerul, Navi Mumbai 400 706
  E-mail: vivamumbai@vivagroupindia.net, Tel. 27721273, 27721274
- Jamals Fazal Chambers, 26 Greams Road, Chennai 600 006
  E-mail: vivachennai@vivagroupindia.net, Tel. 28290304, 28294241
- B-103, Jindal Towers, 21/1A/3 Darga Road, Kolkata 700 017
  E-mail: vivakolkata@vivagroupindia.net, Tel. 22836381, 22816713
- 7, Sovereign Park Apartments, 56-58, K. R. Road, Basavanagudi, Bangalore 560 004
  E-mail: vivabangalore@vivagroupindia.net, Tel.26607409, 26607410
- 101-102 Mughal Marc Apartments, 3-4-637 to 641, Narayanguda, Hyderabad 500 029
  E-mail: vivahyderabad@vivagroupindia.net, Tel. 27564481, 27564482

ISBN 81-7649-498-4

Printed and bound by Sanat Printers, Kundli -131028.

Contents

Preface

Aim

The aim of this book is to provide a new kind of complementary Grammar for adult and young adult learners—one that *actively* involves the learner in understanding concept and structure before providing practice.

It is principally intended to be used as support for teacher-directed courses at Elementary level. However, because of the active-learning approach, it can be used for independent study.

Need

Most 'grammars' are either purely for reference, or reference with practice. This book actively guides the learners towards discovering the language for themselves—thus making it more memorable and engaging. Then the language point is consolidated with meaningful practice.

Used as a complementary support to a course book, this book can help learners to 'fill the holes' in their knowledge, consolidate, or preview important aspects of English grammar.

Approach

The book has forty-six Units, each covering a grammatical concept found in course books at Elementary level. Each Unit is based on the same format—reflecting the way a teacher in the classroom would focus on concept and structure before going on to give practice.

- **Concept and structure:** The learner actively discovers concept and structure for him/herself through motivating activities. Examples of what is required are given to help overcome the difficulty at this level of understanding written instructions. Answers and explanations are provided (Appendix 2)—providing the learner with a clear reference. The answers the student is expected to give are shown in accessible *handscript*.

- **Exercise:** Varied and meaningful practice activities help confirm understanding and give plenty of opportunity for consolidation. A key is provided (Appendix 3). In addition to controlled written practice there are activities providing the opportunity for communicative oral practice.

- **'Test Yourself' Exercises:** For each 'Part' (see Contents) a set of self-testing exercises is included. A combined answer and study/revision guide (Appendix 4) enables the learner to identify weak areas requiring further study or revision.

- **'Further Practice' Exercises:** 'Further Practice' exercises are provided for each *Unit* to enable the learner to 'revisit' areas of difficulty. A key is provided (Appendix 5).

Teachers' notes

- **Complementary use with any general English course book.** The contents of this hook cover, comprehensively, grammar areas included in course books at Elementary level. Having presented an element of grammar in your own way you may use this book for consolidation, revision or recycling. Alternatively, especially with *mixed ability* groups you may choose to ask students to preview material *before* dealing with it in class.

- **Organisation.** Most Units are independent of others and could be used in any order. Those Units making use of prior knowledge to convey concept and structure only do so within a logical teaching sequence (for example, past simple before present perfect).

- **Self-study.** The active-learning approach encourages learner autonomy, giving plenty of support for self-study.

- **Pairwork.** The activities under the heading 'Communicative Activities' could be used for in-class consolidation of homework or outside class in independent study.

Students' notes

Is this book for me? This book is intended for you if you are beyond the 'Beginner' level i.e. you have a little English, which you want to improve.

How do I use it? You can start at the beginning and work through, or pick out areas you find difficult using the Map of the book (page vi) or Index (page 209). If you are not sure what you need to work on you can do the 'Test Yourself' exercises (page 94) to find out where your weak areas are. Alternatively, your teacher may direct you to Units, which will help you. Working at home, this book will help and guide you like a teacher.

Map of the Book

UNIT 1

Present tense of the verb 'to be' (am/is/are)

Talking about **people**, **places** and **objects**

Concept

Complete the gaps with 'am', 'is' or 'are'.

Example: I am Kavita.

I ____ from Panaji.

His name ____ Ravi.
He ____ from Rajasthan.

You ____ in Class 2A.

They ____ from Rome.
They ____ Italian.

I ____ John.
My name ____ Steve.
We ____ friends.

This ____ a school.
It ____ in Kolkata.

This ____ Sudeshna.
She ____ a student.

Structure

Usually we don't say ***'I am*** Susan'—we say 'I'm Susan'—this is a *contraction*.
Write these sentences again with *contractions*.

Example:
I am from London. I'm from London.

You are in my class. ____________
She is from Poland. ____________
He is a student. ____________
It is in London. ____________
We are German. ____________
They are from Denmark. ____________

Negative

Make the sentences *negative* (in *two* different ways).

Examples:
You're in my class.
You're not in my class.
You aren't in my class.

She's from Poland.
____
____

He's a student.
____
____

It's in London.
____
____

We're German.
____
____

They're from Denmark.
____
____

I'm from London.
____
(only one possibility here)

Keys, Answers and Explanations Page No. 146

Exercise

UNIT 1

> ***Example:***
> "My name *is* Preeti Arora.
> I am a teacher. I *am*
> 27 years old and I *am not*
> married.
> Here *are* some photographs of my friends and family ..."

1. Match with the photographs and complete the gaps.

A. This ______ my brother. He ______ very tall and thin. He ______ a teacher too.

B. My mother and father ______ quite young. They ______ both photographers. At the moment they ______ in India. They _____ on holiday in Africa.

C. My house ______ in Allahabad. It ______ quite old, but it ______ very big.

2. Write full sentences about Preeti's friends and family.

Example:	
Sudha/my sister.	Sudha is my sister.
very beautiful	*She* is *very beautiful.*
doctor	*She* is a *doctor.*

My father's name/Rohit
photographer
from Allahabad

Nita and Ria/my friends
very intelligent
not very rich
actresses

My mother/called Shanti
photographer
49 years old

3. Find the mistakes in these sentences and correct them.

Example:	
She are 27 years old. ×	*She is 27 years old.*
I'm a doctor ✓	

(a) They from India.
(b) My house it's quite old.
(c) We're actresses.
(d) He's not very tall.
(e) I'm not a student, I are a teacher.
(f) She's very intelligent.
(g) He's called Stephen.
(h) His name Peter.

4. Communicative Activities.
See Pg 128.

UNIT 2

Verb 'to be': questions (am I?/are you? is he?)

***Is* he French?**

Asking questions about people, places and objects

Concept

There is a party at the International School of English.

Match each *question* with a suitable *answer*:

Example:
(a) 'Is he French?' 3 No, he isn't.

(b) 'Are we friends now?' ______
(c) 'Where are you from?' ______
(d) 'What's your name?' ______
(e) 'Is she from Japan?' ______
(f) 'Are you a model?' ______

Structure

Complete these other conversations at the party.

Examples:
I/you
'Am I boring?' 'No, you aren't/you're not'.
'Are you tired?' 'Yes, I am.'

He/She/It

'Is she your sister?' 'Yes, ______ ______'

____ ____ from Venezuela? 'No, he isn't/he's not.'

We

'______ ______ late?' 'No, we aren't/ we're not'.

They

'Are they married?' 'Yes, ______ ______'

Complete the rules with these words: *negative (x2) positive before after*

Normally we put the verb 'to be' ______ the subject, but to make questions with the verb 'to be' we put the verb ______ the subject.

	Subject + Verb		Verb + Subject
Example:	You'**re** Polish.	=	**Are** you Polish?

To make ______ short answers we *contract* but to make ______ short answers we do NOT *contract*.

Example: No, **I'm not**/Yes, **I am.**

______ short answers can contract two different ways (except 'No, I'm not')*

Example: No, **he's not** or No, **he isn't.**

*See Unit 1

Keys, Answers and Explanations Page No. 146

Question words—We can ask questions *with* or *without* a question word [who/what/why/how/when/where/which].

Example:	
Are you a model?	Yes, I am.
Why are you a model?	Because the money is good!

Make questions *with* and *without* question words to match the answers.

1. She is very rich. a) ______________________? Yes, she is.
   b) Why ______________________? Because she is a supermodel.
2. Warsaw is in Poland. a) ______________________? Yes, it is.
   b) Where ______________________? In Poland.
3. They are both 16. a) ______________________? Yes, they are.
   b) How old ______________________? They are both 16.
4. We are late. a) ______________________? Yes, we are.
   b) Why ______________________? I forgot the time.

Exercise

1. Rosa is a student at the International School of English, in London. In Brazil, she is a doctor. She is thirty two years old. She is married with two children—Juliana is six and Pedro is three. Her husband's name is Paulo. He's a teacher. He's not in London now. It is not the holidays so Paulo and the children are at school.

Write questions and *short* answers about Rosa and her family.

Example:	
Rosa/student?	Is Rosa a student? Yes, she is.
Where/Rosa/student?	Where is Rosa a student? In London.

a) Rosa/teacher? ______________? ______________
b) The International School of English/in France? ______________? ______________
c) **Where**/Rosa/doctor? ______________? In ______________
d) Rosa/forty years old? ______________? ______________
e) **How old**/Rosa? ______________? ______________
f) Rosa/married? ______________?______________
g) Juliana/six? ______________? ______________
h) Pedro/six? ______________? ______________
i) **How old**/the children? ______________? ______ and ______
j) **What**/her husband's name? ______________? ______________
k) Paulo/in London now? ______________? ______________
l) **Where**/Paulo and the children? ______________? ______________

2. Read these conversations and correct any mistakes you find.

Example:	
Mita: 'Hello. My name **are** Mita'	X name is Mita.

Hari: Pleased to meet you. My name's Hari.
Mita: Sorry, are you my brother's friend?
Hari: No, I aren't. I'm Ria's friend.
Mita: You are a doctor?
Hari: No, it isn't.
Mita: Sorry!

Ramesh: Mita's my sister.
Sita: What her boyfriend's name?
Ramesh: Tony. He's a teacher too.
Sita: They is married?
Ramesh: No, not yet.

Ria: Who is that over there?
Jay: That is Kishore. He are very famous.
Ria: Why are he famous?
Jay: He is a singer.

Mita: Are where Ria and Jay?
Ramesh: In the kitchen.
Mita: Are they hungry?

This/that/these/those

this is your room and *that is* ours

Near or **far**?

Concept 1: this/that

Rina is going to stay with her English penfriend, Amanda.

(1)

(2)

Look at the photographs and match the words with the pictures.

(**a**) This = (**1**) or (**2**)? ___________

(**b**) That = (**1**) or (**2**)? ___________

Concept 2: these/those

(1)

(2)

Look at the photographs and match the words with the pictures.

(**c**) These = (**1**) or (**2**)? ___________

(**d**) Those = (**1**) or (**2**)? ___________

Structure

Complete the form with *is* or *are*.

Examples:
This <u>is</u> the bathroom.
That <u>is</u> the kitchen.

This room ______ beautiful.
That bag ______ mine.
(So, are this/that *singular* or *plural*?) ___________

Examples:
These <u>are</u> my children.
Those <u>are</u> my bags.

These apples ______ green.
Those chairs ______ uncomfortable!
(So, are these/those *singular* or *plural*?) ______

Make *negative statements* and *questions* from the following:

Example:		
This is your room.	This isn't your room.	Is this your room?

That's your daughter.	___________	___________
These are his keys.	___________	___________
Those are our bicycles.	___________	___________
This room is beautiful.	___________	___________
That room is John's.	___________	___________
These curtains are very nice.	___________	___________
Those chairs are uncomfortable.	___________	___________

Keys, Answers and Explanations Page No. 147

Exercise

1. Amanda has a dinner party for her friends and Rina.

a) Complete with *this* or *these*.

b) Complete with *that* or *those*.

2. Rina and Amanda are in a music shop. **Put the words in the correct order to make their dialogue.**

Example:
R:/'REM' CD/new/is/the/this = This is the new 'REM' CD.

A: /that/your/is/band/favourite/?/= ______________
R: /is/yes/it/,/= ______________
A: /that/their/best/CD/is/?/ ______________
R: /it/no/is not/./= ______________
/is/this/= ______________
A: /is/very/expensive/that/= ______________

3. Rina and Amanda are in a clothes shop. **Complete the dialogue with [this/these/are/is]**

Example:
R: This is a good shop.

R: ______ shoes ______ lovely!
A: Well, I think ______ ______ better.
R: But ______ ______ brown. ______ shirt ______ the same colour.
A: OK. Try them on.
R: Ahh. ______ ______ uncomfortable.
A: So ______ ______ better! And ______ ______ a lovely colour.

4. **Complete the sentences using *this/that/these/those* and *is/are/isn't/aren't*.**

How much are those?

This isn't very good.

This is very cheap!

How much ________?

______ the last one!

______ very fashionable.

______ the new REM CD?

________ fresh!

Why ____ ____ so expensive?

______ good for you.

______ English newspapers.

A: ______ shoes ______ lovely!
R: No, I think ____ ____ nicer.

5. **Communicative Activities**
See Pg 133

UNIT 4

Singular and plural nouns

child/child*ren*, desk/desk*s*

Concept

(a)

(b)

Find twelve differences between the pictures and complete the sentences with '*a*' or a number *2–10*.

1. In picture (**a**) there is a dictionary. In picture (**b**) there are two dictionar**ies**.
2. In picture (**a**) there is ______ teacher. In picture (**b**) there are ______ teacher**s**.
3. In picture (**a**) there are ______ key**s**. In picture (**b**) there is ______ key.
4. In picture (**a**) there are ______ desk**s**. In picture (**b**) there is ______ desk.
5. In picture (**a**) there are ______ **people**. In picture (**b**) there are ______ **people**.
6. In picture (**a**) there is ______ pen. In picture (**b**) there are ______ pen**s**.
7. In picture (**a**) there is ______ bus. In picture (**b**) there are ______ bus**es**.
8. In picture (**a**) there are ______ wom**en**. In picture (**b**) there are ______ wom**en**.
9. In picture (**a**) there is ______ m**an**. In picture (**b**) there are ______ m**en**.
10. In picture (**a**) there are ______ sandwich**es**. In picture (**b**) there is ______ sandwich.
11. In picture (**a**) there is ______ book (not the dictionary). In picture (**b**) there are ______ book**s** (not the dictionaries).
12. In picture (**a**) there are ______ child**ren**. In picture (**b**) there are ______ child**ren**.

Structure **Complete the table with the nouns in singular and plural forms.**

	SINGULAR		PLURAL
a)	book	◄——►	books
	desk	◄——►	desks
	table	◄——►	______
	______	◄——►	teachers
	pen	◄——►	______

RULE: Most nouns add ______ in the plural.

b)	______	◄——►	buses
	sandwich	◄——►	______

RULE: When the last SOUND of the noun is /s/ /S/ /tS/ /dz/ we add ______ in the plural.

	SINGULAR		PLURAL
c)	dictionary	◄——►	____________

RULE: When the noun ends consonant + y the 'y' changes to ____________.

d)	______	◄——►	keys

RULE: When the noun ends vowel + y the 'y' does NOT change to -ies, we add ______ (like Rule a).

e)	man	◄——►	______
	______	◄——►	women
	person	◄——►	______
	child	◄——►	______

RULE: Some nouns (not only these four) are irregular.

Keys, Answers and Explanations Page No. 148

Exercise

1. Complete with *is* or *are*

(a) There are ten children.
(b) There ______ a teacher.
(c) There ______ two balls.
(d) There ______ a dog.
(e) There ______ a sandwich.
(f) There ______ a bus.
(g) There ______ two houses.
(h) There ______ five girls.
(i) There ______ a book.
(j) There ______ two pens.

2. Complete the information about India today.

Example:
There are 1,02,70,15,247 [person] people.

There are 495.7 million [woman] ______.
There are 531.3 million [man] ______.
There 742 million [person] ______ in villages.
There are 285 million [person] ______ in town and cities.
There are 339,969,048 literate [male] ______.
There are 226,745,947 literate [female] ______.

There are 56 important national [highway] ______.
There are 7 international [airport] ______.
There are 11 major [part] ______.
There are 7,100 railway [station] ______.
There are about 16,125 telephone [exchange] ______.
There are 1,54,551 post [office] ______.

3. Read these sentences and correct the mistakes you find.

Example:
a) There is 495.7 million women in India × are

b) There is a child in the classroom.
c) In Mumbai the bus are red.
d) There are 100 people in the church.
e) There is an old men in the shop.
f) There are 56 important national high-way in India.
g) This is my houses.

4. Read these sentences and correct the spelling mistakes you find. (there is *one* in *every* sentence)

Example:
a) Are the childs happy? × children

b) The sandwichs are fresh.
c) Why are the buss late?
d) The teacheres are tired.
e) There are five churchs in the town.
f) Indian Railways has 7,000 locomotive.
g) There are 10 boies and 12 girls in the class.

5. Communicative Activities.

See Pg 128

UNIT 5

Present simple tense

Talking about **general present time**

Concept

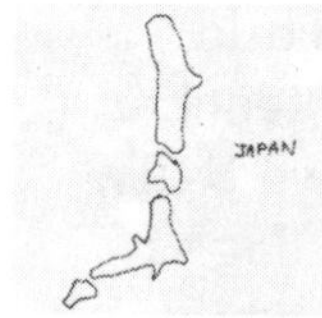

Japan is in the Pacific Ocean. It has four main islands. The capital is Tokyo—six million people live there.

The Japanese make good televisions, cars and computers. They work very hard and get up early—on average at 6.30 am. The working day finishes at about 7 pm.

Mr Koshura gets up at 6.00 and has breakfast—bread and eggs. At 7.00 he goes to work on the train. He works for Toyota. He likes his job and usually stays late at the office in the evenings. At the weekends he plays baseball.

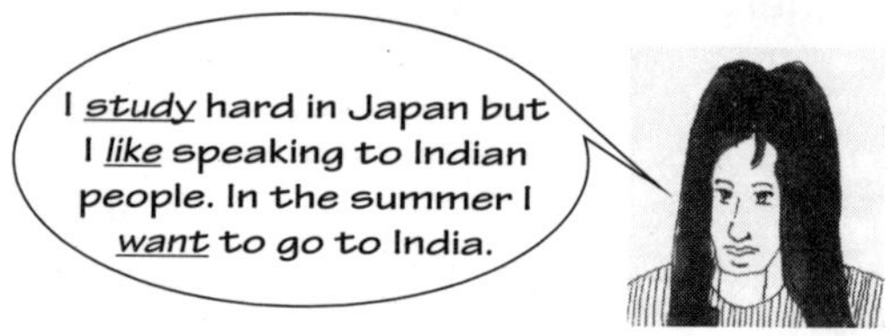

Yuko is a student. She studies English at Hiroshima Shudo University. She works hard but at the weekend she likes going shopping and, in the winter, she goes skiing.

Look at the underlined verbs—this is the present simple tense. Do we use the present simple tense to talk about *now, at this moment* or about things that are *generally true*? ______________

Structure

Can you complete the table?

	be	**make**	**work**	**go**	**finish**	**have**	**play**	**study**
I		make						
you	are	make			finish			
he/she/it		makes						studies
we		make				have		
they		make						study

What do you notice about the **form** of the verb after **he/she/it**? = We usually add ______.

There are some *irregular* verbs too [goes/has/am, is, are] and sometimes the *spelling* changes.

Spelling

Complete the table with the *infinitive* or the *he/she/it* form.

	Infinitive	**He/She/It**	**Infinitive**	**He/She/It**
(a)	work	works	get up	____________
	make	makes	____________	lives

Rule: Most verbs add ______ after he/she/it.

(b) ____________ finishes

watch ____________

Rule: When the last SOUND of the verb is /s/ /S/ /tS/ /dz/ we add ____________ after he/she/it.

(c) study ____________

Rule: When the verb ends *consonant* + y the 'y' changes to ____________.

(d) ____________ plays

Rule: When the verb ends *vowel* + y the 'y' does NOT change to -ies, we add ______ (like Rule (a)).

(e) go ____________

____________ has

be ____________

Rule: Some verbs (not many) are ***irregular.***

Keys, Answers and Explanations Page No. 148

Exercise

1. Complete using the verbs in brackets ( ).
Devon (be) is in the southwest of Britain. The countryside (be) ______ very beautiful and many tourists (go) ______ there in the summer. They (swim) ______ in the sea, (lie) ______ on the beach and (walk) ______ in the hills.

Mr Swinnon (live) ______ in Torquay. He (work) ______ in a hotel. In the morning he (get) ______ up early, (go) ______ for a walk on the beach and then he (cook) ______ breakfast for the visitors.

2. Complete using these verbs: have (×2)/live/rain/like/be/eat/come/make/study/watch/play/think/go/enjoy.

Portugal ______ in the southwest of Europe. It ______ many kilometres of beaches so the Portuguese ______ a lot of fish. They ______ very good wine too.

Jorge ______ from Angola but he ______ in Lisbon, the capital of Portugal. He ______ medicine at the university. At the weekend he ______ to the beach and ______ volleyball. When it ______ he ______ football on the television.

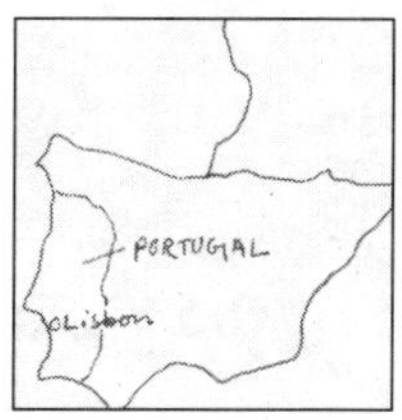

3. Correct the mistakes you find.

St Petersburg is in Russia, near the Baltic Sea. It is a beautiful old city, on forty-four small islands. It snow a lot in the winter and night comes very early, but in the summer the sun never go down.

Irena works as a tourist guide. She take visitors to the *Hermitage* Museum of Art. She gets up early and have breakfast—tea and bread and jam. Then she goes to work and meets the first group of tourists at 9.30 am. She works hard and she walk a lot—the *Hermitage* is very big—20 kilometres to see everything!

4. Correct the spelling mistakes in *every* sentence.

a) Irena finishs work at 6.00.
b) Jorge plaies volleyball.
c) Yuko studys hard.
d) Mr Koshura workes for Toyota.
e) Irena gos to work at 9.00.
f) Jorge haves a lot of friends in Lisbon.
g) Jorge watchs football on the television.

5. Communicative Activities.
See Pg 128.

Present simple auxiliaries: do/does — *Do* we stop at Allahabad?

Asking questions and **making negatives** and **short answers** using the present simple

Concept

Complete the gap with the right *INFINITIVE: leave/know/go/stop/go/arrive/buy*

Now write the sentences above in the right column

Questions	Negatives	Short Answers
What time does the train leave ?	Sorry, I don't know.	Yes, we do.
______________________________ ?	____________________	
______________________________ ?		
______________________________ ?		
______________________________ ?		

Structure

Look at *your examples* and complete the rules:

- To make a **question** in the present simple tense with most verbs (go, arrive, etc.) we use:

  [QUESTION WORD] + __________ OR __________ + SUBJECT + INFINITIVE

- To make a **negative** in the present simple tense with most verbs we use:

  SUBJECT + __________ OR __________ + INFINITIVE

- To make a **short answer** in the present simple tense with most verbs we use:

  YES/NO + SUBJECT + ________OR ________ (positive)/ ________ OR ________ (negative)

- When the subject is **I**, **you**, **we**, **they**, we use __________ (positive) or __________ (negative)
- When the subject is **he**, **she**, **it**, we use __________ (positive) or __________ (negative)

Keys, Answers and Explanations Page No. 148

Exercise

1. *The train from New Delhi to Kolkata.* Put the words in the right order to make questions.

> ***Example:***
> (a) The train to Kolkata leaves New Delhi in the evening.
> [the/when/train/Kolkata/to/leave/does?] <u>When does the train to Kolkata leave?</u>

(b) It costs about Rs 150. [it/cost/does/how much?] ______________________

(c) It arrives thirty-three hours later [it/when/arrive/does?] ______________________

(d) It goes through Uttar Pradesh, Bihar and West Bengal.
[states/how many/it/go through/does?] ______________________

(e) You need to buy your food from the pantry.
[do/where/buy/need to/food/your/you?] ______________________

(f) They also sell food at stations.
[sell/they/where/else/do/food?] ______________________

2. Write *short answers* about the train from New Delhi to Kolkata.

> ***Example:***
> (a) Does the train to Kolkata leave in the evening? <u>Yes, it does</u>

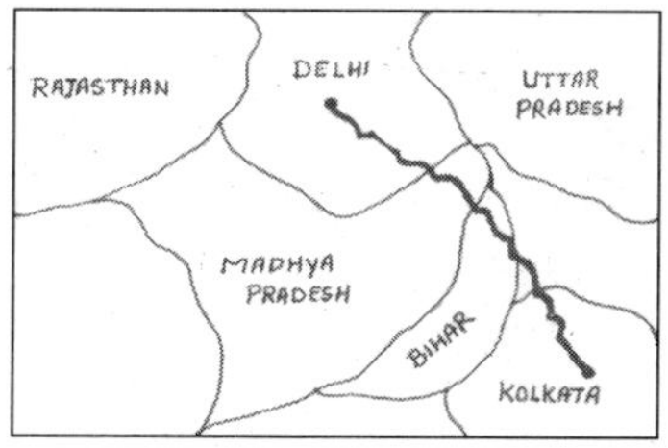

(b) Does it arrive thirty-three hours later? ______________________

(c) Does it go through Rajasthan? ______________________

(d) Do you get to buy food in the train? ______________________

(e) Does it go through Bihar? ______________________

(f) Do they sell food at stations? ______________________

(g) Does the *ticket* cost Rs. 150? ______________________

3. ***Conversations on the train.*** **Complete the questions using *do/does/do not/does not* and these INFINITIVES: *check/stop/like/go/know/cost/arrive***

> ***Example:***
> 'When <u>do</u> we <u>arrive</u> in Patna?' — 'Six o'clock'

'______ you often ______ to Kolkata?	'Yes, I ______.'
'______ you ______ travelling?'	'I love it!'
'______ the train ______ in Benares?'	'No, it ______.'
'How much ______ it ______ to travel 1st class?'	'I ______ ______.'
'Oh no! I ______ ______ a reservation.'	'Thirty-three hours is a long time to stand up!'
'Where ______ you ______ your food?'	'At the pantry.'

4. Correct any mistakes you find.

'Do you have a ticket?'	'Yes, I does.'
'Where does the train stops?'	'In Mughal Sarai, Allahabad and Patna.'
'When we arrive in Patna?'	'I not know.'
'Does the ticket inspector check the tickets?'	'Yes, he do!'
'I don't speak Hindi.'	'I do.'
'We don't stop in Benares.'	'Yes, I knows.'

5. Communicative Activities.

Asking for Information: Student A turn to page 134; Student B turn to page 141.

Adverbs I: frequency

He *never* drives a car

How often? **always/never/sometimes**

Concept

Mr Joshi is very rich. He goes out every night to a restaurant or a club. He is very fat because he does not like exercise much. He likes travelling and goes on holiday every month. Once or twice a month he likes to smoke a cigar—but his wife doesn't like it!

Mr Raj is not very rich. He stays at home every night and watches the television because it is cheap. He likes exercise though—he runs in the park three times a week. He does not have a car and he cannot drive so he goes to work by bus every day. Holidays are expensive—he goes on holiday every five or six years. He enjoys going to football matches—he does not go every week but he goes when he has the money.

Complete with *always/often/sometimes/rarely/never.*

> ***Example:***
> Mr Joshi is never at home in the evenings.

He __________ visits clubs and restaurants.
He __________ goes on holiday.
He __________ takes exercise.
He __________ smokes a cigar.

Mr Raj is __________ at home in the evenings.
He __________ runs in the park.
He __________ drives a car.
He __________ goes on holiday.
He __________ goes to watch a football match.

Now put the adverbs *in order* on the line:

ALWAYS (100%) ____________ ____________ ____________ NEVER (0%)

Structure

Look at these examples:

(a) Mr Joshi *never stays* at home in the evenings.
(b) Mr Joshi *is never* at home in the evenings.

Now answer these questions to find the rule for word order:

What is the **verb** in sentence (a)? __________
What is the **verb** in sentence (b)? __________

With a verb like stay/go/drink, etc does the **frequency adverb** (never, always, etc) *usually** go **before** or **after** the verb? __________

With the verb 'to be' (is/are, etc) does the **frequency adverb** *usually** go **before** or **after** the verb? ______ [*'*Usually*' because sometimes a different word order is possible but this one is *always* correct.]

Keys, Answers and Explanations Page No. 149

Exercise

1. Put the words in the correct order to make sentences.

> ***Example:***
> (a) Sunita/gets up/at/7.30/always Sunita always gets up at 7.30.

(b) eats/she/breakfast/never ______

(c) she/often/a cup of/has/coffee ______

(d) work/always/she/to/drives ______

(e) late/is/she/sometimes ______

(f) The traffic/bad/always/is ______

(g) often/in the evenings/watches/Suraj/old films/on the television ______

(h) he/gets up/always/late ______

(i) he/never/to bed/goes/before 2.00 am ______

2. Rewrite the sentences using adverbs of frequency.

> ***Example:***
> (a) Shyam goes running every morning. Shyam always goes running.

(b) He goes swimming *nearly every week*. He ______ swimming.

(c) He is vegetarian *so he doesn't eat meat*. He ______ meat.

(d) He is very healthy *all the time*. He ______ very healthy.

(e) Suresh gets up at 5.00 *every day*. Suresh ______ at 5.00.

(g) He is tired *all the time*. He ______ tired.

3. Correct the *word order* mistakes you find.

Mina is a nurse and works during the night at the hospital.

Interviewer: 'What time do you finish work, Mina?'

Mina: 'Well, I finish often (X often finish) about 6.00 am, but it is sometimes later. I do not get often home until 8.00 am—then always I go straight to bed!'

Interviewer: 'What time do you get up?'

Mina: 'I get up usually at about 3.00 pm to do some shopping and cooking. I get up rarely later than 4.00 pm because the children always come home from school then. I always am busy in the evening but my husband often helps me to cook the dinner and he puts sometimes the children to bed.'

4. Communicative Activities.

See Pg 129.

Subject and object pronouns: I/me, he/him

Let *us* watch a movie

Referring to peope and objects **without naming them**

Concept

Ravi: 'Harish, **I** (a) like **you** (b) because **you** (c) are a good friend. Will **you** (d) accompany **me** (e) to the movie?'

Harish: '**I** (f) want to see it but **I** (g) need to ask **my** (h) parents first.'

Ravi: 'Do **you** (i) think **your** (j) father will agree?'

Harish: '**I** (k) think **he** (l) will, provided **we** (m) promise to return home early. What about **your** (n) father?'

Ravi: '**I** (o) have already asked **him** (p). **He** (q) also expects **me** (r) home early.'

Harish: '**I** (s) will ask **my** (t) parents tonight.'

Match the pronouns with who (or what) they *refer to.*

Choose from these answers: Ravi, Harish, Harish's father, Ravi and Harish, Ravi's father.

Example:
(a) I = Ravi

(b) you =
(c) you =
(d) you =
(e) me =
(f) I =
(g) I =
(h) my =
(i) you =
(j) your =
(k) I =
(l) he =
(m)we =
(n) your =
(o) I =
(p) him =
(q) He =
(r) me =
(s) I =
(t) my =

Structure

subject	verb	object	
I	like	***you***	**I** is the **subject** pronoun, **you** is the **object** pronoun
You	like	***me***	**You** is the **subject** pronoun, **me** is the **object** pronoun

Write if the pronoun is *subject* or *object.*

Examples:
(a) I = Subject

(b) you =
(c) you =
(d) you=
(e) me =
(f) I =
(g) I =
(h) my =
(i) you =
(j) your =
(k) I =
(l) he =
(m)we =
(n) your =
(o) I =
(p) him =
(q) He =
(r) me =
(s) I =
(t) my =

Complete the table of subject and object pronouns

Subject pronouns		Object pronouns	Subject pronouns		Object pronouns
I	◄······►	me	it	◄······►	______
______	◄······►	you	______	◄······►	us
he	◄······►	______	you	◄······►	______
______	◄······►	her	______	◄······►	them

Keys, Answers and Explanations Page No. 149

Exercise

1. Complete the sentence with the correct *object pronoun*.

> ***Example:***
> (a) Ravi likes Harish because he is his good friend.

(b) It is a good movie and both of them want to see ___________

(c) Ravi thinks Harish's family likes ___________

(d) 'We are Harish's family—why doesn't Ravi often visit ___________?'

(e) 'Harish's family is very good. I like ___________ very much.'

(f) 'I like to accompany ___________. Why don't you come with ___________?'

2. Choose *subject* or *object* pronoun.

Harish: 'Ravi wants **I/me** to accompany **he/him**. What do you think?'

Harish's father: 'Do you like **he/him**?'

Harish: I *like* **he/him**. Do you like him?'

Harish's father: 'Well, **he/him** seldom visits **we/us** ... and his family is not very cordial—**they/them** do not welcome an unfamiliar face.'

Ravi: 'Harish's father doesn't want him to accompany **I/me**.'

Jay: 'Good! I don't like **he/him. He/His** is boring.'

Ravi: 'But, Jay, **he/his** is very good and **I/me** like **he/him**!'

Jay: 'Maybe, but there are lots of good boys ... look at **they/them.'**

3. The text is very strange because it says 'Ravi' and Harish', etc *too many times*. **Write it again but *replace* the underlined words with a *subject* or *object* pronoun.**

> ***Example:*** Harish like Jai but he doesn't like him ...

Ravi likes Harish doesn't like Harish. Ravi wants Harish to accompany him to the cinema, but Jay has to ask his family. Ravi thinks Harish's family is strange. Ravi never visits Harish's family and he thinks Harish's family don't like him. Maybe Ravi's right!

4. Correct any mistakes you find in these sentences.

(a) Jay thinks Harish is boring. He doesn't like he.

(b) Jay likes the other boys in the class. He thinks them are friendly and he wants to speak to they.

(c) Harish likes Ravi but he doesn't want to accompany him.

(d) Ravi likes Harish and him thinks he is friendly.

(e) 'I like you, do you like I?'

(f) Harish is unhappy because Jay doesn't like he.

5. Communicative Activities.
See Pg 129.

UNIT 9

Possessive adjectives and 's

it's my.../your.../his.../Ritu's...

Talking about **possession of**, or **relation to**, people and objects

Concept

Ritu: 'This is **my(a)** grandfather—**your(b)** great-grandfather.'
Debesh: 'Who is this?'
Ritu: 'That is **his(c)** eldest son—Uncle Hari. And this is Uncle Hari's wife. They live in Australia now.'
Debesh: 'What is **her(d)** name?'
Ritu: 'Aunt Mita.'
Debesh: 'Are these Uncle Hari and Aunt Mita's children?*'
Ritu: 'Yes, and this is **their(e)** dog. **Its(f)** name is Spot!'
Debesh: '**Our(g)** dog's name is Spot too!'

(*Notice that we **do not** usually say Hari's and Mita's.)

Complete the gaps with the *noun(s) it refers to.*
Possessive adjective ...'s

Examples:
(a) my = Ritu's
(b) your = Debesh's
(c) his = Great-grandfather's

(d) her = ____________
(e) their = ____________
(f) its = the ____________
(g) our = ____________

'Who**'s** this**'** ***means*** 'Who **is** this'
'And this is Harry**'s** wife' ***means*** **possession**. It does NOT ***mean*** **'is'.**

Look at the dialogue again and decide if *'s* means *is* or *possession.*
Ritu: 'This is my grandfather—your great-grandfather.'
Debesh: 'Who**'s** (a) this?'
Ritu: 'That**'s** (b) his eldest son—Uncle Hari. And this is Uncle Hari**'s** **(c)** wife. They live in Australia now.'
Debesh: 'What**'s** **(d)** her name?'
Ritu: 'Aunt Mita.'
Debesh: 'Are these Uncle Hari and Aunt Mita**'s** **(e)** children?'
Ritu: 'Yes, and this is their dog. Its name**'s** **(f)** Spot.'
Debesh: 'Our dog**'s** **(g)** name**'s** **(h)** Spot too!'

Examples:
(a) is
(b) is
(c) possession

(d) ____________
(e) ____________
(f) ____________
(g) ____________
(h) ____________

Structure

Complete the table of possessive adjectives

I	my	he	________	it	________	they	________
you	________	she	________	we	________		

Keys, Answers and Explanations Page No. 150

Exercise

1. Complete the sentences about the family tree.

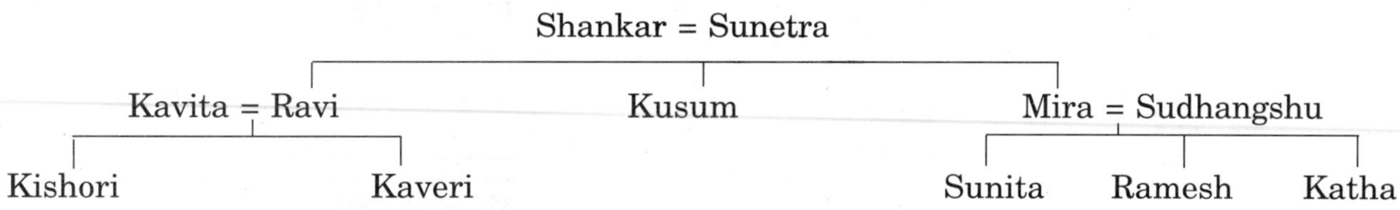

> ***Example:***
> a) Kusum's Shankar and Sunetra's daughter.

(b) Kishori ______ ______ sister.
(c) Ramesh ______ ______ and ______ cousin.
(d) Ravi ______ ______ and ______ brother.
(e) Sudhangshu ______ ______ husband.
(f) Kishori and Kaveri ______ and ______ daughters.
(g) Sunetra ______ ______ wife.
(h) Kusum ______ ______ and ______ sister.

2. Does *'s* mean *is* or *possession*?
(a) Kaveri's (is) Kishori's (possession) sister.
(b) Mira's (______) Sudhangshu's (______) wife.
(c) Ravi's (______) a journalist.
(d) Kavita's (______) Kaveri and Kishori's (______) mother.
(e) Sunita's (______) sister's (______) name's (______) Katha.
(f) Shankar's (______) son's (______) a journalist.

3. These texts sound strange because there are *too many repetitions*. Change the underlined words for a *possessive adjective*.
Kavita and Kavita's (her) husband live near Ahmedabad. They have two children. The children's (______) names are Kishori and Kaveri. They have a cat. The cat's (______) name is Ruby. Sudhangshu has three children. Sudhangshu's (______) son's name's Ramesh and Sudhangshu's daughters' names are Sunita and Katha. Ramesh and Sunita and Katha's (______) cousin's names are Kishori and Kaveri. Shankar and Sunetra live near Indore. Shankar and Sunetra's (______) house is very old.

4. Kaveri is writing a letter to her friend about her family but she has forgotten to put in any apostrophes ('). **Correct her letter.**

> Dear Lekha,
> Let me tell you about my family. My fathers names Ravi and my mothers names Kavita. My fathers a journalist. I have one sister, her names Kishori. Shes OK but I like our cat better. Its names Ruby ...

5. Read these sentences and correct the mistakes you find.

> ***Examples:***
> (a) Whos Kishori's sister? × Who's
> (b) Kaveri likes his sister Kishori. × her

(c) Ruby's Kaveri and Kishori cat.
(d) Kishori and Kaveri are sister's.
(e) My mother's name's Mira.
(f) Sudhangshu lives with her wife, Mira.
(g) Katha's sister's name's Sunita.
(h) Where's Shankar and Sunetras house?
(i) 'My name's Katha. What's you name?'

5. Communicative Activities.
See Pg 129.

UNIT 10

Possessive pronouns: mine/yours

Is this *yours*?

Talking about things which **belong to someone** or which **they are connected with**

Concept

'Whose is this?'
'I think it is her bag' (**hers**)

'Is this his suitcase?'

'These are our suitcases.'

'Where are your bags?'

'I think these are their bags!'

'Look! Mini's bag is here now.'

'This is not my suitcase.'

'Ramesh? Is this your trolley?'

Replace the *underlined words* using the words in the box:

Mini's	his	hers	yours	theirs	mine	yours	ours

Structure

Complete the table

Possessive adjective + noun		Possessive pronoun
my suitcase(s)	◄····►	mine
Your bag(s)	◄····►	______
______ suitcase(s)	◄····►	his
her bag(s)	◄····►	______
______ bag(s)	◄····►	ours
their suitcase(s)	◄····►	______
's + noun		**'s**
Mini's bag(s)	◄····►	______

*Note: Do you remember **'it's'** from Unit 9? It's (the cat's) name is Ruby.*
*There is **no** possessive pronoun for 'it's' (you **have** to use the noun)*

> ***Example:***
> It's name is Ruby (**not** 'it's' is Ruby)

Keys, Answers and Explanations Page No. 150

Exercise

1. Replace the possessive adjective and noun (*your suitcase)* with the possessive pronoun (*yours*).

Example:
(a) 'Is this **your suitcase**?' (yours)

(b) 'No, I think it is **his suitcase.**' (____________)
(c) 'This is not **my bag**.' (____________)
(d) 'Is it **your bag**?' (____________)
(e) 'No, it is not **my bag.**' (____________)
(f) 'Perhaps it is **their bag**.' (____________)
(g) 'Have you got **our bags**? (____________)
(h) 'No, I have got **my bag** (____________) but I do not know where (i) **our bags** (______) are.'
(j) 'This is not **my suitcase** (____________)'
(k) 'No, it is **their suitcase** (____________)'

2. Choose the correct word.

(a) 'This is not (***mine/my***) bag. (***My/Mine***) is bigger.'
(b) 'Are these (***your/yours***) glasses?'
(c) 'Have you got (***our/ours***) bags?'
(d) 'It is (***my/mine!***)'
(e) 'I think (***my/mine***) bag is lost!'
(f) 'Can you help me carry (***my/mine***) bags?'
(g) 'Is that (***her/hers***?)'
(h) (***Their/Theirs***) bags are heavy.'

3. Rewrite the sentences *without the names*.

(a) Give me **Mini's** bag. Give me her bag.
(b) Is that **Shyam's**? ______________________________?
(c) **Shyam and Rina's** bag is red. ______________________________
(d) Are those **Hari and Rani's**? ______________________________?
(e) **Ruby's** is over there. ______________________________
(f) Are those **Suraj's gloves**. ______________________________?
(g) **Nidhi's** umbrella is green. ______________________________
(h) **Kishor's** is blue. ______________________________

4. Correct any mistakes you find.

Example:
(a) 'This is not my!' × mine

(b) 'Is that your newspaper?'
(c) 'Mine parents are retired.'
(d) 'Their children are eight and ten.'
(e) 'There is a party at his house tonight.'
(f) 'They know our family but we don't know their.'
(g) 'Can you take a photo with my camera?'
(h) 'Your camera is better than my.'
(i) 'Is that hers coat?'

5. Communicative Activities.

See Pg 129.

Articles

a, an, the or nothing [o]

Which one do you use?

Concept

Complete the text with '*a*', '*an*', '*the*' or '*nothing [o]*'.

> ***Example:***
> Rajesh lives in o London.

It is a big city. It is ________ capital of ________ Britain. It is ________ expensive city but Peter has ________ good gob. He is ________ lawyer. He has ________ big house near ________ Thames. ________ house was very expensive but it is beautiful.

Now *look at the comments* and *answer the questions* to discover the *rules*:
RULES

1. London and Britain are places. **So, generally do we use '*a*' '*the*' or '*nothing*' with *places*?** ____________
2. The Thames is a river. **So, do we use '*a*', '*the*' or '*nothing*' with *the names of rivers*?** ____________
3. Lawyer is a job. **So, do we use '*a*', '*the*' or '*nothing*' with *jobs?*** ____________
4. Is there more than one capital of Britain? ____________
   So, do we use '*a*', '*the*' or '*nothing*' when there is *only one*? ____________
5. Are there ***many*** big cities in Britain, or only ***one***? ____________
   Are there ***many*** expensive cities, or only ***one***? ____________
   Are there ***many*** good jobs, or only ***one***? ____________
   Are there ***many*** big houses, or only ***one***? ____________
   So, do we use '*a*', '*the*' or '*nothing*' when we talk about *one of many*? ____________
6. The first time the text talked about Peter's house it was one of many [*He has **a** big house*], but the second time [***The** house was very expensive*] did you know *which* house? ____________
   So, when we know *which* thing we mean do we use '*a*', '*the*' or '*nothing*'? ____________

Structure and Pronunciation

'A' or 'An'?
Look at these examples:

an expensive house ***an*** apple ***a*** lawyer ***a*** policeman ***an*** icecream
a university ***an*** umbrella ***a*** big house ***an*** orange ***a*** hospital ***an*** hour

Complete the rules:

We use ____________ when the first **sound** of the next word is a *vowel* sound. [ae/e/i/i:/au, etc]
We use ____________ when the first **sound** of the next word is a *consonant*. [b/d/f/t/g/h, etc]
Sometimes the letter '________' is pronounced/ju:/ so we **don't** use 'an' [Example: a university]
Sometimes the letter '________' is silent so we **do** use 'an' [Example: an hour]

Keys, Answers and Explanations Page No. 151

Exercise

1. Peter is a **lawyer**. Here are some more jobs. **Write '*a*' or '*an*' next to the job.**

> ***Example:***
> an artist a doctor

____ electrician ____ politician ____ teacher ____ university professor
____ dentist ____ secretary ____ manager ____ housewife ____ shop assistant

2. Complete the gaps in the text with '*a*', '*an*', '*the*' or '*nothing*[*O*]'.

> ***Example:***
> (a) O London is (b) a big city. (c) The centre is very busy.

(d) ____ Oxford Street is (e) ____ good place for shopping. You can also go to (f) ____ department store, like 'Harrods', (g) ____ very famous shop.

If (h) ____ weather is nice, you can go in (i) ____ boat on (j) ____ Thames, or walk in (k) ____ park.

It is difficult to find (l) ____ cheap hotel in (m) ____ London but, if you are rich you can stay in (n) ____ expensive hotel like the Park Lane Hilton—with (o) ____ restaurant on (p) ____ top floor of (q) ____ hotel.

3. Now match the letters above with the numbers of the rules on page 22.

> ***Examples:*** (a) = Rule 1 [We generally use *nothing* with the names of places.]
> (b) = Rule 5
> (c) = Rule 4

(d) = Rule ____ (h) = Rule ____ (l) = Rule ____ (p) = Rule ____
(e) = Rule ____ (i) = Rule ____ (m) = Rule ____ (q) = Rule ____
(f) = Rule ____ (j) = Rule ____ (n) = Rule ____
(g) = Rule ____ (k) = Rule ____ (o) = Rule ____

4. This is part of a letter from Peter's friend, Beata. She is Polish, and in Polish there is no '*a*' or '*the*', so she has some problems!
Correct any mistakes with '*a*', '*an*' '*the*' or '*nothing*' that you find.

> Dear Peter,
> How are you? I'm fine. I'm living in the Warsaw now. I have small flat in centre. It is very nice. I also have a new job. I'm secretary now in a big company. A company sells computers. I am a expert now about computers!
> Weather is very nice now in the Poland. It's sunny and warm...

5. Communicative Activities.
See Pg 130.

UNIT 12

Relative pronouns: who/which/that

an animal *which* eats grass

Defining people and things

Concept

Match the words and the definitions.

Example: A person who has children ...	a parent

An animal **that** has a very long nose ...
A house **which** only has one floor ...
A man **who** is married ...
An animal **which** eats grass ...
A book **that** students use ...
A person **that** can play the piano ...

a dictionary
a husband
a cow
a parent
a bungalow
a pianist
an elephant

Bungalow

Look at the examples above and complete with (a) (b) or (c).

- We can use **who** to define (**a**) people (**b**) things (**c**) people and things (a) people
- We can use **which** to define (**a**) people (**b**) things (**c**) people and things ___________
- We can use **that*** to define (**a**) people (**b**) things (**c**) people and things ___________

(*It is possible to use 'that' for people but we usually prefer 'who'.)

So, to say more about **what sort of** *person* it is we use ___________ (or sometimes ___________)
To say more about **what sort of** *thing* it is we use ___________ or ___________

Structure

We can use relative pronouns to do two things:

- to say more about *what sort of thing or person* it is (to *define*)
- to *join* two ideas together

Look at the examples:

1. A parent is a person. (*What sort of person?*)—*He / She* has children.

A parent is a person *who* has children.

What happens to 'he/she'? We *replace* 'he/she' with ___________________

2. A dictionary is a book. (*What sort of book?*)—Students use *it*.

A dictionary is a book *that* students use.

What happens to 'it'? We *replace* 'it' with ___________

Make the sentences in the same way.

> ***Example:***
> A wife is a woman. She has a husband.
> A wife is a woman who has a husband.

A mechanic is a person. He/She repairs cars.

____

A Maruti 800 is a car. It has four wheels.

____

Concorde is a plane. It goes very fast.

____

Keys, Answers and Explanations Page No. 151

Exercise

1. Choose the *correct* relative pronoun.

> ***Example:***
> (a) I do not like people (**which/who**) are unfriendly. I don't like people who are unfriendly.

(b) An express is a train (**that/who**) goes fast. ____________________

(c) I know someone (**that/which**) can play the violin really well. ____________________

(d) I like children (**who/which**) do not make too much noise! ____________________

(e) Do you know the woman (**which/that**) lives upstairs? ____________________

(f) I like films (**which/who**) have a happy ending. ____________________

(g) This book is about a man (**who/which**) went to Antarctica. ____________________

(h) He has a bicycle (**that/who**) costs Rs 500! ____________________

2. Complete the sentences with *who/that/which.*

> ***Examples:***
> (a) A giraffe is an animal that (or which) has a very long neck.
> (b) The man who works in that office is not very friendly.

(c) Is this the train ____________________ is always late?

(d) Can you write a sentence ____________________ uses a relative pronoun?

(e) Do you know the children ____________________ live in that house?

(f) A suitcase is a big bag ____________________ you take on holiday.

(g) Perfume is something ____________________ make you smell nice.

(h) A briefcase is a bag ____________________ business people use.

3. Join the two sentences. Use *which/who/that.*

> ***Example:***
> (a) Chips are potatoes. *They* are cut and fried.
> Chips are potatoes that (or which) are cut and fried.

(b) Football is a game. *It* has eleven players.

____

(c) A typewriter is a machine. *It* writes.

____

(d) A waiter is a person. *He/She* works in a restaurant.

____

(e) Tea is a drink. People drink *it* in India.

____

(f) A watch is a thing. *It* tells the time.

____

(g) A husband is a man. *He* is married.

____

UNIT 13

Have got: I have got/he has got

Talking about **possessions**

He has *got* more than a million

Concept

Many people collect things—stamps, dolls, coins. Vijay Sharma is a playing cards collector. He has got more than 500,000 playing cards.
'Mr Sharma, exactly how many playing cards **have you got**?'
'I have got 652,000. This is a big collection but my friend, Mr Kapoor **has got** even more!'
'How many **has he got**?'
'Oh, **he has got** more than a million.'
'And do you have all the cards you want?'
'No, **I have not**. **I have not got** a complete set of "Janus' Artifacts". Mr. Kapoor **has not got** it either. They are very rare cards ...'

Structure

Look at the examples above and complete the form.

Positive sentences	Negative sentences	Questions	Short answers
Example: I have got	***Example:*** I have not got	***Example:*** Have I got ?	***Example:*** Yes, I have/No I have not
You ___ ___	You ___ ___	___ you ___ ...?	Yes, you ___ /No, you ___.
He/She/It ___ ___	He/She/It ___ ___	___ he/she/it ___ ...?	Yes, he/she/it ___.
			No, he/she/it ___.
We ___ ___	We ___ ___	___ we ___ ...?	Yes, we ___/No, we ___.
They ___ ___	They ___ ___	___ they ___...?	Yes, they ___/No, they ___.

We can use **'have'** with **'got'**, or as a **normal present simple verb (see Unit 5)**

'And *do you have* all the cards you want?' has the same meaning as **'And *have you got* all the cards you want?'**

Change the sentences from *have got* to *have*.

Examples:
He has got more than a million. = He has more than a million.
How many have you got? = How many do you have?
I have not got a complete set. = I do not have a complete set.

How many has he got? = ______________________
He has not got it. = ______________________
I have got 625,000. = ______________________

Choose the correct *short answer*.

Example: (✓) (×)
Have you got a big collection? Yes, I have/Yes, I do

Does he have all the cards he wants? No, he has not./No, he does not.
Has he got more than 100,000 cards? Yes, he has./Yes, he does.
Do you have a complete set? No, I have not./No, I do not.

Keys, Answers and Explanations Page No. 152

Exercise

1. Change these sentences from *have* to *have got.*

> ***Example:***
> (a) How many sisters do you have? How many sisters have you got?
> (b) I do not have any. I have not got any.

(c) Does he have a car? ______________________________

(d) No, he does not. ______________________________

(e) I have a big house in the country. ______________________________

(f) How many bedrooms does it have? ______________________________

(g) Do you have any pets? ______________________________

(h) Yes, I have a dog. ______________________________

(i) They have three children. ______________________________

(j) Do they have any grandchildren? ______________________________

(k) Yes, they do. ______________________________

2. Look at the table and complete the sentences with *have not got* or *has not got.*

	a car	*a flat*	*a house*	*children*	*a television*	*a dog*
Vinay and Kiran	✓	×	✓	✓	×	✓
Subodh	×	✓	×	✓	×	×
Nidhi	×	×	✓	✓	×	×
Shama and Kedar	×	✓	×	×	×	✓

> ***Example:***
> (a) Vinay and Kiran have got a car

(b) Nidhi ______ children.

(c) Shama and Kedar ______ a television.

(d) Subodh ______ a house.

(e) Vinay and Kiran ______ a dog.

(f) Nidhi ______ a flat.

(g) Shama and Kedar ______ a car.

(h) Nidhi ______ a car.

(i) Subodh ______ a dog.

(j) Vinay and Kiran ______ a house.

3. Complete the questions and write short answers *using the table above.*

> ***Example:***
> (a) Has Nidhi got a house? Yes, she has.

(b) ____ Subodh ____ a dog? ______

(c) ____ Kedar and Shama ____ Children? ______

(d) ____ Nidhi ____ a car? ______

(e) ____ Vinay and Kiran ____a television? ______

(f) ____ Kedar and Shama ____ a flat? ______

(g) ____ Subodh ____ children? ______

4. Communicative Activities.

A: turn to page 134; B: turn to page 141.
You both have a table like the one above—but you both have **different information**. Ask your friend questions to complete your table.

Countable and uncountable nouns

chocolate/bananas

What can you count?

Concept

Look at the advertisement.

What can you **count?**
Write the noun and the letter.

Eggs[b] ______ ______
______ ______

THESE ARE **COUNTABLE** NOUNS.

What **can't** you **count**?

milk[a] ______ ______ ______
______ ______

THESE ARE **UNCOUNTABLE** NOUNS.

What can you **sometimes count** and **sometimes not count**—with a ***different meaning***?
Chocolate[f] Chocolates[g] ______ ______

SOME NOUNS CAN BE COUNTABLE **AND** UNCOUNTABLE—*WITH A DIFFERENT MEANING.*

Structure

Look at the examples and complete the rules:

'I would like a banana.'
'Bananas are yellow.'
'He ate six bananas.'

Is 'banana' *countable* or *uncountable?* ________
Can we use *a/an* with *countable nouns*? Yes/No
Can we use *a number* with *countable nouns*? Yes/No
Can we make *countable nouns plural*? Yes/No

'Milk is good for you.'
'I would like some milk.'

Is 'milk' *countable* or *uncountable*? ____________
Can we use *a/an* with *uncountable* nouns? Yes/No
Can we use *a number* with *uncountable* nouns? Yes/No
Can we make *uncountable nouns plural*? Yes/No

Keys, Answers and Explanations Page No. 152

Exercise

1. Look at the picture. What can you count? Write the names of the food in the *correct columns:*

COUNTABLE	UNCOUNTABLE
Eggs	Milk
________	________
________	________
________	________
________	________
________	________

2. Write *a/an* or *nothing (O)* before the nouns.

Example:
an apple

______ mineral water ______ potato ______ orange

______ sugar ______ egg ______bread

______ orange juice

3. Write the plural form next to these words—*if possible.*

(a) rice not possible
(b) egg eggs
(c) banana ____________
(d) bread ____________
(e) milk ____________
(f) potato ____________
(g) apple ____________
(h) money ____________
(i) orange ____________
(j) orange juice ____________
(k) flour ____________
(l) salt ____________
(m) sugar ____________
(n) rupee ____________

4. Communicative Activities.
See Pg 130.

UNIT 15

'Some' and 'any'

there are *some* bananas/is there *any milk?*

Talking about an **indefinite** quantity

Concept

Read the dialogue and decide *which recipe* Bob and Marcia can make for dinner.

Bob: 'There isn't much food in the house, Marcia. What can we have for dinner?'
Marcia: 'What have we got?'
Bob: 'Well, there are **some** potatoes.'
Marcia: 'Is there **any** rice?'
Bob: 'Yes, there is, and there's **some** pasta, but there isn't **any** cheese.'
Marcia: 'Are there **any** onions?'
Bob: 'Yes, we've got **some** onions but we haven't got **any** peppers. There are **some** tomatoes though.'
Marcia: 'And is there **any** meat? If there is we can make ...'

Spaghetti in tomato sauce
Ingredients:
onions/pasta/tomatoes/cheese

Shepherds' pie
Ingredients:
onions/potatoes/meat

Paella
Ingredients:
rice/tomatoes/peppers/onions

Look at the examples above and answer the questions:

When we say **'some'** or **'any'** do we know *exactly* how many potatoes, peppers and onions there are? ____
Are **potatoes, peppers** and **onions** *countable* or *uncountable?* ____
Do we use **is**, or **are**, with plural countable nouns? ____
When we say **'some'** and **'any'** do we know exactly how much rice, pasta and meat there is? ____
Are **rice**, **pasta and meat** *countable* or *uncountable*? ____
Do we use **is** or **are** with uncountable nouns? ____
Do we usually* use **some**, or **any**, with positive sentences? ____
Do we usually* use **some**, or **any**, with negative sentences? ____
Do we usually* use **some**, or **any**, with questions? ____
[*'usually' because, **with a different meaning**, we can use 'some' in questions and 'any' in positive sentences]

Structure

Complete the table with *is/are* *some/any/a*

	countable nouns	**uncountable nouns**
positive	***Singular*** There is a pepper. ***Plural*** There __ ____ peppers.	There is some rice.
negative	***Singular*** There __ n't __ pepper. ***Plural*** There __ n't __ peppers.	There __ n't __ rice.
questions	***Singular*** ___ there ___ pepper? ***Plural*** ___ there ___ peppers?	___ there ___ rice?

Keys, Answers and Explanations Page No. 153

Exercise

1. Change these sentences from *singular* to *plural*.

> ***Example:***
> (a) There's a grapefruit. There are some grapefruits.

(b) Is there an egg? ______________________________

(c) Do you have a lemon? ______________________________

(d) There isn't a pepper in the fridge. ______________________________

(e) Give me an apple. ______________________________

(f) Isn't there an orange on the table? ______________________________

(g) We need an onion. ______________________________

2. Look at the picture and complete the sentences about it.

> ***Example:***
> (a) There are some onions but there aren't any potatoes.

(b) There ______ ______ milk and ______ water.

(c) There ______ n't ______ peppers.

(d) There ______ ______ egg.

(e) There ______ ______ apples.

(f) There ______ n't ______ grapefruit.

(g) There ______ ______ rice but there ______ n't. ______ pasta.

(h) There ______ n't ______ cheese or ______ bread.

3. Complete the questions and short answers *about the picture above.*

> ***Example:***
> (a) Is there a banana? No, there isn't.

(b) ______ there ______ peppers?
____

(c) ______ there ______ apples?
____

(d) ______ there ______ milk?
____

(e) ______ there ______ pasta?
____

(f) ______ there ______ potatoes?
____

(g) ______ there ______ grapefruit?
____

(h) ______ there ______ cheese?
____

(i) ______ there ______ onions?
____

(j) ______ there ______ egg?
____

5. Communicative Activities.

A turn to page 134. B turn to page 142.

You each have a picture of a fridge. **Don't show your picture to your friend.**
There are **twelve** differences. **Tell your friend about your picture and ask questions to find the differences.**

> ***Example:*** 'In my fridge there are six eggs. Are there ***any*** eggs in your fridge?'

Much/many/a lot

how much/many?

Talking about quantitty

Concept

Customs Officer: 'Excuse me, madam. Have you got anything to declare?
Passenger: 'No, I haven't.'
Customs Officer: 'Have you got any cigarettes?'
Passenger: 'Er … yes.'
Customs Officer: **'How many?'**
Passenger: **'Not many**—about 600, I think.'
Customs Officer: '600?!! That's **a lot!** Please open your bags. **How many** cigars have you got here?'
Passenger: **'Not a lot**, really. Only 10.'
Customs Officer: 'That's OK. **How much** wine have you got?'
Passenger: **'Not much**—only one bottle. Look.'
Customs Officer: 'I see. **How much** perfume have you got?'
Passenger: **'Not a lot**—only a litre. Is that OK?'
Customs Officer: 'No it isn't! That's a lot. Please come with me …'

Are cigarettes countable? ____________
Are cigars countable? ____________
What question do we use with *countable* nouns? *How much …? or How many…?* ____________

Is wine countable? ____________
Is perfume countable? ____________
What question do we use with *uncountable* nouns? *How much …? or How many …?* ________

Structure

Write the sentences under the *correct* picture.

a lot of …   not a lot of …   a lot of …   not much …   not a lot of …   not many …

COUNTABLE

positive

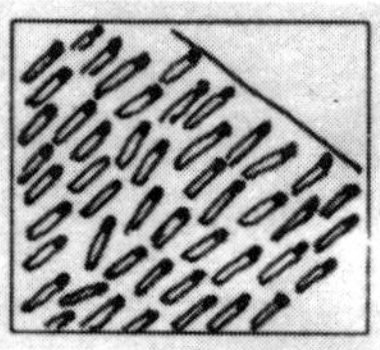

a lot of
cigarettes

negative

not a lot of
cigarettes
not many
cigarettes

UNCOUNTABLE

positive
____

____
perfume

negative
____

____
perfume
____
perfume

Compare: *That's a lot! That isn't a lot!* [**Without** a noun]
*That's a lot **of** perfume! That isn't a lot **of*** perfume! [**With** a noun]

Keys, Answers and Explanations Page No. 153

Exercise

1. Complete the questions about the picture using *How much/How many.*

(a) How much shampoo have you got?
(b) __________ t-shirts have you got?
(c) __________ books have you got?
(d) __________ money have you got?
(e) __________ cassettes have you got?

2. Look at the picture again and *answer* the questions.

(a) shampoo? A lot.
(b) t-shirts? Not a lot or not many (2)
(c) books? __________ or __________ (2)
(d) money? __________
(e) cassettes? __________ or __________ (2)

3. Complete the sentences about the picture using *is(n't)/are(n't)* and *much, many* or *a lot of.*

(a) There is a lot of shampoo.
(b) There ______________________________ cassettes.
(c) There ______________________________ money.
(d) There ______________________________ books.
(e) There ______________________________ t-shirts.

4. Correct the mistakes you find.

(a) There aren't much books.

____

(b) He hasn't got a lot of t-shirts.

____

(c) How much money have you got?

____

(d) There's a lot of money.

____

(e) There aren't a lot of cassettes.

____

(f) How many books is there?

____

5. Communicative Activities.

A: Turn to page 134; B: Turn to page 142.
You both have a picture of a suitcase.
They are similar but *not the same*.
Ask questions to find the differences.

Example:
A: 'How much shampoo have you got?'
B: 'A lot. Three bottles.'
A: 'I haven't got much - 1 bottle.'

UNIT 17

'Too' and 'not enough'

it is *too* big/it is not small *enough*

Talking about an **unsatisfactory** amount

Concept

This is the 'Splendido' Language School in New Delhi. It is a terrible language school!

What problems can you see?

Is the size of the *class* (number of students) OK? No

Is it *more* than is good or *less* than is good? more

So, the class is **too** big.

Is the size of the *room* OK? No

Is it *more* than is good or *less* than is good? less

So, the room **is not** big **enough.**

Is the number of students OK? Yes/No

Is it *more* than is good or *less* than is good? ______

So there are **too many** students.

Is the amount of noise OK? Yes/No

Is it *more* than is good or *less* than is good? ______

So, there is **too much** noise.

Is the number of chairs OK? Yes/No

Is it *more* than is good or *less* than is good? ______

So, there are **not enough** chairs.

Is the amount of light OK? Yes/No

Is it *more* than is good or *less* than is good? ______

So, there is **not** enough light.

When there is **more** than is good do we use ***too*** or ***not enough***? ______________________

When there is **less** than is good do we use ***too*** or ***not enough***? ______________________

Structure

With adjectives:

Look at the examples and answer the questions.

The class is **too** big.

The room is **not** big **enough.**

TOO

Does 'too' come **before**, or **after** the adjective? ______

ENOUGH

Does 'enough' come **before**, or **after** the adjective? ______

Does 'not' come **before**, or **after** the adjective? ______

With nouns:

There is **too much** noise.

There **is not enough** light.

There are **too many** students.

There **are not enough** chairs.

When do we use '*much*' and '*many*'*

—with '*too*' or with '*enough*'? ______

*For more information about 'much' and 'many' see Unit 16.

Keys, Answers and Explanations Page No. 154

Exercise

1. Here are some student complaints about the 'Splendido' Language School.
Rewrite the sentences *so they have the same meaning* using the adjectives in brackets ( ).

Examples:	
(a) The class (number of students) is too *big* (small).	The class isn't small enough.
(b) The room isn't *light* enough (dark).	The room is too dark.

(c) The teacher is too *inexperienced* (experienced). ______________________

(d) The lessons are too *easy* (difficult). ______________________

(e) The course isn't *cheap* enough (expensive). ______________________

(f) My hostel isn't *near* enough (far). ______________________

(g) The school is too *dirty* (clean). ______________________

(h) The lessons aren't *long* enough (short). ______________________

2. Look at some more problems and complete the sentences about them using *too much, too many* or *not ... enough.*

Examples:	
(a) 'The teacher never gives us homework!'	There isn't enough homework.
(b) 'The teacher gives us five hours of homework every day!'	There is too much homework.

(c) 'We only have one book for five students!' There are ____________ books.

(d) 'We have a break every fifteen minutes!' There are ____________ breaks.

(e) 'We never have a break!' There are ____________ breaks.

(f) 'There are only two desks for twenty students!' There are ____________ desks.

(g) 'We never have listening practice!' There is ____________ listening practice.

(h) 'We do writing practice all the time!' There is ____________ writing practice.

3. Some people are *never* happy. Suman lives in Mumbai but she hates it. **Read the conversation between Suman and her friend Ritu. Complete it with *too/enough/too much/too many*.**

Example:
Suman: 'I don't like Mumbai. It's too dirty. There is too much pollution.'

Ritu: 'But it is very exciting—there are lots of shops.'

Suman: 'Well, yes, but the shops are ______ expensive for me. I do not have ______ money and there are ______ people. It is so crowded!'

Ritu: 'What about transport? Don't you like the red buses?'

Suman: 'They look nice, but they are not cheap ______. It costs me Rs 30 a week to go to work! My house is ______ far from the centre.'

Ritu: 'Do you have a nice house?'

Suman: 'No, it is not big ______. I live with four students and they have parties every weekend. It is ______ noisy for me.'

Ritu: 'So why don't you go out at the weekend? There is so much to do in Mumbai! There are lots of theatres and cinemas.'

Suman: 'Yes, but there are ______ theatres and cinemas—I cannot decide where to go!'

4. Communicative Activities.
See Pg 135.

UNIT 18

Present continuous tense

Talking about **now**

She is *speaking* Chinese

Concept

Does she speak French?	Yes/No
Is she speaking French?	Yes/No
Does she speak Polish?	Yes/No
Is she speaking Polish?	Yes/No
Does she speak Chinese?	Yes/No
Is she speaking Chinese?	Yes/No

***Match* the sentence and the definition.**

1. She speaks French (= (a) or (b)?)
2. She is speaking Chinese (= (a) or (b)?)

(a) Now, at this moment. PAST NOW FUTURE

(b) Generally, but maybe not at this moment. PAST NOW FUTURE

Structure

Complete the following using the present continuous tense.

Examples:	
I/eat/dinner	I am eating dinner.
You/look/well	You are looking well.
She/speak/Chinese	She is speaking Chinese.

He/drink/coffee ____________________

It/rain ____________________

We/sit/down ____________________

They/feel/ill ____________________

I am eating dinner

How is the present continuous *formed*? *Subject* + ________ + ________

Question and Negative

Examples:

Is she speaking Polish? No, she is not.

Is it raining? Yes, it is.

(see Units 1 and 2—Questions and negatives using the present tense of the verb 'to be')

Spelling

Generally we add **-ing** to the infinitive of the verb. But sometimes the spelling changes:

A. bite—biting
smoke—smoking (**What happens to the *-e*?**)
write— writing

B. lie—lying
die—dying (**What happens to the *-ie*?**)

C. run—running
hit—hitting (**What happens to the last letter?**)
swim—swimming

Keys, Answers and Explanations Page No. 154

Exercise

1. Write sentences describing what is happening in the picture.

Example:
a) The dog/run <u>The dog is running.</u>

b) The children/swim
c) Grandmother/sleep
d) Father/lie down
e) The birds/sing
f) Mother and Father/talk
g) Grandfather/eat
h) Sun/shine
i) The baby/cry
j) The tree/die

2. Write questions and short answers about the same picture, using 'What' and 'Who'.

Example:
a) Who/smoke? Q: <u>Who's smoking?</u> A: <u>Father is.</u>

b) Who/sleep? Q:__________ A:__________
c) Who/cry? Q:__________ A:__________
d) Who/eat? Q:__________ A:__________
e) Who/swim?* Q:__________ A:__________
f) What/die? Q:__________ A:__________
g) Who/wear shorts? Q:__________ A:__________
h) What/sing? Q:__________ A:__________

(**careful: In this case 'Who' is followed by 'is' even if the answer is plural*)

3. Make questions about the picture and write true answers.

Example:		
a) Grandmother/talk?	Q: <u>Is Grandmother talking?</u>	A: <u>No, she is not.</u>
b) Where/the children/swim? (lake)	Q: <u>Where are the children swimming?</u>	A: <u>In the lake.</u>

c) The birds/sing
d) What/Grandfather/eat?
e) The sun/shine?
f) The dog/sleep?
g) Who/Mother/talk/to?
h) Father/write/a letter?

4. Some of these sentences contain spelling mistakes. Correct any you find.

Example:
a) 'Help! The dog is bitting me!' × The dog is biting me.

b) 'John is eating an icecream. I want one!'
c) 'You are runing too fast for me.'
d) 'Mary is swiming really well.'
e) 'Why is Father lying down?'
f) 'Mother is talkking to Father.'
g) 'I love slepping in the afternoon.'

5. Communicative Activities: A: turn to page 135, B: turn to page 143. You have two pictures that are similar but not identical. Ask questions using the present continuous tense to find the differences.

Example: 'In your picture, **is** the dog **sleeping**?' 'No, **he's running**.'

Present *simple* and present *continuous*

Choosing **which tense** to use

***I live* in England/**
***I am visiting* France**

Concept

Write the sentences under the correct pictures.

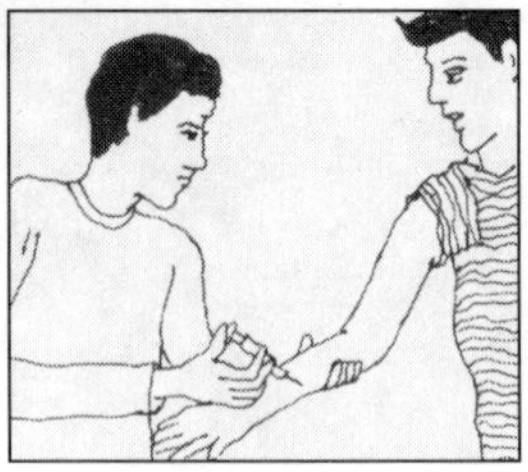

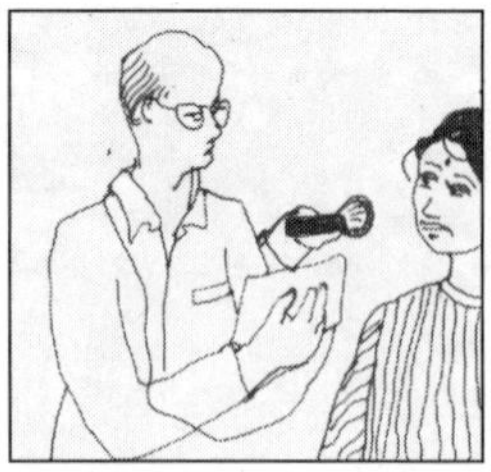

Example:
(i) Paul is a doctor.
(a) He works in a hospital.
(d) He is giving an injection.

(a) He works in a hospital.
(b) He is thinking about going home.
(c) John is a journalist.
(d) He is giving an injection.
(e) He teaches small children.
(f) He is interviewing someone.
(g) Ram is a teacher.
(h) He writes for a national newspaper.
(i) Paul is a doctor.

All these sentences are about the **present** but which sentences **emphasize NOW**?
(b) ____ ____
Are these sentences **present simple** or **present continuous**? __________

Which sentences are about the present ***in general***? (a) ____ ____ ____ ____ ____
Are these sentences **present simple** or **present continuous**? __________

Structure

For present simple see Unit 5.
For present continuous see Unit 18.

Exercise

Write similar sentences about these pictures:

Satyam/mechanic ____________________
He/mend/cars ____________________
He/have/lunch ____________________

Rekha/secretary ____________________
She/type/letters ____________________
She/answer/the phone ____________________

Keys, Answers and Explanations Page No. 155

Suresh/postman ____________________
He/deliver/letters ____________________
He/run/away from a dog ____________________

Rita/pilot ____________________
She/fly/planes ____________________
She/go/home ____________________

Vikram/writer ____________________
He/write/books ____________________
He/read/a book ____________________

John/painter ____________________
He/paint/houses ____________________
He/have/a cup of tea ____________________

2. Choose the correct sentence.

Example:
(a) *Japan is* in the Pacific Ocean <u>Correct</u>
Japan is being in the Pacific Ocean <u>Wrong</u>

(b) *Ria has* ten cups of tea every day. ______________
Ria is having ten cups of tea every day. ______________
(c) We cannot go out—*it rains.* ______________
We cannot got out—*it's raining.* ______________
(d) I cannot hear you because *I listen* to music. ______________
I cannot hear you because *I am listening* to music. ______________
(e) Where is Julia? *She reads* a book. ______________
Where is Julia? *She's reading* a book. ______________
(f) *I* usually *get up* early. ______________
I am usually *getting up* early. ______________
(g) *I* never *eat* chocolate—it makes you fat! ______________
I am never *eating* chocolate—it makes you fat! ______________

3. Make questions with the *present simple* or the *present continuous*.

Example:
(a) What/Sally/do? <u>What does Sally do?</u>
She is a policewoman.
(b) What/you/do? <u>What are you doing?</u>
I am reading a book.

(c) 'What languages/you/speak?'
____
'Marathi, Telugu and Oriya.'
(d) 'Where/you/usually/go/on holiday?' ____________________
'Greece—but not this year.'
(e) 'How many sisters/you/have?' ____________________
'Two.'
(f) 'Where/you/go/now?' ____________________
'To the shops—do you want anything?'
(g) 'What/you/eat?' ____________________
'Cake. It is delicious. Would you like some?'

4. Communicative Activities.
See Pg 130.

UNIT 20

Prepositions of place: in/on/next to

Where?

in **the box/*****on*** **the table/*****next to*** **the door**

Concept

Complete the gaps using these *propositions of place:* on/next to/in front of/opposite/behind/in/under

Where's the cat?

Example:
It is in front of the fire.

It is ______ the table.

It is ______ my feet.

It is _____ the television.

It is ______ a box.

It is ______the dog.

It is ______ the chair.

It is _____ the bowl.

It is ______ a cushion.

It is ______ my feet.

It is ______ the television.

It is ______ a box.

Structure

Things to remember about prepositions of place.

Which preposition is this? ______ **to**
Which preposition is this? **in** ______ **of**
Can we say opposite **to**? ______

Keys, Answers and Explanations Page No. 155

Exercise

1. Look at the pictures and *choose the correct preposition.*

(a) The box is (*in front of / next to*) the plant.

(b) The chair is (*opposite / in front of*) the table.

(c) The saucer is (*on/under*) the cup.

(d) The book is (*on / in*) the table.

(e) The plant is (*near / behind*) the television.

(f) The cup is (*on / near*) the saucer.

(g) The picture is (*next to / on*) the mirror.

(h) The cushion is (*behind / on*) the sofa.

(i) The glass is (*near / next to*) the apples.

2. Look at the picture of the room and decide if these statements are TRUE or FALSE. If they are *false*—correct the statement.

Example:
(a) The lamp is next to the television.
False—the lamp is on the television.
(b) The chocolates are on the table. True

(c) The newspaper is on the sofa.
____

(d) The videos are on the television.
____

(e) The curtains are in front of the television.
____

(f) The apples are behind the calendar.
____

(g) The cat is near the shoes.
____

(h) The cat is on the table.
____

(i) The plant is next to the table.
____

3. Complete these sentences about the same room.

(a) The glasses are next to the bottle.
(b) The apples are ____________ the bowl.
(c) The radio is ____________ the table.
(d) The photograph is ____________ the lamp.
(d) The shoes are ____________ the floor.
(f) The calendar is ____________ the apples.
(g) The table is ____________ the sofa.
(h) The remote control is ____________ the sofa.

4. Communicative Activities
A: Turn to page 136
B: Turn to page 143

You each have a picture of a different room.
A: Describe your room to B (*don't* show it)
B: Draw what A describes. Now look at the picture. Does it look the same? Now change roles.

UNIT 21

Prepositions of time: in/at/on

At 6 o'clock /*on* Friday/*in* the evening

Talking about **when**

Concept and Structure

at 6.00
at Dussehara
on my birthday
on 16th August
last night
at Christmas

in 1966
on Friday evening
at night
in April
at the moment

in the evening
in (the) summer*
in the afternoon
in the future
at teatime

on Independence Day
at midnight
in the 1980s
next week
at noon

on Saturday
at the weekend
in the past
in the 20th century

*You can say in summer/winter/autumn/spring, or in ***the*** summer/winter/autumn/spring

Put the examples above next to the correct *rule* below:

At

We use **at** for:
the time of day at 6.00 ___________ ___________
festivals of more than one day ___________ ___________
mealtimes ___________
and three more you need to remember ___________ ___________ ___________

In

We use **in** for:
year in 1966 ___________ ___________
periods of the day ___________ ___________
seasons ___________
months ___________
and two more you need to remember ___________ ___________

On

We use **on** for:
days on Saturday ___________
special days ___________ ___________
dates ___________

No preposition

When there is an *adjective* (this/next, etc) we *do not* use preposition ___________ ___________

'The'* or *'nothing?'
Write 'the' when necessary before these time expressions.

AT	IN	ON
at ______ Christmas	in the future	on ______ Friday
at ______ moment	in ______ April	on ______ Tuesday morning
at ______ 11.00	in ______ 15th Century	on ______ 15th December
at ______ midnight	in ______ morning	on ______ Republic Day
at ______ weekend	in ______ winter	on ______ Saturdays

Keys, Answers and Explanations Page No. 155

Exercise

1. Complete the sentences about holidays and festivals in India with *in, at, on* or *no preposition.*

(a) Teacher's Day is ______ 5th September.
(b) Flag Day is ______ December.
(c) Indians celebrate Gandhi Jayanti ______ 2nd October.
(d) National Youth Day is celebrated ______ 12th January.
(e) Children's Day is celebrated ______ 14th November, birthday of Pt. Jawaharlal Nehru.
(f) Some people go to church ______ midnight ______ Christmas Eve.
(g) There is usually a ten day holiday in schools ______ Dussehara.
(h) Most people don't work ______ the weekends.

2. Look at Ruby's diary and complete the sentences about her week with *in, at, on* or *no preposition.*

(a) ______ Monday morning ______ 9:00 Ruby is going to the Dentist.
(b) She is meeting Rita ______ lunch-time ______ Tuesday.
(c) ______ the evening ______ 14th March she is going out for dinner.
(d) She has a meeting ______ 3:00 ______ the afternoon ______ Thursday.
(e) ______16th March she has a meeting ______ noon.
(f) She is having a party ______ her birthday.
(g) She is not working ______ the weekend.
(h) ______ Sunday she is visiting Rita's parents.
(i) Shiela's birthday is ______ next week ______ 21st March.
(j) Ruby is very busy ______ the moment.

Ruby's Diary

3. Correct any mistakes you find in these sentences.

(a) I was born on the 1970s.
(b) Are you very busy this week?
(c) I cannot sleep in the night.
(d) Are you going on holiday on Christmas?
(e) We got married in 1975.
(f) Do you think life will be very different on the future?
(g) Life was different in past.
(h) My birthday is on 29th November.
(i) Is it cold in Shimla at winter?
(j) I'm learning Urdu in moment.
(k) The telephone rang on midnight.
(l) I'm going on holiday in next week.

4. Communicative Activities.
See Pg 131.

UNIT 22

Prepositions of movement

Where **to**?

Concept

Complete with the correct preposition of movement. Choose from this list:

to from out of into on off up down over
under through round along across past

..... the barracks

..... the barracks ..... the river

..... the bridge

..... the river-bank

..... the hill

..... the hill

..... the park

..... the statue

..... the post-office

..... the road

..... the railway bridge

Then jump ..... this box

and jump ..... the box—20 times!

Then you can go ..... the barracks and rest.

Keys, Answers and Explanations Page No. 156

Exercise

1. Match the *descriptions* with the *correct* map.
(four small maps, showing same area but different routes)

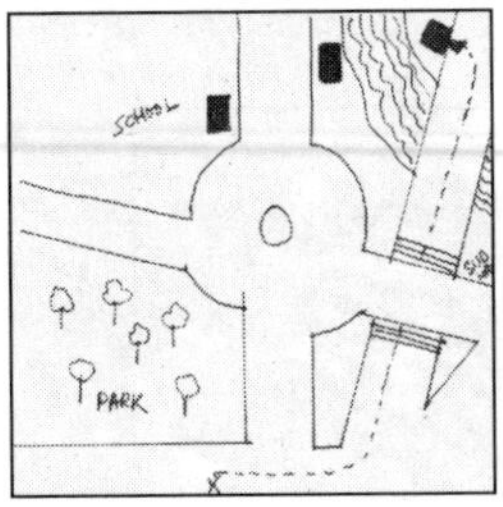
A

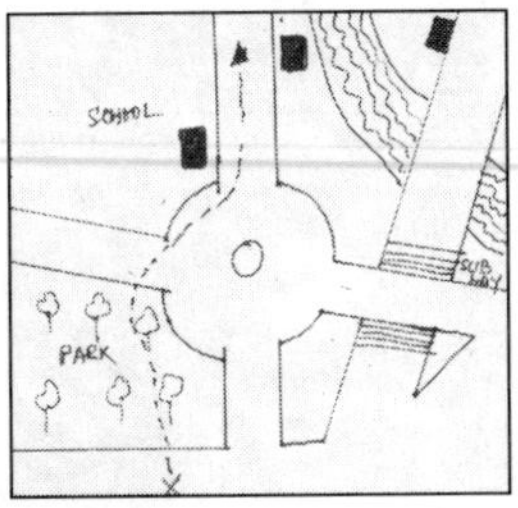
B

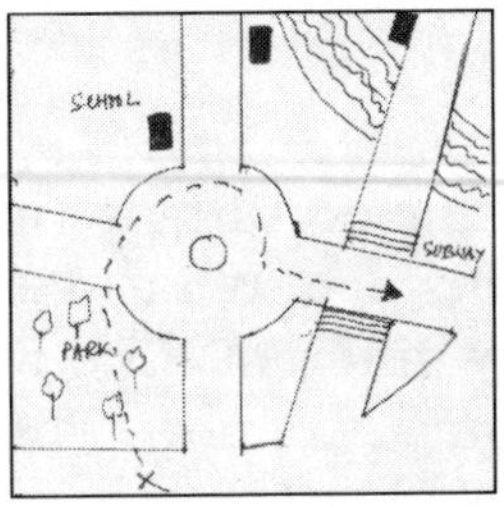
C

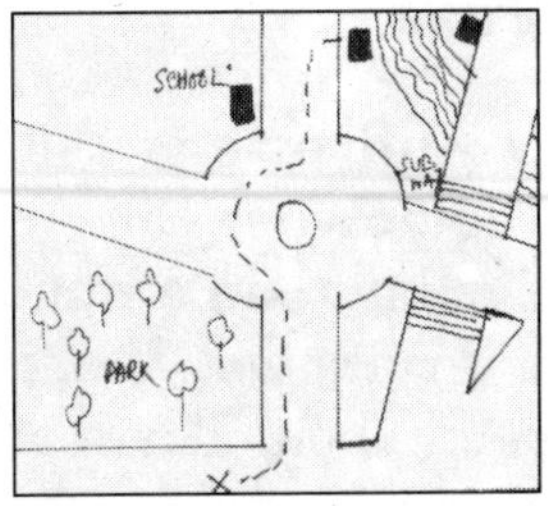
D

(a) Go across the road, then through the park, round the roundabout and past the school. B
(b) Go along the road, under the subway, across the bridge and into the building on your left. _____
(c) Go over the road, through the park, round the roundabout then over the bridge. _____
(d) Go across the road, round the roundabout, past the school and into the building on your right. _____

2. Choose the correct preposition.

(a) Go (across/ round) the road.

(b) How do I get (from/to) the post-office (from/to) the bank?

(c) Go (into/ under) the hotel.

(d) Get (on/ over) the bust.

(e) Go (through/ down) the hill.

(f) Go (along/ past) the road.

(g) Go (through/ round) the shopping centre.

(h) Go (over/ past) the supermarket.

(i) Go (out of/ under) the subway.

3. Complete the dialogue with the correct preposition.
Use these prepositions: off/out of/to/from/round/over/on/along

A: 'How do I get ___________ the school ___________ the post office?'
B: 'Go ___________ the school, ___________ the road, ___________ the roundabout, then turn left. Go ___________ the bridge and it is the building on your left.'
A: 'Is it a long way?'
B: 'About half an hour. You could get ___________ a number 9 bus outside the school and get ___________ next to the bridge.'

4. Communicative Activities.
See Pg 136.

Past simple tense of verb 'to be'

was/were

Talking about **the past** using the verb **'to be'**

Concept

Bill Andrews is 100 today.
Interviewer: 'Bill Andrews, I expect life is very different today than a hundred years ago. What **was** it like?'
Mr. Andrews: 'Yes, it is very different. Life **was** much quieter then. There are so many cars now. There **weren't** any cars when I was a boy.'
Interviewer: '**Were** you happy as a child?'
Mr. Andrews: 'Oh yes, I **was** very happy—but I am still happy now!'
Interviewer: 'Tell me about your family.'
Mr Andrews: 'Well, my father **was** a postman and my mother **was** a cook. We **were not** rich—but we **were not** poor either. There **were** five children. My brothers and sisters **were** all younger than me but I'm the only one still here.'

Structure

Look at the examples above and complete the table of the verb *'to be'* in the simple past.

SIMPLE PRESENT			SIMPLE PAST		
Positive	**Negative**	**Question**	**Positive**	**Negative**	**Question**
I am	I am not	Am I ...?	I was	I was not	Was I ...?
You are	You are not	Are you ...?	You ______	You ______	______you ...?
He is	He is not	Is he ...?	He ______	He ______	______ he ...?
She is	She is not	Is she ...?	She ______	She ______	______ she ...?
It is	It is not	Is it ...?	It ______	It ______	______ it ...?
We are	We are not	Are we ...?	We ______	We ______	______ we ...?
They are	They are not	Are they ...?	They ______	They ______	______ they ...?

[any problems with the verb 'to be' in the ***simple tense***—see Units 1 & 2]

Keys, Answers and Explanations Page No. 156

Exercise

1. Choose *was* or *were*.

(a) He (**was/were**) a policeman. He was a policeman.
(b) We (**was/were**) very happy. ______
(c) (**Was/Were**) you busy? ______
(d) They (**was not/were not**) interested in it. ______
(e) I (**was/were**) at school. ______
(f) It (**was not/were not**) expensive. ______
(g) (**Was/Were**) she your teacher? ______

2. Complete the text with *was* or *were*.

Interviewer: 'What was it like during the First World War, Bill?'
Bill: 'It ______ a terrible time. I ______ a young man, so I ______ in the army. We ______ in France.'
Interviewer: 'Where ______ your wife and children?'
Bill: 'They ______ in London. That ______ dangerous too. There ______ bombs and there ______ not a lot of food. The children ______ very young and they ______ very frightened.'

3. Are these statements *true* or *false*? Correct the *false* statements using *was not* or *were not.*

Example:
(a) Bill was an old man during the First World War False—Bill was not an old man during the First World War
(b) Bill was in the army. True

(c) Bill was in France ______
(d) Bill's wife and children were in France ______
(e) It was dangerous in London ______
(f) There was a lot of food in London ______
(g) The children were quite old ______
(h) The children were frightened ______

4. Make questions about the text using *was* or *were*.

Example:
(a) How old/Bill/during the First World War? How old was Bill during the First World War?

(b) /Bill/in the army? ______?
(c) Where/Bill ______?
(d) Where/Bill's wife and children? ______?
(e) /It dangerous in London? ______?
(f) /there bombs? ______?
(g) /there a lot of food? ______?
(h) How old/the children? ______?
(i) /the children frightened? ______?

5. Communicative Activities.

See Pg 131.

Past simple tense

Talking about the **past**

They *built* a small aeroplane

Concept

The story of flight

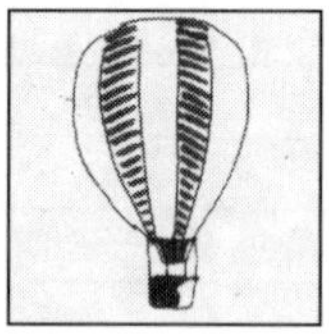

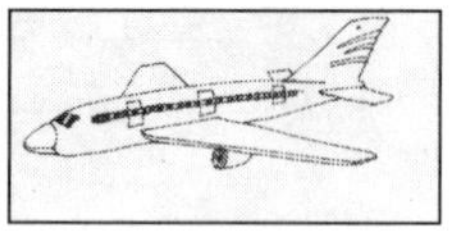

The first flight in the history of man **was** in a hot air balloon. Two brothers called Montgolfier **made** a balloon from linen and paper. They **decorated** it in bright colours. Two passengers **got** in. Then they **lit** a fire underneath the balloon and it **rose** up into the air.

The first men to fly an aeroplane **were** the brothers Wilbur and Orville Wright. They **built** a very small aeroplane. It only **stayed** up in the air for a few seconds. Later, a Frenchman, Louis Bleriot, **flew** an aeroplane across the English Channel.

This story is about the **past** so the verbs are in the **past tense**. Write their **infinitive** form.

Example:
was— be

made	-	lit	-	built	-
decorated	-	rose	-	stayed	-
got	-	were	-	flew	-

Structure

- 'Decorate' and 'stay' are **regular** verbs. So, to form the past tense of regular verbs what do we add to the infinitive? ___________
- The other verbs are **irregular**. They are formed in different ways, which are sometimes difficult to guess. Do you know the past tense forms of these useful verbs?

Infinitive	**Past Simple**	**Infinitive**	**Past Simple**
Example: begin ◄-----►	began		
break ◄-----►	___________	buy ◄-----►	___________
can ◄-----►	___________	do ◄-----►	___________
drink ◄-----►	___________	go ◄-----►	___________
have ◄-----►	___________	say ◄-----►	___________
see ◄-----►	___________	take ◄-----►	___________
write ◄-----►	___________		

(A list for you to learn and/or use for reference is in Appendix 1)

Spelling of regular verbs

Look at the examples and complete the rules.

(a) carry—carried
study—studied
When the verb ends consonant (b, c, d, etc) + y the 'y' changes to _______

(b) play—played
enjoy—enjoyed
When the verb ends vowel (aeiou) + y, the 'y' does not change to 'i', we add _______

(c) travel—travelled
stop—stopped
When the verb ends consonant + vowel + consonant we double the final _______

BUT: say—said/pay—paid (these are *irregular* verbs)

Exercise

1. Complete this crossword with the past tense forms of the verbs. (Appendix 1 will help)

Down		**Across**	
1.	Bring	3.	Take
2.	Rise	5.	Sing
4.	Drink	6.	Begin
6.	Blow	7.	Know
8.	Write	9.	Steal
9.	Stand	10.	Be
11.	Swim	13.	See
12.	Hate	14.	Think
15.	Give	16.	Make
17.	Eat	18.	Ride

2. Complete this story with the past tense forms of the verbs in brackets.

THE STORY OF MOTOR CARS

> ***Example:***
> Carl Benz (invent) invented the petrol engine.

Another German, Daimler, (design) ____________ a car with an engine. This (be) ____________ the start of the modern car. At first, there (be/not) ____________ many cars. In England, a man (have) ____________ to walk in front of every car with a red flag. Then, in America, Henry Ford (build) ____________ a cheaper car, (call) ____________ the Model T Ford, which ordinary people (can) ____________ buy.

3. Complete this story with appropriate past tense forms, choosing from the verbs in the box.

THE STORY OF THE RAILWAY

> ***Example:***
> George Stephenson invented

the first steam train, ____________ "Locomotion". Steam engines ____________ coal and ____________ water. The hot water ____________ steam and the steam ____________ the wheels go round. Railways ____________ very popular. Trains ____________ faster. They ____________ passengers, parcels, letters and food.

carry	*become*	*travel*	*invent*	*heat*	*produce*
make	*call*	*burn*			

4. Communicative Activities.

See Appendix Pg 131.

UNIT 25

Past simple auxiliary: did/didn't

***Did* you go? I *didn't* eat it**

Asking questions and **making negatives** using the past simple

Concept

What do you know about World History?

Complete the questions with the correct *infinitive*. Choose from:

die invade bring invent speak kill give up have

Examples:
1 When **did** Alexander the Great invade India?
2 When **did** Queen Victoria die?
3 **Did** Mughal Emperor Babur speak Hindi?

4 What **did** Thomas Alva Edison ________?
5 **Did** Queen Victoria ________ nine children?
6 Why **did** Nicholas II, the Czar of Russia ________ the throne?
7 **Did** the Italians ever ________ their leader?

Now match the *questions* with the *correct answers*.

Example:
(a) Electric bulb 4

(b) No, **he didn't** (only Persian)
(c) In 326 BC
(d) Yes, **she did** ________
(e) Because of the Bolshevik Revolution ________
(f) In 1901 ________
(g) **Yes, they did** (Benito Mussolini) ________

True or false?

Example:
Henry the Eighth didn't have six wives. FALSE

Subhash Chandra Bose didn't form the 'Azad Hind Fauj'. ________
Sikandar Lodhi didn't build the Taj Mahal at Agra. ________
The Duke of Wellington didn't win the Battle of Waterloo. ________
The American people didn't like President George Washington. ________

Structure

Write the examples from above in the table below:

QUESTIONS

	[Question words] +	**did** +	**subject** +	**infinitive** +	**(other)**
Examples:					
1.	When	did	Alexander the Great	invade	India?
2.	When	did	Queen Victoria	die?	________
3.	________	Did	Babur	speak	Hindi?
4.	________	________	________	________	________
5.	________	________	________	________	________
6.	________	________	________	________	________
7.	________	________	________	________	________

NEGATIVES

Subject +	**didn't** +	**infinitive (+)**
Example:		
Henry VIII	didn't	have six wives
________	________	________
________	________	________
________	________	________
________	________	________

SHORT ANSWERS

Yes/No +	**subject** +	**did/didn't**
Example		
No	he	didn't
________	________	________
________	________	________

Exercise

Queen Victoria was born in 1819. She didn't have any brothers or sisters so she was probably quite a lonely child. She studied with a private teacher, Fraulein Lehzen, at home. She had lessons every day from 9.30 until 5.00. From 5.00–6.00 she learned poetry in English, French and German. She had an interesting hobby—she collected dolls and made clothes for them. She had 132 dolls.

When she was only eighteen her uncle, William IV, died and Victoria became Queen. She married her cousin, Prince Albert, in 1840 and they had nine children (five girls and four boys). She loved Albert very much and when he died in 1861 she was very unhappy and wanted to die. However, she was Queen for another forty years until she died in 1901.

1. Make *Yes/No* questions about the text. Answer the questions with *short answers*.

Example:
(a) Victoria/have/any brother or sisters? Did Victoria have any brothers or sisters? No, she didn't.

(b) she/go to school? ______________________? ____________
(c) she/speak/French and German? ______________________? ____________
(d) William IV/die/in 1837? ______________________? ____________
(e) Victoria and Albert/get married/in 1840? ______________________? ____________
(f) she/love/her husband? ______________________? ____________
(g) they/have/ten children? ______________________? ____________
(h) she/die/in 1861? ______________________? ____________

2. *Complete* the questions *to match* the answers

Examples:
(a) Where did Victoria study? At home
(b) When did she have lessons? Every day from 9.30–5.00

(c) What ______ collect?	Dolls
(d) How many dolls ______________?	132
(e) When ______ William IV ______?	When Victoria was 18
(f) When ______ Victoria ______ Queen?	In 1837
(g) When ______________ Albert?	In 1840
(h) How many children ______ they ______?	Nine
(i) When ______ Albert ______?	In 1861

3. Correct the sentences that are NOT TRUE with a full sentence using *'didn't'*.

Example:
(a) Victoria studied at home. True
(b) Victoria went to school. Victoria didn't go to school

(c) Victoria spoke French and German.
____
(d) Victoria spoke Chinese. ______________________
(e) Victoria had 200 dolls. ______________________
(f) Victoria became Queen when she was twelve.
____

(g) Victoria and Albert got married in 1845.
____
(h) Victoria and Albert had nine children.
____
(i) Victoria and Albert had five sons.
____
(j) Albert died in 1861.
____
(k) Victoria died in 1861.
____

4. Communicative Activities.

You are going to read two texts about William Shakespeare—but with different information. Ask your friend questions to find out more information. A: Turn to page 136. B: Turn to page 144.

UNIT 26

Would like

Would you like a cup of tea?/ I would like some chocolate, please

Offering something **to** someone; requesting something **from** someone

Concept

Read the dialogues and answer the questions.

Rita: (a) '**Do you like** chocolate?'
Kishan: 'Oh yes! I like chocolate more than anything!'
Rita: (b) '**Would you like** some* chocolate?'
Kishan: 'No thanks. I am on a diet. **I would like** an apple, please.'

Does Kishan like chocolate? ___________
Does Kishan like apples? ___________
Does Kishan want chocolate **now**? ___________
Does Kishan want an apple **now**? ___________

When Rita asks '**Do you like** chocolate?' is she talking about *now* or *in general*? ___________
When Rita asks '**Would you like** some chocolate?' is she talking about *now* or *in general*?
____
Which question **means the same** as 'Do you want ...?'-(a) or (b) ______
**Notice that we use 'some' with 'would you like ......?'*

Ravi: (c) '**Do you like** going to the theatre?'
Sreya: 'Yes, I do.'
Ravi: (d) '**Would you like** to go to the theatre with me next Friday?'
Sreya: 'Oh! Er ... sorry, I cannot, I am busy.'

Does Sreya like going to the theatre? ___________
Does she want to go with Ravi on Friday? ___________
Which question **means the same** as 'Do you want ...?'-(c) or (d) ___________

Structure

Write the *contractions*.

I would like ___________

Example:	
You would like	You'd like

He would like ___________
She would like ___________
We would like ___________
They would like ___________

Make *questions*.

Example:	
You would like	Would you like?

He would like ___________
She would like ___________
We would like ___________
They would like ___________

Complete with *-ing* or *to+infinitive*.

Example:
I like (cook) cooking.
I would like (cook) to cook dinner tonight.

He likes (watch) ______ television.
He would like (watch) ______ the football this afternoon.

She likes (go) ______ to the cinema.
She would like (go) ______ and see a film tonight.

We like (play) ______ tennis.
We would like (play) ______ tennis this afternoon.

Keys, Answers and Explanations Page No. 158

Exercise

1. Match the questions to the answers.

Example:
(a) Do you like tea?

(b) Would you like a cup of tea?
(c) Do you like going to the cinema?
(d) Would you like to go to the cinema?

1. Yes, I do/No, I do not.
2. Yes, please/No, thanks.
3. Yes, I would love to/Sorry, I cannot.
4. Yes, I do/No, I do not.

2. Choose *like* or *would like.*

Example:
(a) **Do you/Would you** like a coffee? Yes, please. Would you

(b) **I** like/**I would** like to go and see the new film at the Roxy Cinema this weekend.
(c) What **do you/would you** like to do tonight?
(d) **Do you/would you** like getting up early? No, I hate it!
(e) **I would** like/**I** like getting up late on Saturdays.
(f) **Do you/Would you** like London? It is OK, but it rains all the time!
(g) When he is older, **he would** like/**he** like to be a doctor.
(h) Why are you a teacher? Because **I** like/**I would** like teaching.
(i) **Would you/Do you** like to go out to dinner? Yes, I would love to.

3. Complete with *-ing* (cooking) or to + *infinitive* (to cook).

Example:
(a) Would you like (go) to go to the beach?

(b) Do you like (play) ________ tennis?
(c) What do you like (do) ________ on holiday?
(d) I really like (lie) ________ on the beach and (do) ________ nothing! My wife likes (sightsee) ________.
(e) I like (cook) ________ but I do not like (do) ________ the washing up.
(f) I would like (see) ________ "Macbeth" tonight. I really like (go) ________ to the theatre.
(g) Would you like (dance) ________? No, sorry, I don't like (dance) ________.

4. Complete the dialogues using *would like (to + infinitive)* or *like (-ing).*

Example:
A: 'What would you like to do (do) today?'

B: 'Well, I think I ________ (go swimming) in the sea. It's a lovely day. So, what ________ (do) today, then?'
A: 'I ________ (visit) the Castle.'
B: 'But it's so hot! Why don't we go to the castle later?'

A: 'Do you ________ (play) tennis?'
B: 'No, not much.'
A: 'What sports do you ________?'
B: 'I ________ (run).'
A: 'Oh, good! Would you ________ (go) running with me this evening?'
B: 'Sorry, I can't. I'm going to the cinema.'

4. Communicative Activities.

See Pg 137.

UNIT 27

Requests and permission: can/could/may *could* you help me?/*can* I go?

Making **requests** and asking **permission**

Concept

(a) '**Can** you give me a lift?'
(b) '**Can** I have some more dessert, please?'
Both these sentences use '**can**'.
Which sentence is *asking someone to do something*? (a) or (b) ______
Which sentence is *asking permission*? (a) or (b) ______

Look at these dialogues and answer the questions.

Raj: 'Can you pass me the salt, please?'
Geeta: 'Here you are.'
Raj: 'Could you lend me Rs 5 please?'
Geeta: 'Yes, OK. Do not forget to give me it back!'

What **two** words can you see for *asking someone to do something*? ______ ______
Which is more formal/polite? ______
Why is Raj more polite in the second dialogue? ______

Child: 'Mother, can I watch tv?
Mother: 'Yes, of course.'
Child: 'Mother, may I go to a party on Saturday?'
Mother: 'Well...'

What **two** words can you see for *asking permission*? ______ ______
Which is more formal/polite?* ______
Why is the child more polite in the second dialogue? ______

(*Some people think that 'may' is more correct than 'can', but most people now think 'can' is OK.)

Structure

Requests (asking for something)

Which sentence is correct? (only one)

Can/Could you *to help* me? ______ (× ✓)
Can/Could you *helping* me? ______ (× ✓)
Can/Could you *help* me? ______ (× ✓)

Permission

Which sentence is correct? (only one)

Can/May I *smoking*? ______ (× ✓)
Can/May I *smoke*? ______ (× ✓)
Can/May I to *smoke*? ______ (× ✓)

Keys, Answers and Explanations Page No. 159

Exercise

1. Put the words in the correct order to make sentences.

Example:	
(a) tell/the time/can/me/you/please?	Can you tell me the time, please?

(b) you/that/spell/please/could? ____________________?

(c) I/here/sit/can? ____________________?

(d) smoke/I/may? ____________________?

(e) your/can/pen/borrow/please/I? ____________________?

(f) a lift/you/could/give/please/me? ____________________?

(g) you/can/me/pass/the salt? ____________________?

(h) I/may/to/go/Mother/the disco? ____________________?

2. Divide *the sentences from exercise one* into two columns.

REQUESTS	ASKING FOR PERMISSION
Can you tell me the time, please?	Can I sit here?
____________________	____________________
____________________	____________________
____________________	____________________

3. What do you say?

Example:
(a) You want someone to *open the window*.
Could you open the window, please ?

(b) You are in a train and you want to sit down.
____________________ here, ____________________?

(c) You are in class and you want someone to *say* something again.
____________________ that again, ____________________ ?

(d) You are in class and you want someone to *spell* something.
____________________ that, ____________________?

(e) You are in class and you want to *leave early*.
____________________?

(f) You want someone to *help* you?
____________________ me ____________________?

4. Manuel is a Spanish student staying with an Indian family. **Complete the conversation with his Indian host, Mr Kumar.**

Manuel: '__________ use the kitchen?'
Mr Kumar: 'Yes, you can.'
Manuel: '__________ invite my friends round?'
Mr Kumar: 'Yes, of course, but __________ ask us first?'
Manuel: '__________ give me a key to the house?'
Mr Kumar: 'Yes, but __________ be quiet if you come in late?'
Manuel: '__________ smoke in my room?'
Mr Kumar: 'No, I am sorry. This is a non-smoking house.'

5. Communicative Activities.
See Pg 131.

UNIT 28

Ability (can/could) — I *can* swim/I *could* swim when I was seven

Concept

Match the jobs with what they ***can*** do

Example: a secretary	can	make a cake
a waiter	can	write
a cook	can	type
a translator	can	add up a bill
a journalist	can	speak two or more languages

Ram is a translator

Interviewer: 'Do you like your job?'

Ram: 'It is hard work but very interesting.'

Interviewer: '<u>How many languages **can** you speak</u>?'

Ram: 'Three, <u>**I can** speak French, German and Hindi</u>. My parents are Indian, so <u>**I could** speak Hindi when I was a child</u>.'

Interviewer: '<u>**Could** you speak Hindi well then</u>?'

Ram: '<u>Yes, I **could**</u>. We always spoke Hindi at home.'

Interviewer: '**Could** you speak French and German then too?'

Ram: '<u>No, I **could not**</u>. I learnt French at University and <u>**I could not** speak German until I went to live in Germany</u> after University.'

Interviewer: '**Can** you speak any Japanese?'

Ram: '<u>No, I **cannot**</u>. <u>I **cannot** speak any other languages.</u>'

Do we use **can/cannot** to talk about the *past*, or the *present*? ____________

Do we use **could/could not** to talk about the *past*, or the *present?* ____________

Structure

Write the <u>underlined</u> sentences from the dialogue in the table.

	PRESENT	PAST
Question ◄——►	How many languages can you speak?	____________________?
Positive ◄——►	____________________	I could speak Hindi when I was a child.
Positive Short answer	Yes, I can.	____________________
Negative	I cannot speak any other languages.	____________________
Negative Short answer	____________________	____________________

What is the *present tense* form of **can** for I/you/he/she/it/we/they (all persons)? ____________

What is the *past tense* form of **can** for I/you/he/she/it/we/they all persons? ____________

Keys, Answers and Explanations Page No. 159

Exercise

1. Match the verbs to the jobs. Then write sentences using *can*.

type fast   take orders   take dictation   explain grammar   make a speech
serve food   answer the phone   help students   understand politics
write on the board   add up a bill

a teacher   *a politician*   *a waiter*   *a secretary*

Example:
(a) A teacher can write on the board.

(b) A teacher ____________
(c) A teacher ____________
(d) A politician ____________
(e) A politician ____________
(f) A waiter ____________
(g) A waiter ____________
(h) A waiter ____________
(i) A secretary ____________
(j) A secretary ____________
(k) A secretary ____________

2. Two people are applying for a job as a secretary. **Look at the table of what they *can* and *cannot* do and complete the questions and answers.**

Example:
(a) Can Sarah take dictation? Yes, she can

(b) ________ John answer the phone? ________
(c) ________ Sarah use a computer? ________
(d) ________ John type 100 words a minute? ________
(e) ________ Sarah answer the phone? ________
(f) ________ John write shorthand? ________
(g) ________ Sarah type 100 words a minute? ________
(h) ________ John take dictation? ________
(i) ________ Sarah take dictation? ________
(j) ________ John use a computer? ________

	Sarah Smith	John Andrews
type 100 words a minute	×	✓
take dictation	✓	✓
write shorthand	×	✓
answer the phone	✓	✓
use a computer	✓	×

Who do you think should get the job? ________

3. Which of these things can *you* do? Write true sentences using *can/cannot.*

read   play the piano   speak English   play chess   ride a bicycle   cook   take dictation   run   swim
speak your (my) own language   write   drive a car

Example:
I can read

4. Which of these things in exercise 3 could you do when you were ten years old? Write true sentences using *could/could not.*

Example:
I could read

5. Communicative Activities.
See Pg 132.

UNIT 29

Obligation (have to)

I *have to* go home

Talking about something **necessary**

Concept

Suresh: 'I hate my school! We **have to** wear a uniform and I always **have to** do lots of homework.'

Suresh's father: 'You're lucky! When I was at school I **had to** wear a hat! And we **had to** do a lot more homework.'

Suresh: 'But you **didn't have to** eat school dinners. Yeuch! You went home to eat.'

Suresh's father: 'OK, but you **don't have to** study Latin! French is much easier.'

Answer **the questions and** ***complete*** **with: had to/has to/does not have to/did not have to.**

Is it necessary/obligatory for Suresh to wear a uniform? ***Yes/No***
So, Suresh ______ wear a uniform.
Is it necessary/obligatory for Suresh to study Latin? ***Yes/No***
So, Suresh ____________ study Latin.
Is it necessary/obligatory for Suresh's father to wear a hat *now*? ***Yes/No***
Was it necessary/obligatory for Suresh's father to wear a hat when he was at school? ***Yes/No***
So, Suresh's father ______ wear a hat when he was at school.
It is necessary/obligatory for Suresh's father to eat school dinners *now*? ***Yes/No***
Was it necessary/obligatory for Suresh's father to eat school dinners when he was at school? ***Yes/No***
So, Suresh's father ___________ eat school dinners when he was at school.

Structure

Use the example ***above*** **to complete the table.**

PRESENT	**PAST**
NECESSARY	NECESSARY
Example: I <u>have to</u> study French.	***Example:*** I <u>had to</u> study Latin.
You ____________ study French.	You ____________ study Latin.
He/She ____________ study French.	He/She ____________ study Latin.
We ____________ wear a uniform.	We ____________ wear a hat.
They ____________ wear a uniform.	They ____________ wear a hat.
NOT NECESSARY	*NOT* NECESSARY
Example: I <u>don't have to</u> study Latin.	***Example:*** I <u>didn't have to</u> study French.
You ____________ study Latin.	You ____________ study French.
He/She ____________ study Latin.	He/She ____________ study French.
We ____________ wear a hat.	We ____________ eat school dinners.
They ____________ wear a hat.	They ____________ eat school dinners.

Make questions and short answers.

He has to study French.	<u>Does he have to study French?</u>	<u>Yes, he does/No, he doesn't.</u>
They have to wear a uniform.	________________________?	________________
He *had* to wear a hat.	________________________?	________________
They *had* to study Latin.	________________________?	________________

Exercise

1. Look at the 'contract' which a teacher made with her students.

The Teacher	The students
I promise to … —be friendly —give some homework —help the students —speak clearly	We promise to … —work hard —do the homework —be on time —speak English in class

Write sentences about the contract using *have to/has to.*

Example:
(a) The teacher has to be friendly.

(b) The students ______________________

(c) ______________________

(d) ______________________

(e) ______________________

(f) ______________________

(g) ______________________

(h) ______________________

2. *Last year* Reena was a secretary. *Now* she has a new job—she is a travelling salesperson.
Write sentences about her old job and her new job using *has to/had to (+)* and *does not have to/did not have to (-)*

When Reena was a *secretary:*

Example:
(a) She had to type letters (+)

(c) She ____________ travel a lot (-)
(e) She ____________ work at the weekend (-)
(g) She ____________ work from 9.00–5.00 (+)
(i) She ____________ work hard (+)

Now Reena is a *salesperson:*

(b) She does not type letters (-)

(d) She ____________ travel a lot (+)
(f) She ____________ work at the weekend (+)
(h) She ____________ work from 9.00–5.00 (-)
(j) She still ____________ work hard (+)

3. Complete the text with *have to/do not have to/had to/did not have to.*
I am a teacher. I work in the centre of London but I live in the Southeast, quite a long way from the school. So every morning I _________ get up at 7.00. There are no buses so I _________ walk to the train station. I get a train to Victoria Station and then I usually go on the Underground. The school is quite near so I _________ go on the Underground—if the weather is good, I sometimes walk. I _________ be at work at 8.45 because classes start at 9.00.
Yesterday was terrible because there was a train strike, so there were no trains to Victoria. I _________ get up at 6.00 and walk a long way to catch a bus. When I got to the bus stop the buses were all full so I _________ wait a long time. Luckily a friend gave me a lift home at the end of the day so I _________ walk or wait for a bus again.

4. Write questions (using *have to/had to*) and answers about the text.

Example:
(a) What time/she/get up? — What time does she have to get up? — 7.00

(b) Why/she/walk to the train station? ______________________? ________
(c) She/go on the Underground? Does ______________________? ________
(d) What time/she/be at work? ______________________? ________
(e) What time/she/get up *yesterday*? ______________________? ________
(f) Why/she/wait a long time? ______________________? ________
(g) She/walk at the end of the day? Did ______________________? ________

5. Communicative Activities.
See Pg 137.

UNIT 30

Advising (should/should not)

you *should* relax/
you *should not* work so hard

Giving advice

Concept

Are these good or bad things to do if you want to be healthy? ***Tick* (✓) if you think they are good. *Cross* (×) if you think they are bad things to do.**

> ***Example:***
> - smoke ×
> - eat less fat ✓

- eat fruit
- exercise three times a week
- eat a big meal before you go to bed
- walk up the stairs and not take the lift
- drive everywhere
- stay awake all night

Is it a good idea to smoke if you want to be healthy? ______
So, if you want to be healthy you shouldn't **(should not)** smoke.
Is it a good idea to eat less fat if you want to be healthy? ______
So, if you want to be healthy you **should** eat less fat.

Write sentences about the other things using *You should …* or *You should not …*

> ***Example:***
> - You should eat fruit.

- ____________________ exercise three times a week.
- ____________________ eat a big meal before you go to bed.
- ____________________ walk up the stairs.
- ____________________ drive everywhere.
- ____________________ stay awake all night.

Structure

What is the *present tense form* for **should/shouldn't** with I/you/he/she/it/we/they (all persons)? _____
Which is correct? (only one)

- I shouldn't **to smoke** ______ (× ✓)
- I shouldn't **smoking** ______ (× ✓)
- I shouldn't **smoke** ______ (× ✓)

Keys, Answers and Explanations Page No. 160

Exercise

Here is some advice about learning English. **Rewrite the sentences using *should/should not*.**

(a) 
(b) 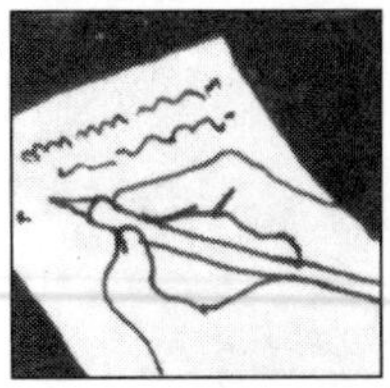
(c) 

> ***Example:***
> (a) It's a good idea to read in English.
> You should read in English.

(b) It is a good idea to write vocabulary in a notebook.
____

(c) It is not a good idea to try and translate every word you read.
____

(d) 
(e) 

(d) It is a good idea to listen to the radio in English.
____

(e) It is not a good idea to speak your own language in your English class. ________________________________

(f) It is not a good idea to forget to do your homework.
____

(f) 
(g) 
(h) 

(g) It is a good idea to watch English films.
____

(h) It is a good idea to study hard!
____

2. Suraj is studying for an important exam. **Complete the advice his friend, Raj, gives him.**

> ***Example:***
> Suraj: 'I am really worried about my exam, Raj.'
> Raj: (not/worry) 'You should not worry. You will be OK.'

Suraj: 'Yes, but I have got too much work to do!'
Raj: '(plan your time) ____________.'
Suraj: 'I know, but I do not have much time. I am going to a party on Saturday.'
Raj: 'Well, (not/go to the party) ________________!'

Suraj: 'But I need to relax sometimes.'
Raj: 'Yes, well, (not/work all the time) ________________. You can work on Sunday.'
Suraj: 'I am going swimming on Sunday.'
Raj: 'I think (work harder) ____________!'

3. Write advice for these people, using *he/she/they*.

(give up smoking)

(not drink so much)

(exercise more)

(not eat so much chocolate)

(speak English in class)

(buy a new car)

(spend less money)

(be careful!)

4. Communicative Activities.
See Pg 137.

UNIT 31

Possibility (may/might)

it *may* rain/I *might* go

Talking about **possibility**

Concept

King: 'Right, then, daughter. Which Prince are you going to marry? You have to make a decision!'
Princess: 'Well ... I **might** marry Prince Humphrey, he is quite goodlooking.'
King: 'What about Prince Alfred, he is quite intelligent.'
Princess: 'Well, I **may**. On the other hand, I *might not* marry either of them. In fact, I **may not** marry anyone!'

Positive

Is the Princess *definitely* going to marry **Prince Humphrey**? ___________
Is she definitely **not** going to marry him? ___________
What *word* does she use to show she is *not sure*? ___________
Is the Princess *definitely* going to marry **Prince Alfred**? ___________
Is she definitely **not** going to marry him? ___________
What *word* does she use to show she is *not sure*? ___________
Do *may*, and *might* have the same meaning when talking about *possibility*? ___________

Negative

Is the Princess definitely **not** going to marry either of the princes? ________
What *word* does she use to show she is *not sure*? ________
Is the Princess definitely **not** going to marry anyone? ________
What *word(s)* does she use to show she is *not sure*? ________
Do *may not* and *might not* have the same meaning when talking about *negative possibility*? ________

Structure

What is the form of **might/mightn't (might not)** for I/you/he/she/it/we/they (all persons)? _________
What is the form of **may/may not** for I/you/he/she/it/we/they (all persons)? _________
Is it possible to write **mayn't** _________

Keys, Answers and Explanations Page No. 161

Exercise

1. Make these sentences *negative*.

> ***Example:***
> (a) The Princess may make a decision. The Princess may not make a decision.

(b) The Princess may want to be rich. ____________________
(c) The Princess might like Prince Humphrey better. ____________________
(d) Her father may like Prince Alfred better. ____________________
(e) Prince Alfred may love someone else. ____________________
(f) Prince Humphrey might love someone else. ____________________

2. The Princess has a lot of important decisions to make about her life—but she is not sure what to do. **Write the answers to her father's questions using *might*.**

> ***Example:***
> (a) 'Who are you going to marry?'
> (Prince Humphrey/Prince Alfred) I might marry Prince Humphrey or I might marry Prince Alfred.

(b) 'When are you going to decide?' (this week/next year) ____________________
(c) 'What will you do if you do not marry either of them?' (travel the world/write a book)
____
(d) 'Where are you going to live?' (Here/abroad?) ____________________

3. Prince Humphrey is thinking about the Princess. He wants to marry her, but he is not sure if it will happen. **Rewrite his sentences using: *may* or *may not*.**

> ***Example:***
> (a) Perhaps the Princess will **marry me.** The Princess may marry me.

(b) Perhaps we will **live in my castle.**	We ____________________
(c) Perhaps she wo**n't like that.**	She ____________________
(d) Perhaps we will **live with her father.**	We ____________________
(e) Perhaps her father does **not like me.**	Her father ____________________
(f) Perhaps I will **build a new castle in her country.**	I ____________________
(g) Perhaps my people will **not like that.**	They ____________________
(h) It is all very complicated! Perhaps she wo**n't marry me.**	She ____________________

4. Tonight there will be a big party at the Princess' castle. Prince Humphrey and Prince Alfred will be there. **Rewrite the sentences using *might/might not*.**

> ***Example:***
> (a) Perhaps the Princess will dance with Prince Humphrey. The Princess might dance with Prince Humphrey.

(b) Perhaps Prince Humphrey will ask the Princess to marry him. ____________________
(c) Perhaps the Princess will say 'No'.____________________
(d) Perhaps Prince Humphrey will be sad.____________________
(e) Perhaps Prince Alfred will be successful.____________________
(f) Then perhaps Prince Humphrey will be angry.____________________
(g) Perhaps Prince Humphrey will hit Prince Alfred.____________________
(h) Perhaps the Princess will be very angry.____________________
(i) Perhaps she won't marry either of them.____________________
(j) Perhaps she won't get married at all.____________________

5. Communicative Activities.
See Pg 137.

Past continuous

I *was reading*

Talking about something happening at a **specific time** in the past

Concept

A man is dead! Someone killed him **at 6.00 yesterday afternoon.**
There are three suspects: Bill Bother, Tom Trouble, Tina Trouble.
The police ask them the question:
'What **were you doing** at 6.00 yesterday afternoon?'

Bill Bother:
'I **was playing** the piano for an Old People's Club dance.'

Tom and Tina Trouble:
'**We were visiting** Tina's grandmother in hospital.'

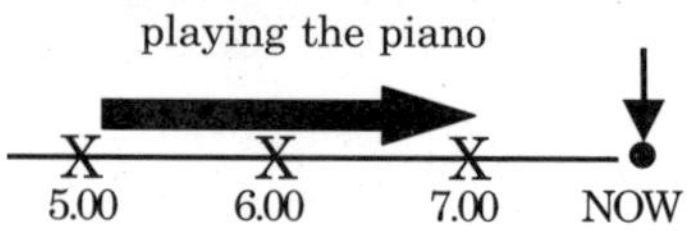

Look at the time-line
What time did Bill start playing the piano? _____
What time did he finish playing the piano? _____

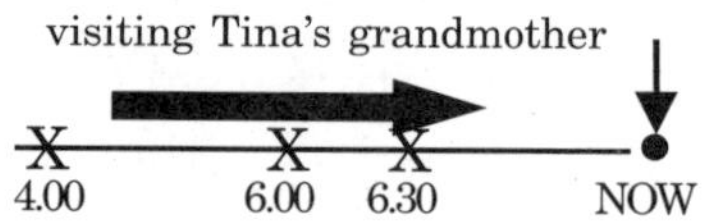

Look at the time-line
What time did Tom and Tina start visiting? ____
What time did they finish visiting? _____

Look at the difference:

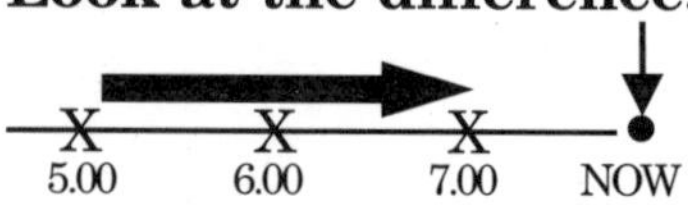

(**a**) I was **playing** the piano.

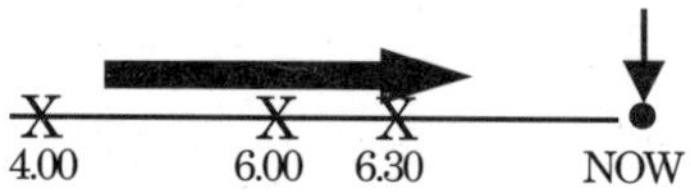

(**b**) We **were visiting** Tina's grandmother.

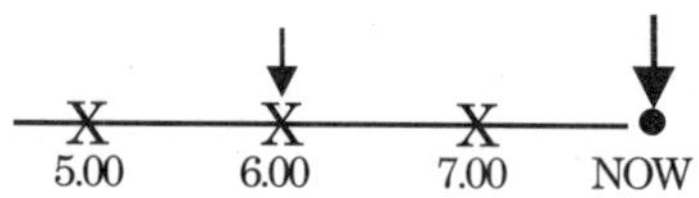

(**c**) Someone **killed** a man.

What tense are sentences (**a**) and (**b**)? ___________
What tense is sentence (**c**)? ______

Structure

Complete the table.

SUBJECT + VERB TO BE (past) + VERB+ing

Example:		
I	was	reading

You	______	speak______
He/She/It	______	eat______
We	______	play______
They	______	work______

Note: for **spelling** rules with '-ing' see Unit 18

Now make *questions*.

Example:	
I/read	Was I reading?

You/speak ____________________
He/eat ____________________
We/play ____________________
They/work ____________________

Now make negative sentences.

Example:
I/read I was not reading.

You/speak ____________________
He/eat ____________________
We/play ____________________
They/work ____________________

Keys, Answers and Explanations Page No. 161

UNIT 32

Exercise

1. Rajiv and Sunita are friends but Rajiv lives in Australia and Sunita lives in Britain. It is difficult for them to telephone each other because the time is so different.

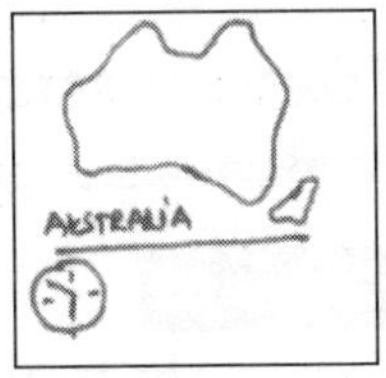

Write sentences about what they were doing yesterday.

Example: *have breakfast / leave work* At 8.00 am in Britain Sunita was having breakfast. But, in Australia Rajiv was leaving work.

have lunch / have a Coke. At 12.00 pm in Britain ________________. But in Australia ________________

go to bed / get up At 10.00 pm in Britain ________________. But in Australia ________________.

read in bed / go to work At 11.00 pm in Britain ________________. But in Australia ________________.

2. **Complete the telephone conversation between Rajiv and Sunita.**

Rajiv: 'Hi, Sunita?'

Sunita: 'Rajiv! I tried to telephone you yesterday but you were never at home. What were you doing?'

Rajiv: 'What time did you ring?'

Sunita: 'Well, first I rang at 8.00 am—that's 5.30 pm in Australia.'

Rajiv: 'I ______ ____________ work.'

Sunita: 'Then I rang at 12.00 pm—that is 9.30 pm in Australia.'

Rajiv: 'Oh, I ______ ____________ coke with my friends.'

Sunita: 'Then I rang at 5.00 pm—oh dear, that's 2.30 am in Australia!'

Rajiv: 'Yes, I ______ ____________—or I was *trying* to sleep!'

3. Rajiv went for dinner last night with his friends. **Look at the picture and complete the sentences about what was happening when he arrived.**

Example:
(a) Tim/talk to Lisa Tim was talking to Lisa

(b) John and Jay/have an argument. ________________
(c) Jane/have a hamburger. ________________
(d) Mary and Louisa/dance. ________________
(e) Peter/drink a coke. ________________
(f) Tim and Jay/have pizza. ________________
(g) Tim and Lisa/sit on a bench. ________________
(h) Rajiv's friends/have a good time! ________________

4. **Write questions and short answers about the picture.**

Example:
(a) Tim/talk to Louisa? Was Tim talking to Louisa? No, he wasn't

(b) Jane/drink a coke? ________________? ____________
(c) Mary and Louisa/dance? ________________? ____________
(d) Tim and Lisa/eat? ________________? ____________
(e) Tim/sit? ________________? ____________
(f) Lisa/stand up? ________________? ____________
(g) Rajiv's friends/have a good time? ________________? ____________

5. **Communicative Activities.**
See Pg 138.

Past continuous and past simple

It *was raining* when I *left*

Contrasting past situations and events

Concept

Read this true story. You need to understand these words:

clamp: Look at the picture. If you park your car in the wrong place or leave it too long someone may put a **clamp** on your car, or **clamp** your car so that you cannot drive away.

steering wheel lock: Look at the picture. You can use a steering wheel lock to stop a thief driving your car away.

strike: If you want more money for doing your job you can **stop working** (or go on **strike**).

fine: If you park your car in the wrong place or leave it too long you may have to **pay some money** (or a **fine**).

I was feeling really tired and annoyed when I finally arrived home, at New Delhi Station. I was twenty four hours late because of a railway strike. I really needed to get home and sleep. I went to the railway car-park to get in my car but as I was walking across the car-park I saw a yellow clamp on my car! I couldn't believe it. The car park attendent was sleeping in his van when I woke him up. 'Take that clamp off my car!' I said. 'Sorry, sir. Your car has been here for more than twenty four hours. You have to pay a fine of Rs. 40,' he replied …

Match the sentences from the story with the time-line.

(**a**) I was feeling really tired.
= (1) or (2)? ______

(**b**) I finally arrived home.
= (1) or (2)? ______

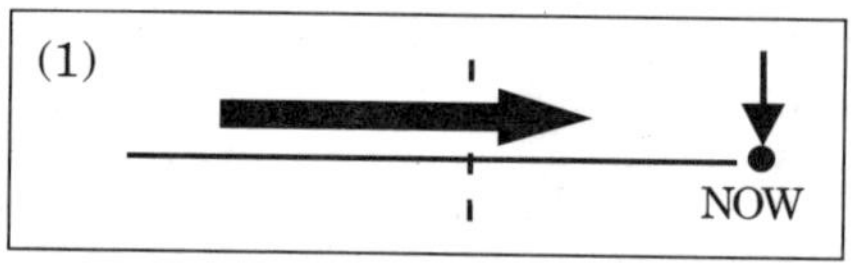

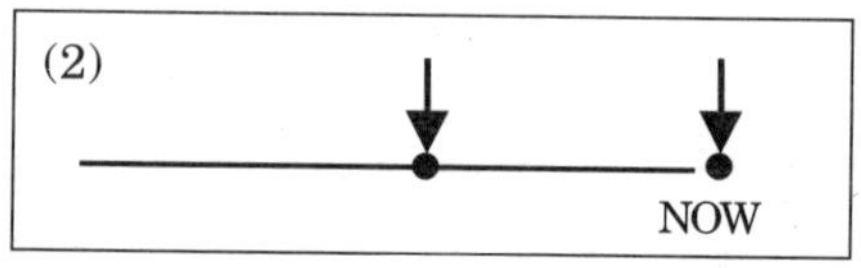

Was he feeling tired *before* the train arrived in New Delhi? Yes/No ______________

Did he *continue* feeling tired after the train arrived in New Delhi? Yes/No ______________

Which sentence describes the *background situation*? (**a**) or (**b**) ______

What *tense* is this sentence? ______________

Which sentence describes an *action* that happened *during* the background situation? (**a**) or (**b**) ______

What *tense* is this sentence? ______________

(**c**) The car-park attendent was sleeping. = (1) or (2)? ______

(**d**) I woke him up.
= (1) or (2)? ______

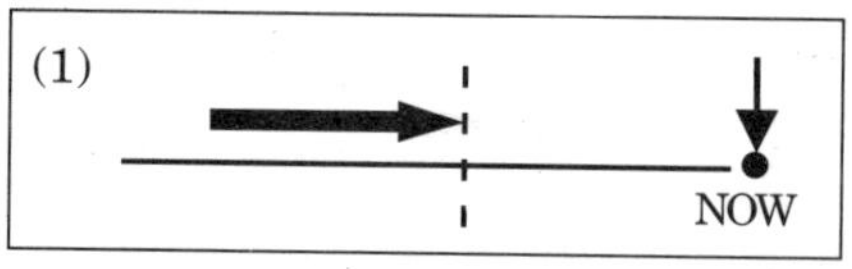

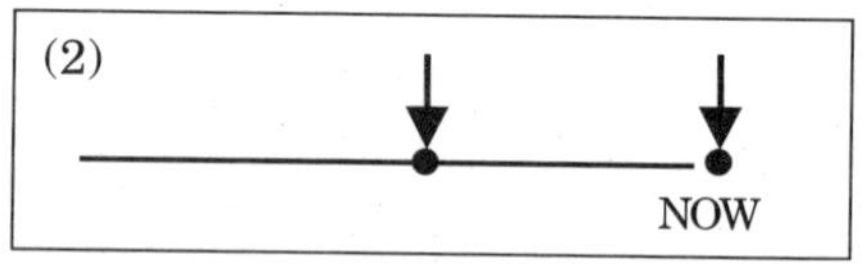

Was the car-park attendant sleeping *before* the man found him? Yes/No ______________

Did he *continue* sleeping after the man found him? Yes/No ______________

Which sentence describes the *background situation*? (**c**) or (**d**) ______

What *tense* is this sentence? ______________

Which sentence describes an *action* that happened *after* the background situation? (**c**) or (**d**) ______

What *tense* is this sentence? ______________

Structure

For the form of past continuous see Unit 32.
For the form of past simple see Unit 24.

Keys, Answers and Explanations Page No. 162

Exercise

1. Choose *past simple* or *past continuous* to complete the story.

… I explained that I was twenty four hours late because there was a railway strike.

'Sorry, sir,' he said, 'Rules are rules—Rs 40 please.'

I was so angry that while (**he was writing/he wrote**) the ticket for the fine (**I was going/I went**) to my car and (**taking out/took out**) my steering wheel lock and (**was locking/locked**) *his* steering wheel. 'Right,' I said. 'Now I can't move my car and you can't move your van!'

'I'll call the police!' he said. 'No, *I* will.' I replied and so we both called them.

But while we were waiting for the police to arrive (**he was saying/he said**), 'OK, you win' and (**he was taking/he took**) the clamp off my car. So I took off the steering wheel lock. I got in my car but as I was leaving (**the police were arriving/the police arrived**) and I had to stop and explain the whole story. They couldn't stop laughing. I don't know what they thought was so funny!'

2. The next morning the car-park attendent went home and told his wife the story.
Complete his story using *past simple* or *past continuous*.

Last night I (feel tired) was feeling tired. I (sleep) ____________ when this man (wake me up) ____________. He was really angry because his car had been clamped. While he (shout) ____________ at me I tried to tell him he had to pay a fine of Rs 40. As I (write) ____________ the ticket he (go) ____________ to his car and came back with a steering wheel lock and he locked my steering wheel! I could not believe it! I called the police—and so did he. While we (wait) ____________ for the police he got angrier and angrier. I felt quite scared so I decided to let him go. He (drive) ____________ away when the police (arrive) ____________ but he stopped to talk to them. For some reason the policemen thought the story was really funny.

3. Look at the examples and answer the questions.

(**a**) He drove away when the police arrived.
(**b**) He was driving away when the police arrived.
Which sentence means he *started* driving *before* the police arrived? ____________
Which sentence means he *started* driving *at the same time* as the police arrived? ____________

(**c**) I was feeling really tired and annoyed when I arrived home.
(**d**) I felt really tired and annoyed when I arrived home.
Which sentence means he *started* feeling tired and annoyed *before* he arrived home? ____________
Which sentence means he *started* feeling tired and annoyed *at the same time* as he arrived home? __________

4. Write sentences using *when* and the past simple and the past continuous to describe these pictures.

Example:
(I/drive home/see an accident) I was driving home when I saw an accident

(It/rain/I/arrive)
____
____

(I/read/the phone/ring)
____
____

(We/dance/the electricity/go out)
____
____

(They/rob a bank/the police/arrive)
____
____

(She/shop/she/meet him)
____
____

5. Communicative Activities.
See Pg 138.

Adjectives I

a *black* cat/a *big* house

Concept

Put the correct *adjective* under each picture.

A ______ cat.

A ______ cat.

(***white/black***)

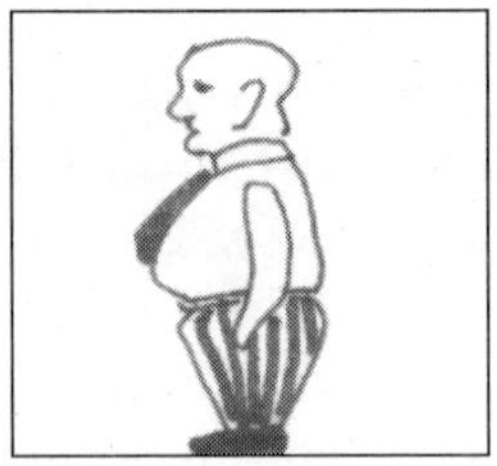

A ______ man.

A ______ man.

(***fat/thin***)

An ______ house.

A ______ house.

(***new/old***)

A ______ woman.

An ______ woman.

(***young/old***)

He is ______.

He is ______.

(***sad/happy***)

We are ______.

We are ______.

(***tall/short***)

Structure

Look at the examples above.
Does the adjective go *before* or *after* the noun? ____________
So, which is correct?—'*a big house*' or '*a house big?*' __________________

We can also make a sentence with the verb **to be** and an adjective:
Make sentences:

Example:	
He/thin	He's thin.

they/rich ________________________
it/cold ________________________
I/hungry ________________________*

*Careful! In English we **do not** say 'I have hunger'—we use an adjective.

Which is the correct plural?
A big house— '***big houses***', or '***bigs houses***'? ________________
So, in English the adjective **does not change** for plural.

Keys, Answers and Explanations Page No. 162

Exercise

1. Write the *opposite* of the adjectives. Choose from this list:

young sad poor hot exciting noisy easy bad fast cheap tall new

(a) quiet	noisy	(e) cold	__________	(i) short	__________
(b) expensive	__________	(f) good	__________	(j) happy	__________
(c) rich	__________	(g) difficult	__________	(k) old (people)	__________
(d) boring	__________	(h) slow	__________	(l) old (things)	__________

2. Rewrite the sentences using the *opposite* adjectives.

(a) The children are very quiet today. The children are very noisy today
(b) He bought an old car. It was very cheap. __________
(c) The weather was hot today. __________
(d) I love cold weather! __________
(e) This TV programme is really boring. __________
(f) This is an easy exercise. __________
(g) My aunt is really old. __________
(h) He wrote a really bad essay. __________
(i) The train is really slow. __________
(j) My brother is quite tall. __________
(k) He bought me a big present. __________

3. Remember we can put the adjective **before the noun (1) *or* use the verb 'to be' (2)**
Write (1) or (2) next to the sentences from exercise 2.

(a) The children are very quiet today. 2
(b) He bought an old car. It was very cheap. 1 and 2
(c) The weather was hot today. _______
(d) I love cold weather! _______
(e) This TV programme is really boring. _______
(f) This is an easy exercise. _______
(g) My aunt is really old. _______
(h) He wrote a really bad essay. _______
(i) The train is really slow. _______
(j) My brother is quite tall. _______
(k) He bought me a big present. _______

4. Put the words in brackets ( ) in the correct order to complete the postcard.

The weather (beautiful/really/is)
is really beautiful.
Brighton (is/an/town/exciting)
____
but it (quite/is/expensive)
__________.
Yesterday I went to see (play/great/a)
__________ at the theatre.
The actors (good/very/were)
__________.
Today I am going shopping. There are some (shops/wonderful) __________.
I want to buy (dress/new/a)
__________.
Then tomorrow we are going on a boat-trip—if (calm/the sea/is)
__________.

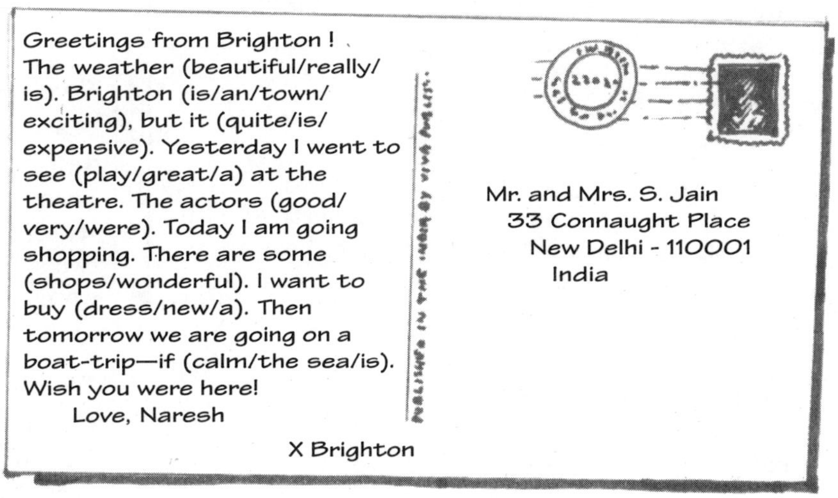

5. Communicative Activities.
See Pg 138.

UNIT 35

Adjectives II: Comparatives

bigger/better/more beautiful

Making **comparisons** between two things

Concept

Brasilia is the capital of Brazil but forty years ago the capital was Rio de Janeiro. Many Brazilians argue about which city is *better*.

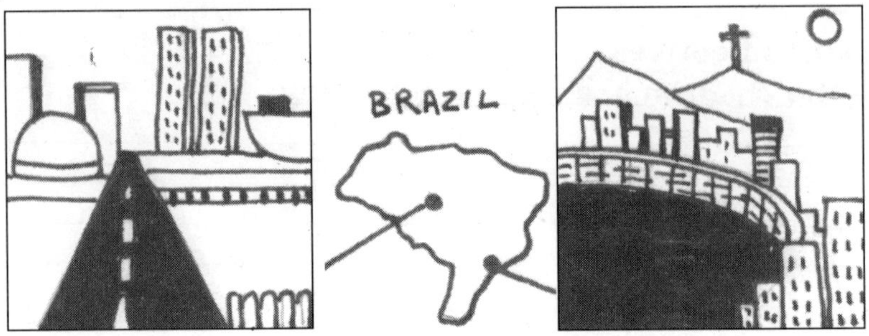

Julia is from Rio.
Rio is a much better place to live than Brasilia. It is bigger and certainly more beautiful. The hotels and restaurants are cheaper and it is hotter and nearer the sea. People say it is more dangerous than Brasilia—but I think Brasilia is worse.

Cristina is from Brasilia.
It is not true that Brasilia is uglier or more boring than Rio. It is just different! It is smaller but it is safer too—and the air is cleaner. It is further from the sea but we have beautiful river beaches. The beaches in Rio are dirtier than ours.

Structure

Write the underlined words from the texts next to the matching adjectives.
Then use the examples to *complete the rule*.

One syllable adjectives
clean *cleaner*
cheap ________
small ________
near ________

Rule: To make a comparative from adjectives with *one* syllable we add ________
Spelling
big ________ What happens to the last letter of the adjective? ________
hot ________ What happens to the last letter of the adjective? ________
safe ________ Do we need two 'e's? ________

-y adjectives
ugly ________
dirty ________
Rule: To make a comparative from adjectives with two syllables that **end in y** we change the 'y' to ________ and add ________

Two or more syllable adjectives
beautiful ________
dangerous ________
boring ________
Rule: To make a comparative from adjectives with two syllables that **DO NOT end in y** we use the word ________ before the adjective.

Irregular adjectives
good *better*
bad ________
far ________
(There are not many irregular adjectives but you need to learn them.)

We often use **'than'** with comparatives:
Rio is a much better place to live **than** Brasilia.
It is not true that Brasilia is uglier or more boring **than** Rio.
The beaches in Rio are dirtier **than** ours.

Keys, Answers and Explanations Page No. 163

Exercise

1. Divide these adjectives into *four* columns:

old easy important good
nice exciting cheap sunny
noisy warm quiet far
expensive tall lucky fast
comfortable heavy bad

-er	-ier	more...	irregular
old	*easy*	*important*	*good*

2. Correct any *spelling* mistakes you find.

Example:
(a) Rio is hoter than Brasilia × hotter

(b) Brasilia is smallier than Rio.
(c) Rio is nearer the sea than Brasilia.
(d) Brasilia is sunnyer than Rio.
(e) Rio is older than Brasilia.
(f) Rio is poorer than Brasilia.
(g) Rio is niceer than Brasilia.
(h) Brasilia is dryer than Rio.

3. Look at the information about York and Manchester.

Manchester
Population 438,500
Distance from London 300km
Cost of train to London £32

York
Population 300,000
Distance from London 320km
Cost of train to London £34

Complete the sentences about York and Manchester.
Use the **comparative form** of these adjectives: ***big/small/clean/dirty/cheap/expensive/far/near***

Example:
(a) Manchester is bigger than York.

(b) Manchester is _______ London than York.
(c) The train ticket from York to London is ______ than from Manchester to London.
(d) Manchester is ______ than York (look at the picture!).
(e) York is ______ than Manchester.
(f) York is ______ from London than Manchester.
(g) The train ticket from Manchester to London is ______ than from York to London.
(h) York is ______ than Manchester.

4. Look at the information about *Faro* and *Oporto*.

Oporto	
Population	700,000
Sunshine hours	1600 per year
Average temperature	58F
Rainfall	A lot

Faro	
Population	500,000
Sunshine hours	3000 per year
Average temperature	64F
Rainfall	Very little

Write sentences comparing Faro and Oporto.
Use the comparative form of the adjectives in brackets ( ).

Example:
(a) (big) Oporto is bigger than Faro.
(b) (small) Faro is smaller than Oporto.

(c) (sunny) ____________
(d) (cloudy) ____________
(e) (hot) ____________
(f) (cool) ____________
(g) (rainy) ____________
(h) (dry) ____________

5. Communicative Activities. Talk together about two cities in your country (countries). Compare them using some of the words in this unit.

UNIT 36

Adjectives III: Superlatives

the *biggest*/the *best*

Comparing something with **two or more other things**

Concept

Father: 'So, where do you want to go for a day out this weekend?'

Shiv: 'Can we go to Bolton Towers? They have got a new rollercoaster and it is **the fastest** in the world! It's much **faster** than the one at Courtney Amusement park—and that's **fast!**'

Father: 'Hmmm, it is probably very **expensive**. Is not Courtney Park **cheaper**? It is only Rs. 8 and Bolton Tower is Rs. 12!'

Mother: 'Well, **the cheapest** is probably Wondsworth Safari Park, that is Rs. 6—and it's much **more educational**. It is also **the nearest** to where we live.'

Shiv: 'Oh, Mother! Bolton Towers is much **more exciting**—all my friends are going there.'

Father: 'Exactly—so it will have **the longest** queues...'

Look at the sentences and answer the questions.

(a) The Courtney Park rollercoaster is **fast.**

(b) The Bolton Towers rollercoaster is **faster** (than the Courtney Park rollercoaster).

(c) The Bolton Towers rollercoaster is **the fastest** in the world.

Which sentence (a), (b) or (c) compares *one* rollercoaster to a *second* rollercoaster? b

Write the comparative adjective* in the sentence. faster

Which sentence compares *one* rollercoaster to *all* the other rollercoasters? ______

What is the superlative adjective in the sentence? ______

Which sentence just describes one rollercoaster? ______ *see Unit 35

What is the adjective** in the sentence? ______ **see Unit 34

(a) Bolton Towers is Rs. 12.	Which is **the most expensive**? ______
(b) Courtney Park is Rs. 8.	Which is **the cheapest**? ______
(c) Wondsworth Safari Park is Rs. 6.	Is Courtney Park **more expensive** than Wondsworth Safari Park? (Yes/No) ______

Structure

Complete the table using the examples from the advertisements and the dialogue.

ADJECTIVE	COMPARATIVE ADJECTIVE	SUPERLATIVE ADJECTIVE	
One syllable adjectives			
fast	faster	the fastest	*To make a superlative adjective from an adjective with one syllable we add* ________
cheap	________	________	
big	bigger	________	
near	nearer	the nearest	
long	longer	________	
Two syllables or more			
exciting	________	________	*To make a superlative adjective from an adjective with two syllables or more we add* ________
________	more expensive	the most expensive	
educational	________	the most educational	
comfortable	more comfortable	________	
Irregular			
good	better	________	
bad	worse	the worst	
far	further	the furthest	

Keys, Answers and Explanations Page No. 163

Exercise

1. Write the *superlative* form of these adjectives.

(a) beautiful the most beautiful.
(b) delicious ________
(c) cheap ________
(d) safe ________
(e) dangerous ________
(f) hot ________
(g) boring ________
(h) good ________
(i) large ________
(j) small ________
(k) relaxing ________
(l) expensive ________
(m) clean ________
(n) bad ________
(o) near ________

2. Look at these holiday advertisements and make sentences.

Hotel Boa Viagem
[5 minutes from the beach]
Recife, Brazil
14 nights Rs. 789

Hotel Thai
[20 minutes from the beach]
Phuket, Thailand
7 nights Rs. 632

Palm Hotel
[15 minutes from the beach]
Key West, Florida
10 nights Rs. 423

(a) Recife is (expensive) the most expensive holiday.
(b) Hotel Boa Viagem is (near) ________ to the beach.
(c) Recife is (long) ________ holiday.
(d) Hotel Thai is (far) ________ from the beach.
(e) Hotel Thai is (big) ________ hotel.
(f) Phuket is (short) ________ holiday.
(g) Key West is (cheap) ________ holiday.
(h) Palm Hotel is (small) ________ hotel.

3. Suresh and Shweta are deciding where to go on holiday: Brazil, Thailand or the United States. **Complete their conversation with the correct *superlative* form.**

Suresh: 'Well, I think (a) (good) the best place to go is Thailand. It is certainly (b) (cheap) ________ country and it has got (c) (beautiful) ________ beaches. The weather is wonderful—Bangkok is (d) (hot) ________ city in the world.'
Shweta: 'But Brazil has beautiful beaches too and I think it is (e) (relaxing) ________ place.'
Suresh: 'Relaxing! It is (f) (dangerous) ________! We will probably get shot!'
Shweta: 'Rubbish! The United States is (g) (bad) ________. Florida is really dangerous for tourists.'
Suresh: 'So, let us go to Thailand. It's (h) (safe) ________. It is (i) (interesting) ________ place too—a completely different culture. And the food is (j) (delicious) ________ in the world.'
Shweta: 'Well, yes, American food is probably (k) (boring) ________ all hamburgers and steaks and it is (I) (expensive) ________ place to go too.'

4. Correct the mistakes you find.

(a) Brazil is the most far place. the furthest
(b) French food is the goodest in the world. ________
(c) Bangkok is the hottest city in the world. ________
(d) Madame Tussauds is the interestingest thing to see in London. ________
(e) Are you the most old in your family? ________
(f) I sat in the comfortablest chair. ________

5. Correct the *spelling* mistakes you find.

(a) Tokyo is the bigest city in Japan. biggest
(b) Jonny is the noisyest student in the class! ________
(c) I answered the easiest question. ________
(d) The fasttest car won the race. ________
(e) Jane and Sue are both thin but Mary is the thinest. ________
(f) Who is the busyest person in the office? ________

6. Communicative Activities.
See Pg 139.

UNIT 37

Adverbs II: Manner

Describing **how** we do something

Don't speak so quickly

Concept

A ghost story: It was a cold night. The wind blew noisily around the house. Mrs Kumar climbed up the stairs slowly. The house was dark and she was holding a long candle. At the top of the stairs she heard a strange voice. 'Welcome', it said, quietly. Mrs Kumar was really frightened. She started to run quickly down the stairs. Suddenly the candle went out. Mrs Kumar screamed loudly...

Divide the underlined words from the story into verbs and nouns

Example:	
night	noun
blew	verb

climbed ____________
house ____________
candle ____________
voice ____________
said ____________
Mrs Kumar ____________
run ____________
went out ____________
screamed ____________

An **adjective** describes a *noun.*
(Problems with adjectives? See Unit 33)
What *adjectives* describe the nouns above?

Example:		
cold	night	(It was a *cold* night.)

__________ house
__________ candle
__________ voice
__________ Mrs Kumar

An **adverb** describes a verb. It says *how* something happens. **What *adverbs* describe the verbs above?**

Example:		
blew	noisily	(The wind blew *noisily* around the house.)

climbed __________
said __________
run __________
went out __________
screamed __________

Structure

Is **'quick'** an adjective, or an adverb? __________
Is **'quickly'** an adjective, or an adverb? __________
What do we usually ***add*** to an ***adjective*** to make an ***adverb***? __________
noisy - noisily: what happens to the *spelling* when the adjective ends in -y? ____________

What are the *adverbs* from these *adjectives?* Careful! They are all *irregular.*

ADJECTIVE	ADVERB
Example:	
I am a **good** tennis player.	I play tennis well.
This is a **fast** car.	He drives __________.
This unit is quite **hard.**	You need to work __________ to learn English!
I am always **late.**	He arrived __________ again.

Does an *adjective* usually go *before*, or *after*, the *noun*? __________
Does an *adverb* usually go *before*, or *after*, the *verb*? __________

Keys, Answers and Explanations Page No. 164

Exercise

1. Make these *adjectives* into *adverbs*.

(a) bad	badly	(e) angry	________	(i) silent	________
(b) good	________	(f) quiet	________	(j) violent	________
(c) easy	________	(g) noisy	________		
(d) careful	________	(h) slow	________		

2. Read the dialogue and write *how* they said the sentences.

'I am really looking forward to our holiday,' she said (happy) happily.

'Er, do you think we have enough money to go on holiday, darling?' he asked (nervous) ______.

'Of course we do!' she said, (confident) ______.

'But, have you forgotten we have got to pay for the new car?' he asked, (quiet) ______.

'I thought you did that last month!' she shouted, (angry) ______.

'No, we had to pay for your new clothes last month—Rs. 500!' he replied, (cross) ______.

'Oh, well, no holiday, then' she said (sad) ______.

3. Use an *adverb* to write another sentence about the situations.

(a) It was an **accident.**	He did it accidentally.
(b) His laugh was **wicked.**	He laughed ________________.
(c) His English is **fluent.**	He speaks English ________________.
(d) She is very **polite.**	She behaves ________________.
(e) They wear **different** clothes.	They dress ________________.
(f) He is **good** at singing.	He sings ________________.
(g) It was **easy** for him to win.	He won ________________.
(h) She was **happy** when she laughed.	She laughed ________________.

4. Choose an *adjective* or *adverb*.

Driving in Kolkata is not (a) (*easy/easily*). The traffic moves very (b) (*slow/slowly*) in central Kolkata—about 12 km per hour. You also need to drive (c) (*careful/carefully*) because some drivers are very (d) (*impatient/impatiently*) and drive (e) (*dangerous/dangerously*.) Another problem is finding a place to park. Car-parks are very (f) (*expensive/expensively.*) It is often better to leave your car outside the city centre and then you can (g) (*easy/easily*) travel into the centre on public transport. The buses and the metro railway are very (h) (*good/well*).

There are lots of (i) (*excellent/excellently*) restaurants in Kolkata and—if you have the money—you can eat very (j) (*good/well*). In Kolkata you can eat Indian, Thai, French, Chinese food ... everything!

5. Communicative Activities.

See Pg 132.

Present tenses for future use

I am meeting Raj tonight/ the train *leaves* at 6 o'clock

Talking about **arrangements;** talking about **programmes** and **timetables**

Concept

***Look* at the dialogues and *answer* the questions.**

Shyam: 'What time are we leaving **(a)** tomorrow?'
Ria: 'Well, the plane leaves **(b)** at 10.00, so we should leave at 6.00.'
Shyam: 'Are we meeting **(c)** John and Susie at the airport?'
Ria: 'No, they are coming **(d)** here first.'

Ritu: 'What are you doing **(e)** tonight?'
Mina: 'I am going **(f)** to the cinema with Wasim.'
Ritu: 'What time does the film start? **(g)**'
Mina: '7.00.'

Hari: 'When is Anuj going **(h)** back to school?'
Radha: 'School starts **(i)** on 6th January.'

What are the names of the two **tenses** underlined above? ________________ and ________________
In these examples are they talking about ***present*** **time** or ***future*** **time**? ____________________

Which sentences are talking about ***an arrangement between people***? (a)___ ___ ___ ___ ___ ___
What *tense* are they? ____________________

Which sentences are talking about ***an event happening at a specific time/on a specific date***?
(b)___ _______ _______
What *tense* are they? ____________________

Structure

For the ***form*** of the present simple and present continuous see Units 5 and 18.

Keys, Answers and Explanations Page No. 164

Exercise

1. Mr Joshi is going on a business trip to Jakarta. **Look at his desk.**

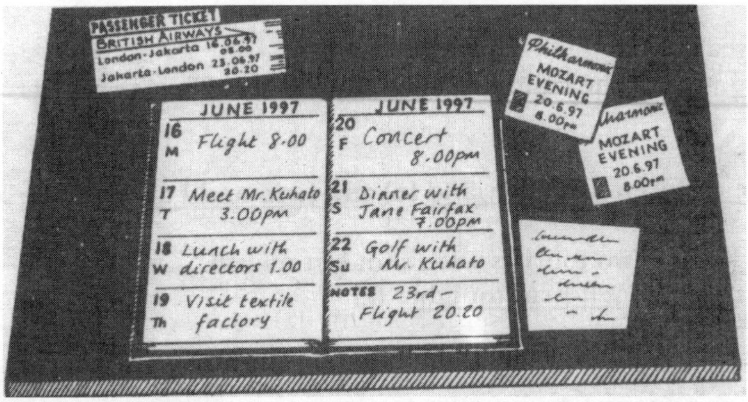

Write sentences about his arrangements using *present simple* and *continuous*.

(a) The plane (leave) <u>leaves</u> at 8.00 on 16th June.
(b) Mr Joshi (meet) ______________ Mr Kuhato at 3.00 pm on 17th June.
(c) He (have) ______________ lunch with the Directors at 1.00 on 18th June.
(d) On 19th June he (visit) ______________ a textile factory.
(e) On 20th June he (go) ______________ to a concert.
(f) The concert (start) ______________ at 8.00pm.
(g) On the 21st June he (have) ______________ dinner with Jane Fairfax.
(h) On the 22nd June he (play) ______________ golf with Mr Kuhato.
(i) The plane back to London (leave) ______________ at 20.20 on the 23rd June.

2. Complete the questions about Mr Joshi's business trip.

(a) What time/the plane/leave London? <u>What time does the plane leave London?</u>
(b) Who/he/meet on 17th June? ______________________________
(c) What/he/do on 18th June? ______________________________
(d) Where/he/visit on 19th June? ______________________________
(e) What time/the concert start? ______________________________
(f) When/he/have dinner with Jane Fairfax? ______________________________
(g) What/he/do on 22nd June? ______________________________
(h) What time/the plane back to London/leave? ______________________________

3. Find the mistakes—*using the wrong tense*—and *correct* them.

Nita: 'When are you leaving for Jakarta?'
Mr Joshi: 'Well, the plane (a) <u>is leaving</u> at 8.00 am so I (b) <u>stay</u> with friends near the airport.'
Nita: 'What time (c) <u>does the plane</u> arrive in Jakarta?'
Mr Joshi: 'About 2.00 pm, local time. I (d) <u>meet</u> Mr Kuhato at 3.00 pm.'
Nita: '(e) <u>Do you visit</u> the textile factory?'
Mr Joshi: 'Yes, on the 19th. I have got lots of meetings but also time for some relaxation. (f) <u>I am playing</u> golf with Mr Kuhato on the 22nd, for example.'
Nita: 'When (g) <u>are you coming back</u>?'
Mr Joshi: 'On the 23rd. The plane (h) <u>is landing</u> at Heathrow Airport at 3.00 am on the 24th. Too early in the morning!'

(a) __________
(b) __________
(c) __________
(d) __________
(e) __________
(f) __________
(g) __________
(h) __________

4. Communicative Activities.
See Pg 132.

UNIT 39

Going to/Will—I

***I am going* to be a doctor/ *I will ring* you tonight**

Decisions taken **previously**, and **now**, about **the future**

Concept

Jay: 'Where are you going on holiday this year?'
Ravi: 'We are going to Florida and Disneyland. **(a)** *[1] The children are really excited. They are going to meet Mickey Mouse!' **(b)**
Jay: 'What are you and Nidhi going to do there?'
Ravi: 'Well, our cousins are going to take the children to Disneyland **(c)** and Nidhi and I are going to lie on the beach.' **(d)**
Jay: 'It is quite dangerous at the beach, you know. Two tourists were shot last month.'
Ravi: 'Really?! We will not go to the beach then! **(e)** I will tell Nidhi tonight.' **(f)**

Look at the underlined sentences.

Which sentences show what Ravi decided **about the future *before*** the conversation with Jay?
(a) ________ ________ ________
Does he use **going to** or **will**? ________
Which sentences show what Ravi decided **about the future *during*** the conversation with Jay?
(e) ________
Does he use **going to** or **will**? ________

Structure

GOING TO

Complete the rule using these words: VERB 'TO BE' (is/am/are) **GOING TO**

To make the **going to** future we use
SUBJECT (I/you/he, etc) + ____________ + ____________ + **INFINITIVE** (eat/drink, etc)

Make these sentences using 'going to' into questions

Example:	
They are going to take the children.	Are they going to take the children?

He is going to lie on the beach. ______________________________?
We are going to visit Disneyland. ______________________________?

WILL

What is the form of will for I/you/he/she/it/we/they (all persons)*[2]? ______________
What is the **negative** form of will? ______________

Write the contractions.

Example:
I will I'll

You will	____________	It will	____________
He will	____________	We will	____________
She will	____________	They will	____________

Which sentence is correct? (only one)

I think I'll **go** to the cinema. ________ (× ✓)
I think I'll **to go** to the cinema. ________ (× ✓)
I think I'll **going** to the cinema. ________ (× ✓)

*[1] When the infinitive is *go* we **do not** usually say 'I am ***going to go*** to Florida' because it is too long! We say '***I am going***' to Florida.
*[2] Some people say '**I shall**' and '**We shall**' but we normally only use 'shall' in offers and suggestions.

Examples:	Shall I open the window?
	Shall we go to the cinema?

Keys, Answers and Explanations Page No. 165

Exercise

1. Fatima is an advertising manager. She works very hard but **next week** she is going on a really relaxing holiday to Sri Lanka. She wants to completely forget about work.

Write sentences about what she *is going to do* or *not going to do*.

(a) lie on the beach — She is going to lie on the beach.
(b) take her mobile phone — She is not going to take her mobile phone.
(c) sleep late every day ______
(d) take her lap-top computer ______
(e) telephone her office every day ______
(f) eat delicious healthy food ______
(g) go scuba diving ______
(h) have a really good time ______

2. These are some of the things Fatima is thinking as she lies on the beach. **Match each one with a verb and write what she *decides to* do.**

go in the shade	have something to drink	go for a swim
have something to eat	put on some suncream	read a book

(a) 'I feel hungry.' — 'I will have something to eat.'
(b) 'The sun is really hot.' ______
(c) 'I feel thirsty.' ______
(d) 'I think I am burning.' ______
(e) 'The sea looks wonderful.' ______
(f) 'I am bored.' ______

3. Choose *going* to or *will* to complete the dialogue.

Minu: 'What (are you going to do/will you do) next week Fatima?'
Fatima: 'Didn't I tell you? (I am going [to go]/I'll go) on holiday.'
Minu: 'You lucky thing! Where (are you going [to go]/will you go?)'
Fatima: 'Sri Lanka. (Are you going [to go]/will you go) anywhere this year?'
Minu: 'I don't know yet. Maybe we (are going to visit/will visit) friends in Wales.'
Fatima: 'Well, (I am going to send/I will send) you a postcard!'
Minu: 'Thanks!'

4. Complete Fatima's postcards with '*will*' or '*am going to*'.

Dear Minu,

Having a lovely time in Sri Lanka. Tomorrow I am going to visit an old palace in the jungle but today it is really hot so I think I ______ just lie on the beach. It is so relaxing! I ______ ring you when I get back, OK?

Love, Fatima

Dear Mother and Father,

I am really enjoying my holiday in Sri Lanka. I ______ stay here three weeks and really relax. Next week I ______ go on a trip into the jungle.—Don't worry! I ______ be very careful!

Love, Fatima

5. Communicative Activities.
See Pg 132.

UNIT 40

Going to/Will—II

Making **predictions**

it's *going to* rain/you'*ll* (*will*) be rich

Concept

Does the gipsy ***know for certain*** the man will get a good job? ______

Does the gipsy ***know for certain*** the man will have a happy and prosperous life? ______

Does the man ***know for certain*** that the crystal ball is going to fall? ______

How does the man know? What can he *see*? ______________________________

In the first picture does she ***know for certain*** that they will have to get some more petrol? ________

In the second picture does she ***know for certain*** that they are going to have to get some more petrol? ________

How does she know? What can she *see*? ______________________________

So, do we use **will** or **going to** when we are ***guessing*** (***or predicting***) about the future? ________

So, do we use **will** or **going to** when we can ***see now*** that something is ***certain*** to happen in the future? ________

Structure

For the form of **going to** and **will** see Unit 39.

Keys, Answers and Explanations Page No. 165

Exercise

1. Look at these pictures from the film *'The Adventurer'*. Complete the sentences about what you can see **is going to** happen and what probably **will** happen.

(a) the train/come
The train is going to come.
the hero/rescue her
The hero will rescue her.

(b) they/fight
___
one of them die
___

(c) they/fall in love
___
they get married
___

(d) he/fall
___
he/die
___

(e) he/ask her to marry him
___
she/say 'Yes'
___

(f) he/give her flowers
___
she/be happy
___

2. Make *questions* from the sentences in exercise 1.

(a) Is the train going to come?
Will the hero rescue her?
(b) ___?
___?
(c) ___?
___?
(d) ___?
___?
(e) ___?
___?
(f) ___?
___?

3. The Director of the film is explaining to the actors what's going to happen in a scene. **Complete the dialogue using *'going to'*.**

Director: 'OK, in this scene the villain (kidnap) is going to kidnap the heroine and he (tie) ___ her to the train tracks. She (scream) ___ very loudly and, before the train comes, the hero (hear) ___ her screaming and rescue her.'
Actor: 'they (fall in love) ___?
Director: 'Yes, but first the hero and villain (fight) ___.'
Actor: 'the hero (win) ___?'
Director: 'Of course!'

4. What do you *think* will happen at the end of the film? Make sentences using *'will'*.

(a) The hero (kill) the villain. The hero will kill the villain.
(b) The villain (apologise) and the hero (not kill) him. ___
(c) The heroine (be) very happy. ___
(d) The hero and heroine (get married). ___
(e) They (live) happily ever after. ___
(f) They (have) two children. ___

5. Communicative Activities.
See Pg 139.

Present perfect I: experience

***Have* you ever *been* to China?**

Talking about a **non-definite** time in the past

Concept

Katha is an English Teacher. She **has been** to lots of different countries.
Look at her photos. Where **has** she **been**? She's **been** to:

Budapest

Prague

Paris

Berlin

Riga

Do you know **when** she went to these places? ***Yes / No*** What **tense** is 'She has been'? ______
'**Been**' is the past participle * of the verb '______'.

*The past participle is the third part of the verb—there is a list of irregular past participles in Appendix 1.

Interviewer: 'Katha, **have** you ever **been** to Paris?'
Katha: 'Yes, **I have.** Actually, **I have been** there five or six times. I first went there in 1985 and fell in love with it!'
Interviewer: 'What other cities **have** you **visited**?'
Katha: 'Well, **I have been** to most of the big cities in Europe, but **I have** never **been** to Moscow. I went to St Petersburg last year though.'
Interviewer: 'Did you visit the Winter Palace when you were in St Petersburg?'
Katha: 'Yes, of course.'
Interviewer: '**Have** you **been** to Seoul?'
Katha: 'No, **I have not. I have not been** to South East Asia. Maybe next year!'

'**I have been** there five or six times.'—Do you know **when**? ***Yes / No***
What **tense** does she use? ***Present Perfect*** or ***Simple Past?*** ______
'I first went there in 1985'—Do you know **when**? ***Yes / No***
What **tense** does she use? ***Present Perfect*** or ***Simple Past***? ______
'Did you visit the Winter Palace when you were in St Petersburg?'
Is the interviewer talking about **a definite time** in the past? ***Yes / No***
'***Have*** you **been** to Seoul?'
Is the interviewer talking about **a definite time** in the past? ***Yes / No***

Structure

Positive
'She **has been** to lots of different countries.'
'**I have been** there five or six times.'
The positive form of Present Perfect is:
Subject + has or ______ + past participle
(been/visited/eaten, etc)

Question
'**Have** you **been** to Seoul?'
'Where **has** she **been**?'
The question form of Present Perfect is:
______ **or** ______ **+ subject +** ______

Negative
I have not been to South East Asia.
The negative form of Present Perfect is:
subject + ______ **or have + not +** ______

Short answers
Yes, **I have.**

Keys, Answers and Explanations Page No. 166

Exercise

UNIT 41

1. Write the past participle of the verbs (Look in Appendix 1 if you are not sure).

> ***Example:***
> (a) be - been (b) break - broken

(c) buy - ______
(d) come - ______
(e) cut - ______
(f) drink - ______
(g) drive - ______
(h) eat - ______
(i) fall - ______
(j) forget - ______
(k) get - ______
(l) give - ______
(m) go - ______ or ______
(n) have - ______
(o) know - ______
(p) make - ______
(q) meet - ______
(r) read - ______
(s) see - ______
(t) speak - ______
(u) steal - ______
(v) take - ______
(w) think - ______
(x) write - ______

2. Look at the table to complete the *questions* and *short answers.*

	eat snails	*read Shakespeare*	*meet the President*	*drive a lorry*	*go to Australia*
Samir	✓	✓	×	✓	×
Katha	✓	×	✓	✓	✓
Rohit and Jaya	×	✓	✓	×	×

> ***Example:***
> (a) Has Samir ever eaten snails?
> Yes, he has.

(b) ______ Katha ever ______ Shakespeare? ________

(c) ______ Rohit and Jaya ever ______ the President? ________

(d) ________ Samir ________ a lorry? ________

(e) ________ Katha ________ to Australia? ________

(f) ________ Rohit and Jaya ________ snails? ________

3. Make questions to match the answers

> ***Examples:***
> (a) You/eat/snails? — Have you (ever) eaten snails? — Yes, I have.
> (b) Where/you/eat them? — Where did you eat them — In France.

(c) Rohit and Jaya/meet the President? ________________? Yes, they have.
(d) When/they/meet him? ________________? Last year.
(e) Samir/read/Shakespeare? ________________? Yes, he has.
(f) What/he/read? ________________? Hamlet.
(g) Katha/drive/a lorry? ________________? Yes, she has.
(h) When/she/drive it? ________________? A few years ago.
(i) You/meet the President? ________________? Yes, I have.
(j) Where/you/meet him? ________________? At Rashtrapati Bhavan.

4. Choose the correct form of the verb.

> ***Example:***
> (a) Have you *went / been* to China? — Have you been to China?

(b) I have *been / went* there last year.
(c) I have never *ate / eaten* sushi.
(d) *Has / have* she been to France?
(e) They *has / have* travelled all over the world.

5. Communicative Activities.
See Pg 139.

Present perfect II: time up to now

I have worked here since November

Talking about something that **started in the past** and **continues up to now**

Concept

Jeetu is Indian but he lives in Venezuela.

Interviewer: 'How long have you lived in Venezuela?'

Jeetu: 'Well, I came here in 1991, so I have been here for six years now.'

Interviewer: 'You must like it here. Are you going to stay?'

Jeetu: 'Yes, I have been married to a Venezuelan since 1993. It is a great country—I love the people, the weather…'

Jeetu ***lives*** in Venezuela. Is this talking about **now,** or the **past** ? ________

Jeetu ***came*** to Venezuela **in 1991**. Is this talking about **now,** or the **past**? ________

Jeetu ***has lived*** in Venezuela **for six years**. Is this talking about **now, the past,** or **now and the past**? ________

Jeetu ***is married***. Is this talking about **now,** or the **past**? ________

Jeetu ***got married*** **in 1993**. Is this talking about **now,** or the **past**?

Jeetu ***has been married*** **since 1993.** Is this talking about **now, the past,** or **now *and* the past**?

____

Match sentences (a) and (b) with time-line (1) or (2).

(a) I have been married **since 1993.** (1 or 2?)

(b) I have been married **for four years.** (1 or 2?)

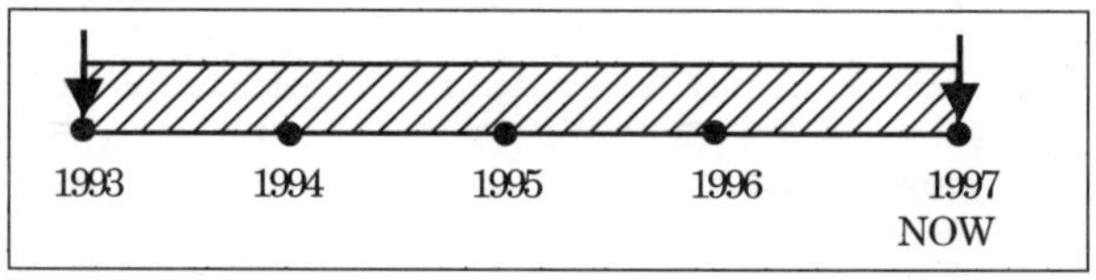

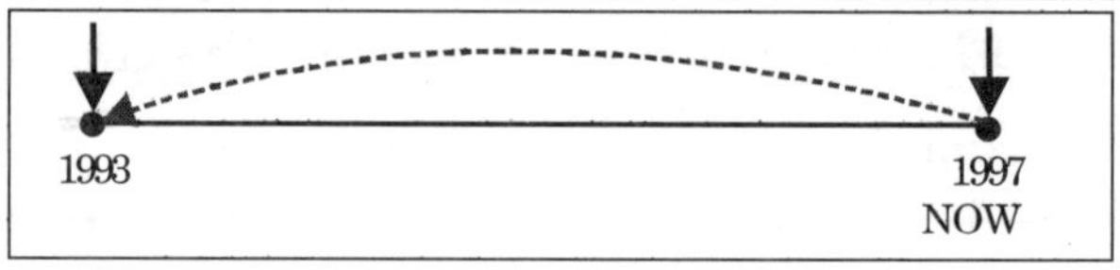

Divide these time expressions into *since* and *for*:

last February	a long time	1989	two months	a week ago	I was born
yesterday	a couple of hours	9.00	three years		

since	**for**
Example: last February	***Example:*** a long time
________	________
________	________
________	________
________	
________	

Structure

For the form of present perfect see Unit 41.

Keys, Answers and Explanations Page No. 166

Exercise

1. Complete the sentences using the underlined verb and *for* or *since*.

> ***Examples:***
> (a) It is June. Ravi is in England. He arrived in England in March.
> Ravi has been in England since March.
> Ravi has been in England for three months.

(b) It is 1997. Deepak and Sumitra know Peter. They met him in 1995.
Deepak and Sumitra ______ Peter ______1995.
Deepak and Sumitra ______ Peter ______ two years.

(c) It is 1997. I have a cat. I bought the cat in 1996.
I ______ a cat ______ a year.
I ______ a cat ______ last year.

(d) It is 1997. Sheila lives in Maldives. She came to Maldives in 1993.
She ______ in Maldives ______ 1993.
She ______ in Maldives ______ four years.

(e) It is November 30th. Shyam is 21. His birthday was 16th November.
Shyam ______21______ two weeks.
Shyam ______ 21 ______16th November.

(f) It is April. We work in Chennai. We started working in Chennai in January.
We ______ in Chennai ______ January.
We ______ in Chennai ______ three months.

2. Make questions about the situations in exercise 1.

> ***Example:***
> (a) How long/Ravi/be/in England? How long has Ravi been in England?

(b) How long Deepak and Sumitra/know/Peter? ______________________
(c) How long/you/have/cat? ______________________
(d) How long/Sheila/live/in Maldives? ______________________
(e) How long/Shyam/be/21? ______________________
(f) How long/you/work/in Chennai? ______________________

3. Make negative sentences using ... not ... long.

> ***Example:***
> (a) He/be married He has not been married long.

(b) We/live in England. ______________________
(c) They/work here. ______________________
(d) I/be a teacher. ______________________
(e) She/have a car. ______________________
(f) He/know her. ______________________
(g) You/be married. ______________________

4. Complete the texts with the verb in the *correct form.*

Jan (has been/is) a teacher for ten years. She (has become/became) a teacher when she left university in 1987. She likes travelling and (went/has been) all over the world. Last year she (went/has been) to China.

My wife and I (got married/have got married) in 1976, so we (have been married/are married) for more than twenty years now. When we got married we (lived/have lived) with my wife's mother but we (have bought/bought) this house fifteen years ago and since then we (have lived/live) here.

5. Communicative Activities.

See Pg 132.

Present perfect III: present result

They *have* lost their keys

Talking about an action in the **past** with a result **now**

Concept

Hari went skiing *last weekend* for the first time. It was terrible!

He fell off the ski-lift and cut his head.

He fell over and broke his leg.

Never again!

Now he is recovering at home.

Look at the pictures and answer the questions.

When did he break his leg? ______________________

Is this talking about the **past** or the **present?**______________________

Is his leg still broken **now?**______________________

Is this talking about the **past** or the **present**? ______________________

He **has broken** his leg.

Is this talking about the **past**, the **present**, or a **past action with a present result?** ______

When did he cut his head? ______________________

Is this talking about the **past** or the **present?** ______________________

Is his head still cut **now?**______________________

Is this talking about the **past** or the **present?** ______________________

'He **has cut** his head.'

Is this talking about the **past**, the **present,** or a **past action with a present result**?

____

Structure

For the form of the Present Perfect Simple see Unit 41.

Keys, Answers and Explanations Page No. 167

Exercise

1. Write the *past participle* of these verbs. (Look up any new words in your dictionary.)

(a) hurt hurt
(b) break ________
(c) burn ________
(d) drink ________
(e) sprain ________
(f) catch (measles) ________
(g) watch ________
(h) cut ________
(i) bump ________

2. Vineet is at the hospital, waiting to see the doctor. **Write sentences about what you can see *has happened* to the other people in the waiting room.** Use the verbs from exercise 1.

(a) He has bumped his head.
(b) ________________ too much television!
(c) ________________ poison by accident.
(d) ________________ measles.
(e) ________________ his ankle.
(f) ________________ his arm.
(g) ________________ his leg.
(h) ________________ her finger.
(i) ________________ her back.

3. Choose *simple past* or *present perfect.*

(a) I (lost/have lost) my keys—I cannot get into my house! I have lost my keys.
(b) I (broke/have broken) my leg, but it is OK again now. ________________
(c) I (ate/have eaten) too much. I feel sick. ________________
(d) He (fell/has fallen) over—help him to stand up! ________________
(e) I (won/have won). Shall we play again? ________________
(f) Duncan (arrived/has arrived) early but he has gone now. ________________
(g) Why are you wet? (Did you go/Have you been) swimming? ________________

4. Complete the sentences with *simple past* or *present perfect.*

(a) '(you/eat) enough? Have you eaten enough?
'Yes, thanks. It was delicious.'
(b) 'Why is the dog barking?'
'Because the post (arrive) ________________'
(c) 'Oh no! It is raining and I (forgot) ________________ my umbrella!'
(d) 'She (dye) ________________ her hair purple but her mother did not like it so she (dye) ________________ it brown again now.'
(e) 'She (miss) ________________ the train so she caught a bus instead.'
(f) 'Your shoes look new. (you/clean) them? ________________'
(g) 'I (feel) ________________ terrible this morning but now my headache (go) ________________'

Communicative Activities.
See Pg 140.

Present perfect IV: 'yet' and 'already'

Happened? or **going to** happen?

I have *already* been to Germany

Concept

Dia is travelling around Central Europe.

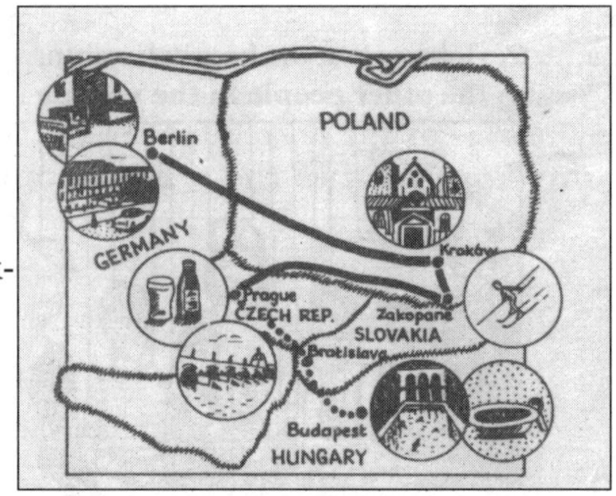

Interviewer: 'Why did you decide to come to Central Europe?'
Dia: 'Oh, I think it is fascinating. There are so many things to do and see.'
Interviewer: 'What have you done so far?'
Dia: 'Well I have **already** been to Germany. I have walked along Unter den Linden and visited Checkpoint Charlie.'
Interviewer: 'Have you been to Poland **yet**?'
Dia: 'Yes I have seen Krakow and been skiing in Zakopane. It was beautiful!'
Interviewer: 'What are you going to do next?'
Dia: 'Well, I have **already** been to Czech but I have not been to Slovakia or Hungary **yet**. I am really looking forward to visiting the Thermal Baths in Budapest and eating lots of goulash!'

Look at the examples of ***yet*** and ***already.***
Which means something *has happened* before now? 'Yet' or 'already'?______
Which means something has *not happened* before now, but it is *going to happen?* 'Yet' or 'already'? ______

Look at the map and the dialogue and complete the chart with the things Dia *has done* or *wants to do*:

ALREADY DONE	NOT DONE **YET**	
walked along Unter den Linden	visited Bratislava	walked along Unter den Linden
______________	______________	visited Checkpoint Charlie
______________	______________	seen Krakow
______________		been skiing in Zakopane
______________		crossed the Charles Bridge in Prague
______________		drunk Czech beverage
		visited Bratislava
		eaten goulash
		visited the Thermal Baths in Budapest

Structure

Look at the examples and complete the form:
'I have already been to Czech' SUBJECT + ______/______+______+ PAST PARTICIPLE
We usually use **already** *in* ***positive sentences.***

'Have you been to Poland yet? ______/______+ SUBJECT + PAST PARTICIPLE + ______?
'I have not been to Hungary yet.' ______ + HAVE NOT/HAS NOT + ______ + ______.
We usually use **yet** *in* ***questions*** *and* ***negative sentences.***

Make sentences about what Dia *has done or wants to do.*

ALREADY DONE	NOT DONE **YET**
She's already walked along Unter den Linden.	She hasn't visited Bratislava yet.
______________	______________
______________	______________
______________	
______________	
______________	

Keys, Answers and Explanations Page No. 167

Exercise

A Weekend in Krakow

Saturday

10.00 am: Tour of the Old Town
1.00 pm: Lunch at Ariel's in Kazimierz, the Jewish Quarter
3.00 pm: Free for shopping (Visit the Sukiennice Market)
6.00 pm: Chopin Concert
8.00 pm: Traditional evening meal at Staropolska Restaurant.

Sunday

10.00 am: Visit Wawel Castle
1.00 pm: Lunch at the Cafe Jama Michalika
2.30 pm: Trip to Wieliczka Salt Mines

1. Dia is spending a weekend in Krakow, Poland. *It is now 8.00 pm on Saturday.* Complete the sentences about her trip using *yet* and *already*.

(a) see the Old Town She has already seen the Old Town.
(b) have lunch at Ariel's ____________________
(c) go shopping ____________________
(d) visit the Sukiennice ____________________
(e) hear the Chopin Concert ____________________
(f) eat at Staropolska Restaurant ____________________
(g) visit Wawel Castle ____________________
(h) have lunch at the Cafe Jama Michalika ____________________
(i) go on a trip to Wieliczka Salt Mines ____________________

2. Make *questions* and write *short answers* about her trip so far using *yet*.

(a) see the Old Town Has she seen the Old Town yet? Yes, she has.
(b) go shopping ____________________? __________
(c) visit Wieliczka ____________________? __________
(d) see Wawel Castle ____________________? __________
(e) hear the Chopin Concert ____________________? __________
(f) have dinner at Staropolska Restaurant ____________________? __________

3. Put the words in the *right order* to *make sentences*.

(a) already/have/seen/I/the museum I have already seen the museum.
(b) you/yet/been/have/to Prague? ____________________
(c) has not/she/eaten/*pierogi*/yet ____________________
(d) lots of photos/have/I/already/taken ____________________
(e) spent/much money/I/have not/yet ____________________
(f) I/already/been/have/to the Castle ____________________
(g) has not/she/the bridge/crossed yet ____________________
(h) Dia/visited/Bratislava/yet/has? ____________________

4. Communicative Activities.

A: You are on a Round the World Trip. Look at the map and the instructions on page 140.
B: You are on a Round the World Trip. Look at the map and the instructions on page 144.

UNIT 45

Questions Revision 1: Asking questions by changing the word order

is/are/was/can/were/will

Concept

(a) Can you play the piano?	(f) Can I borrow Rs. 500?
(b) What are you doing with that gun?	(g) May I go now?
(c) Have you been to Lucknow?	(h) Where were you yesterday?
(d) What are you going to do next?	(i) Would you like some tea?
(e) Are you meeting Ravi tomorrow?	(j) What were you doing?

Find **two** questions asking about someone's plans or arrangements. d ______ [Units 38 and 39]

Find **one** question making a request. ______ [Unit 27]

Find **one** question asking for permission. ______ [Unit 27]

Find **one** question asking politely if someone wants something. ______ [Unit 26]

Find **one** question asking about a non-definite time in the past. ______ [Unit 41]

Find **one** question asking about NOW, this moment. ______ [Unit 18]

Find **one** question asking about ability. ______ [Unit 28]

Find **three** questions asking about the past. ______ [Units 23, 32 and 41]

Structure

All these questions are formed in the same way. Write the questions into the table.

	[QUESTION WORD] +	AUXILIARY VERB +	SUBJECT +	MAIN VERB
(a)	______	Can	you	play the piano?
(b)	What	are	you	doing with that gun?
(c)	______	______	______	______
(d)	______	______	______	______
(e)	______	______	______	______
(f)	______	______	______	______
(g)	______	______	______	______
(h)	______	______	______	______
(i)	______	______	______	______
(j)	______	______	______	______

Keys, Answers and Explanations Page No. 168

Exercise

1. Make these sentences into *Yes/No questions.*

(a) He is a Portuguese builder. Is he a Portuguese builder?
(b) They are dancing. __________
(c) You were late. __________
(d) Ali can dance really well. __________
(e) They are going to the seaside. __________
(f) Your computer was very expensive. __________
(g) You would like to go. __________
(h) He is coming home by train. __________
(i) She could swim. __________
(j) You are feeling better. __________

2. Put the words in the correct order *to make a question.*

(a) you/have/here/lived/how long? How long have you lived here?
(b) pass/you/can/the salt? __________?
(c) he/happy/was? __________?
(d) you/will/do/what? __________?
(e) he/going/where/is? __________?
(f) help/you/can/I/ __________?
(g) Who/going to /you/are/marry? __________?
(h) the film/how long/was? __________?
(i) your bag/is/where? __________?
(j) going/they/where/were? __________?

3. Complete the questions *to match the answers.*

(a) Where are you from? Gujarat.
(b) ________ I use the phone? Yes, of course.
(c) Where ________ ________ ________ on holiday? We are going to Darjeeling.
(d) What ________ ________ like to eat? Dosa, please.
(e) How old ________ you in 1975? Three.
(f) ________ you ever ________ crab? Yes, it was delicious.
(g) Where ________ you going? To the station.
(h) ________ you finished yet? Nearly.

4. Communicative Activities.
See Pg 132.

UNIT 46

Questions Revision 2: Asking questions by using an extra auxiliary do/does/did

Concept and Structure

Make these sentences into questions.

A.

1. Elephants eat leaves.
   Do elephants eat leaves?
2. He comes from Ecuador.
   Where________________________?
3. I went to the office.
   Where________________________ ?
4. She gave up smoking.
   ________________________?
5. They like strong coffee.
   ________________________?
6. I have three children.
   How many children ________________?

B.

1. Tigers can run very fast.
   Can tigers run very fast?
2. The Galapagos Islands are near Ecuador.
   Where ________________________?
3. I have forgotten my book.
   What ________________________?
4. She is going to give up smoking.
   ________________________?
5. They would like some tea.
   ________________________?
6. He has got three cars.
   ________________________?

What **three words** do we use to **make questions** in column **A**?_____ _____ _____
These three words are *auxiliaries.* Write the auxiliaries used in the questions in column **B.**

1. *can* 2. _________ 3. _________ 4. _________ 5. _________ 6. _________

[Any problems? See Unit 45.]

We use **do, does** and **did** to make a question when there is **no other auxiliary,** only a main verb.
Which one do we use to talk about the past? *did*
Which one do we use with *he, she, it* to talk about the *present?* _____
Which one do we use with *I, you, we, they* to talk about the *present?* _____

Exercise

1. Read the story and *make questions* to match the answers.

Once upon a time there was a poor woman who lived in a little house in the wood with her two daughters—Snow White and Rose Red. Snow White had blond hair and Rose Red had dark hair but they were both very pretty. One cold winter's day someone knocked on the door and Rose Red answered it. There was a big brown Bear outside but he said he was hungry so they let him come in. They gave him some food and the Bear fell asleep by the fire. He came back every day through the winter.

The spring came and one day Snow White and Red Rose were out walking in the forest when they saw a Dwarf with a long white beard. His beard was caught in a tree. The girls tried to help him but they could not free him. So Snow White took out some scissors and cut off the beard. The Dwarf was not grateful. 'You stupid girl!' he said and picked up a big bag of gold that was in the tree. Then he walked off.

The next day the girls saw the Dwarf again. He was fishing in the river but his beard was caught on the fishing-line and he could not free himself. They tried to help him but they could not free him.

Keys, Answers and Explanations Page No. ???

So Snow White took out some scissors and cut off the end of his beard. The Dwarf was free but very angry. 'You stupid girl! Look at my beard!' he said, and picked up a bag of jewels that was at the end of his fishing line. Then he walked off.

A few days later they saw the Dwarf again. This time he was counting a big pile of jewels and gold. 'What are you looking at?' he shouted. Suddenly the Bear jumped out from behind a tree. 'Are you stealing my treasure?' he shouted at the Dwarf. 'Oh! No, sir.' said the Dwarf. 'Do not eat me! Eat these nice young girls!' But the Bear hit the Dwarf and killed him. Then the Bear turned into a Prince. He explained that the Dwarf had turned him into a bear and stolen his treasure. Snow White married the Prince and Rose Red married his brother. They all lived happily ever after.

(a) In a little house in the wood — Where/live where did the poor woman and her children live?
(b) blond — What colour hair/have ______________?
(c) On a cold winter's day — When/knock on the door ______________?
(d) That he was hungry — What/say ______________?
(e) some food — What/give the bear ______________?
(f) a Dwarf — Who/see in the forest______________?
(g) a bag of gold — What/find in the tree______________?

2. Make the sentences about the story into questions.

(a) Snow White *took out* some scissors. — What did Snow White take out?
(b) She *cut off* the end of his beard. — What ______________?
(c) He *picked up* a bag of gold. — What ______________?
(d) The next day they *saw* him again. — When ______________?
(e) 'You stupid girl!' he *said.* — What ______________?
(f) He *explained* that the Dwarf had turned him into a bear. — What ______________?
(g) Rose Red *married* the Prince's brother. — Who ______________?

3. Write 'Yes/No' questions about these sentences.

(a) The bear *killed* the Dwarf. — Did the Bear kill the Dwarf?
(b) The Bear *hit* the Dwarf. ______________?
(c) They *tried* to help him. ______________?
(d) The Bear *fell asleep* by the fire. ______________?
(e) He *came back* every day. ______________?
(f) He *walked off.* ______________?
(g) The Dwarf *stole* the treasure. ______________?

4. Put these questions into the present tense.

(a) Did Snow White have some Scissors? — Does Snow White have some scissors?
(b) Where did the family live? ______________?
(c) Did the Bear eat people ? ______________?
(d) Did the Dwarf steal the Prince's gold? ______________?
(e) Did the Dwarf like fishing? ______________?
(f) Did Snow White and Rose Red love their husbands? ______________?

Test Yourself Exercises

Identifying areas for study *or* revision

***Note: for answers and study/revision guide, see Appendix* 4 (page 192)**

Part one: (Units 1-4) Talking about people, places and objects **Answers Page 192**

TEST YOURSELF

1. Put the words in the *right order* to make QUESTIONS.

> ***Example:***
> teacher is a he <u>Is he a teacher</u>?

(a) this is what ____________
(b) expensive are these ____________
(c) Post Office is the this ____________
(d) we are late ____________
(e) sister that is your ____________
(f) they German are ____________
(g) shoes these her are ____________

2. Complete the conversation.

> ***Example:***
> Sushil: Hello. What'<u>s</u> your name?
> Jaya: Jaya.

Sushil: (a) ______ you Ravi's sister?
Jaya: Yes, that's right.
Sushil: Is (b) ______ your party?
Jaya: No, it (c) ______. It's Hari's.
Sushil: Is (d) ______ your friend over there?
Jaya: Yes, it (e) ______ and, she's very nice.
Sushil: Oh.

3. Make these sentences *plural.*

> ***Example:***
> This is a woman. <u>These are women.</u>

(a) That child is very intelligent. ________________
(b) Is this your bag? ________________
(c) This is an English dictionary. ________________
(d) Is this a cheese sandwich? ________________
(e) The bus is red. ________________
(f) This is your key. ________________

4. There are *mistakes* in some of the sentences below. Find them and correct them.

> ***Example:***
> Is these your children? <u>Are these your children?</u>

(a) What's your job? ________________
(b) I like childs. ________________
(c) I are an artist. ________________
(d) Are that your sisters? ________________
(e) No, he isn't. ________________
(f) Those are factories. ________________
(g) We aren't very happy? ________________
(h) That's very interesting. ________________
(i) He's is my friend. ________________
(j) These are good photographs. ________________
(k) These photographs are good. ________________
(l) Is your this husband? ________________

5. Choose the *right word* to complete the sentences.

> ***Example:***
> Italy *is / are* a very beautiful country <u>is</u>

(a) We *are / is* French.
____

(b) *This / These* are my parents.
____

(c) What *am / is* your name?
____

(d) The people *is / are* happy.
____

(e) Yes, it *isn't / is*.
____

(f) The men *is / are* in the field.
____

(g) Are you a student? No, *I / I'm* not.
____

(h) What's *that / those?*
____

 Answers Page 192

1. Complete the following sentences using the correct form of the verb in brackets ( ).

(a) Many tourists go to Spain. (go)
(b) The Japanese ______ very good cars. (make)
(c) I ______ in Devon. (live)
(d) Yuko ______ to go to England. (want)
(e) In the winter he ______ skiing. (go)
(f) Sita and Ria ______ breakfast at 8 am. (have)
(g) Gita ______ work at 6 pm. (finish)
(h) She ______ French in the evening. (study)
(i) Priya ______ at 6 am every day. (get up)

2. Make these sentences *negative*.

(a) Alessandra comes from Lisbon. Alessandra doesn't come from Lisbon.
(b) Tony and Vicky live in Italy. ______
(c) We get up early on Sundays. ______
(d) Rina studies medicine at University. ______
(e) I stay late at the office in the evenings. ______
(f) Priya likes going shopping. ______

3. Make *questions* to match the answers.

(a) 'When/the train to Bhopal/leave?' When does the train to Bhopal leave?
'At 8.30.'
(b) 'How much/a ticket/cost?' ______?
'Rs. 375.'
(c) 'You/like/living in Bhopal?' ______?
'Yes, I do.'
(d) 'She/work/for Toyota?' ______?
'No, she doesn't.'
(e) 'Where Mina and Raj/study?' ______?
'At the University of Calcutta.'
(f) 'When/the plane/arrive in New Delhi?' ______?
'At 9.30 am.'

4. Rewrite these sentences using adverbs of frequency (always/often/sometimes/rarely/never)

(a) I go swimming every morning.
I always go swimming.
(b) Once or twice a week Sarah gets up early.
Sarah ______
(c) Sheila can't drive and doesn't have a car.
Sheila ______
(d) They are very happy all the time!
They ______
(e) Emma travels once or twice a year.
Emma ______
(f) I go running four or five times a week.
I ______

5. Put the words in the *right order* to make sentences.

(a) often/Ann and Tony/on holiday/go Ann and Tony often go on holiday.
(b) never/Jo/tea/drinks ______
(c) to watch/Ravi/sometimes/goes/a football match ______
(d) often/swimming/go/I ______
(e) to the cinema/rarely/goes/Debbie ______
(f) hungry/Jim/always/is ______

6. Correct any mistakes you find.

(a) Do you likes bananas? X-like
(b) Jean and Brian go always to Spain on holiday.
(c) The buses never are late.
(d) When the sun shine, I go swimming in the sea.
(e) The train doesn't stop in Cambridge.
(f) What time gets up Mr Kumar?
(g) Ram finishes work at 5.30.
(h) What do Shiv do at the weekend?
(i) He plaies football.
(j) Minu never go to the cinema.

Part three: (Units 8–12) Referring to people, places and objects

Answers Page 193

TEST YOURSELF

1. Choose the correct pronoun (eg *he/him*) or possessive adjective (eg *his*)

(a) Do you like *he / him / his?* him
(b) No, but I like *she / her / hers.* ______
(c) *We / Us / Our* don't live in *we / us / our* old house now. ______
(d) Is that car *you / your / yours?* ______
(e) No, it's *she / her / hers.* ______
(f) *They / Their / Theirs* daughter is a doctor. ______
(g) Where does *she / her / hers* live? ______
(h) Where is *she / her / hers* house? ______
(i) Please write to *I / me / my* soon. ______
(j) That book isn't *my / mine.* ______
(k) I don't think that house is *their / theirs.* ______

2. Rewrite the sentences *without using the names.*

(a) Suman and Jackie's flat is in central Chennai.
Their flat is in central Chennai.
(b) What floor is Dipak's flat on?
______
(c) Rani and Kavita are Ria's friends.
______
(d) Ria's flat is near Rini and Kavita's.
______
(e) Is that Mithi's?
______
(f) No, it's Joy's.
______

3. Decide if 's = *is*, or *possession*.

(a) Is that Peter's car? possession
(b) Ravi's a doctor. ______
(c) John and Mary's house is in London. ______
(d) My daughter's interested in tennis. ______
(e) The British Queen's one of the richest women in the world. ______
(f) Mother and Father's wedding anniversary is in June. ______

4. Rewrite the sentences in exercise 3 *without using the name* of the person.

(a) Is that **Peter's** car? Is that his car?
(b) **Ravi's** a doctor. ______
(c) **John and Mary's** house is in London. ______
(d) **My daughter'**s interested in tennis. ______
(e) The British **Queen's** one of the richest women in the world. ______
(f) **Mother and Father's** wedding anniversary is in June. ______

5. Complete the sentences with *a, the* or *nothing*.

My parents live in **(a)** a small house. **(b)** ______ house has only one garage but they have two cars, **(c)** ______ Maruti 800 and **(d)** ______ Fiat Padmini. **(e)** ______ Maruti 800 is quite new and **(f)** ______ Fiat Padmini is older. So they keep **(g)** ______ Maruti 800 in **(h)** ______ garage.

My brother is **(i)** ______ businessman. He works in **(j)** ______ London, but he lives in **(k)** ______ Henley, near **(l)** ______ River Thames.

His wife is **(m)** ______ teacher in **(n)** ______ school in **(o)** ______ Henley. They have **(p)** ______ eight year old son, Marcus.

6. Correct the mistakes you find in these sentences.

(a) Vijay wants to be doctor when he grows up.
Vijay wants to be a doctor ...

(b) Oh no, it's raining. Can you lend me a umbrella?
______

(c) He often gives she flowers.
______

(d) Is that hers house?
______

(e) Can you give me your address?
______

(f) A pet is an animal who lives in your house.
______

(g) River Nile is the longest in the world.
______

(h) I don't want to speak to him.
______

(i) What's the answer to question 7?
______

(j) He travels all over world.
______

(k) The Prime Minister is the person which governs India.
______

(l) I'd love to meet the President of India.
______

(m)I make breakfast for our children.
______

(n) That's mine car, over there.
______

7. Choose *who* or *which*.

(a) A clerk is a person who works in a bank or an office.

(b) I like food ______ tastes good.

(c) A wife is a woman ______ is married.

(d) That's the man ______ works in my office.

(e) She's the woman ______ lives next door.

(f) A tram is a type of bus ______ uses electricity.

(g) A fountain pen is a pen ______ uses liquid ink.

(h) ______ is your favourite book?

Part four: (Units 13-17) Amounts Answers Page 194

1. Complete the dialogues using these words: *too/enough/much/many/some/any/have/has/got.*

Ravi: 'Which hotel do you think we should stay in—the Grand or the Seafront?'
Priya: '(a) ______ the Grand got a swimming pool?'
Ravi: 'No, but it's (b) ______ a sauna.'
Priya: 'How (c) ______ does it cost?'
Ravi: 'Rs. 520 a night. I think that's (d) ______ expensive! The Seafront is cheaper.'

Shopkeeper: 'Can I help you?'
Customer: 'I'd like (e) ______ apples please.'
Shopkeeper: 'How (f) ______ would you like?'
Customer: 'Four please.'

Priya: '(g) ______ you got (h) ______ money?
Shyam: 'Yes ...'
Priya: 'Can I borrow (i) ______ please?'
Shyam: 'How (j) ______ do you want?'
Priya: 'Rs.15?'
Shyam: 'Sorry, I haven't got (k) ______.'

Theresa: 'How (l) ______ children have you (m) ______ ?
Sheila: 'Four—two boys and two girls. What about you?'
Theresa: 'I haven't got (n) ______'

John: 'What's your town like?'
David: 'Well, I think it's (o) ______ small. There isn't much to do.'
John: 'Are there (p) ______ cinemas or theatres?'
David: 'No, there are (q) ______ pubs though.'

TEST YOURSELF

2. Choose *is* or *are*.

(a) How many strawberries ______ there?
(b) There ______ n't enough eggs.
(c) There ______ some coffee in the jar.
(d) Rice ______ quite cheap.
(e) Tomatoes ______ very good for you.
(f) Bread ______ delicious.
(g) How much flour ______ there?
(h) There ______ six eggs in this cake.
(i) ______ there any sugar?

3. Complete the dialogues with *too/much/many/enough*.

Father: 'How are you getting on at school, Shiv?'
Shiv: 'Ok, but there's (a) ______ ______ homework.'
Father: 'How (b) ______ homework do you get?'
Shiv: 'About an hour a night.'
Father: 'That isn't (c) ______! You should do at least two hours! I'm going to speak to your teacher ...'

Ritu: 'Do you like your new job, Sonali?'
Sonali: 'It's OK, but the hours are (d) ______ long—I work from 8.00–6.30.'
Ritu: 'How (e) ______ do you get paid?'
Sonali: 'Not (f) ______!'

Priya: 'Oh no! I'm making a cake and I haven't got (g) ______ eggs!'
Hari: 'How (h) ______ do you need?'
Priya: 'Four and I've only got two.'

4. Choose the correct *word* to complete the text.

Ravi lives in a big house near the sea. He (a) (*have / has*) got a swimming-pool. He (b) (*have / has*) got (c) (*many / a lot of*) money but he (d) (*hasn't / haven't*) got (e) (*many / much*) friends.

Peter and Pamela live in a flat. The flat (f) (haven't/hasn't) got (g) (some/any) good furniture and it looks bare. They (h) (*haven't / hasn't*) got (i) (*much / many*) money but they still enjoy life.

Part five: (Units 18–19) Talking about now

Answers Page 194

1. Write sentences describing what *is happening* in the picture.

Example:
(a) The sun/shine   The sun is shining.

(b) Grandmother/sit on the sofa ______________________
(c) The dog and cat/eat ______________________
(d) The baby/cry ______________________
(e) Grandfather/lie down ______________________
(f) Father/read a book ______________________
(g) The children/play ______________________
(h) Grandfather/sleep ______________________
(i) Mother/write a letter ______________________

2. Make *questions* for the following *answers*.

> ***Example:***
> (a) Who/cry?
> Who's crying? The baby.

(b) Who/read a book?
____________________ ? Father.

(c) What Father/read?
____________________ ? A book.

(d) Who/sit on the sofa?
____________________ ? Grandmother.

(e) The children/play?
____________________ ? Yes, they are.

(f) What/Mother/write?
____________________ ? A letter.

(g) Father/read a newspaper?
____________________ ? No, he isn't.

(h) Grandfather/sleep?
____________________ ? Yes, he is.

3. Write *short answers* to these questions.

> ***Example:***
> (a) Is the baby crying? Yes, it is.

(b) Is Grandmother writing a letter? __________

(c) Is the sun shining? __________

(d) Are the children lying down? __________

(e) Is Father sleeping? __________

(f) Are the cat and the dog eating? __________

4. Make questions with the *present simple* or *present continuous* to match the answers.

> ***Example:***
> (a) What/languages/you/speak?
> What languages do you speak? German, Japanese and Italian.

(b) What/the children/do?
____________________________ ? They're in the garden, I think.

(c) What/Raj/do?
____________________________ ? He's a nurse.

(d) How many CDs/you/have?
____________________________ ? About two hundred.

(e) What/you/drink?
____________________________ ? Orange juice. It's delicious. Would you like some?

(f) What time/you/usually get up?
____________________________ ? During the week at about 7.30, but later at the weekend.

(g) What/you/listen to?
____________________________ ? The new Oasis album. If you don't like it, we can listen to something else.

5. Choose *present simple* or *present continuous* to complete the sentences.

> ***Example:***
> (a) 'It's so hot this summer that all the plants in the garden *die / are dying*.' are dying

(b) 'Shyam *runs / is running* in the park every day.'
(c) 'I can't answer the door, I *talk / I'm talking* on the phone!'
(d) 'Sshh! Quiet! The baby *sleeps / is sleeping*.'
(e) 'Where *do you go / are you going* this afternoon?' 'Shopping. Do you want anything?'
(f) 'Where's Grandmother?' 'She *sits / is sitting* on the sofa.'
(g) 'What *do you eat / are you eating*?' 'Pizza. Do you want some?'
(h) 'What *is Ratan doing? / does Ratan do!*' 'He's a teacher.'

6. Correct any *spelling* mistakes you find.

Example:	
(a) Rima's writting a letter to Jim.	writing

(b) John's really tired. He's lieing down.
(c) You naughty boy! Why are you hitting your sister?
(d) The children are swiimming in the sea.
(e) It's a beautiful day, the sun's shineing.
(f) Who are you talking to?
(g) I'm telephonning my mother.

Part six: (Units 20–22) Prepositions

Answers Page 195

1. Look at the pictures and decide if the statements are *true* or *false*. If they are *false*— correct the statement.

(a) The dog is on the table.
False - the dog is under the table.

(b) The chair is opposite the TV. __________________

(c) The cup is next to the oranges. __________________

(d) The CD is under the book. __________________

(e) The bus is behind the chair. __________________

(f) The post office is next to the bank. __________________

(g) The clock is in front of the picture. __________________

(h) The dog is opposite the chair. __________________

(i) The apples are in the box. __________________

2. Look at the maps and complete the directions using a *preposition of movement:* (*across, round, into, under, over, through, down, along, past, up*).

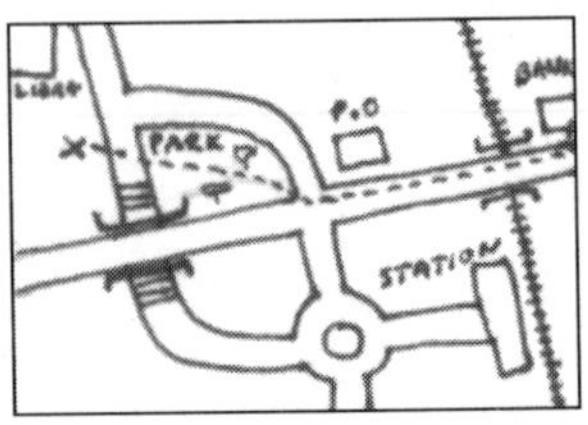

Go (a) across the road, (b) __________ the park, (c) __________ the Post Office, (d) __________ the railway bridge and (e) __________ the building on your left.

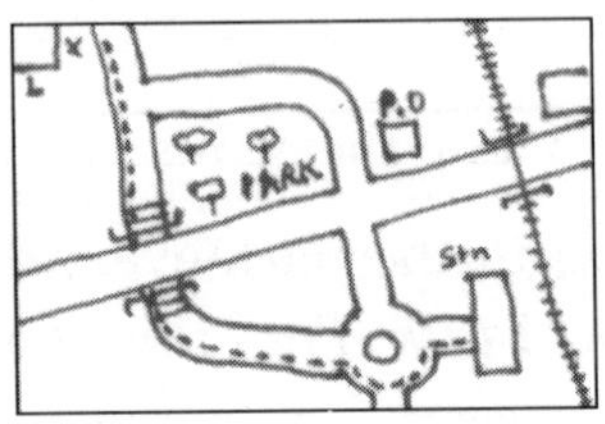

Go (f) __________ the road, (g) __________ the steps, (h) __________ the subway, (i) __________ the steps, (j) __________ the roundabout and (k) __________ the railway station.

3. Choose the *correct word* to complete the dialogue.

A: How do I get (a) (from/*in*) the railway station (b) (*into/to*) the library?

B: The library? It's quite a long way. Go (c) (*along/past*) the road, (d) (*under/round)* the roundabout, (e) (*over/under*) the subway, (f) (*past/up*) the park and it's the building on your left.

A: Is there a bus?

B: Yes, you could get (g) (*on/down*) a number 12 bus and get (h) (*in/off*) opposite the park.

4. Complete the following sentences with *in/at/on* or *nothing*.

(a) Shyam's birthday is <u>on</u> the 27th September.
(b) The train leaves______10.30 pm.
(c) Shiela is going to Spain______next week.
(d) India won the Cricket World Cup______1983.
(e) John and Alison went to the cinema ______ last night.
(f) Rajiv's cleaning his car ______ the moment.
(g) Are you having a party ______ your birthday?
(h) The Beatles were very popular ______ the 1960s.

TEST YOURSELF

5. Correct the mistakes in *some* of these sentences.

(a) At the future, there will be more computers.
<u>X in the future</u>
(b) I usually get home from work 6.00.
(c) All the shops are closed on Diwali.
(d) Sue's going to visit her grandmother in the weekend.
(e) Rina is coming to England in next month.
(f) Life was very different in the 18th Century.
(g) It's very cold in night now.
(h) On the past not many people had telephones.

6. 'The' or 'nothing'? Write 'the' if *necessary* in these sentences

(a) Minu always goes running in the morning.
(b) On______New Year's Day, Sheila got four cards!
(c) At______midnight it started raining.
(d) I'm studying English at______moment.
(e) On______Saturdays I stay in bed late.

Part seven: (Units 23–25) Talking about the Past I

Answers Page 197

1. Choose *was* or *were*.

> ***Example*:**
> (a) She was/were an only child. ***<u>She was an only child.</u>***

(b) I rang Justin and Sue but they *was/were* away on holiday.
(c) The bank *was/were* in the main square.
(d) *Was/Were* you at home last night?
(e) No, I *was/were* out.
(f) We *was/were* really excited about going on holiday.

TEST YOURSELF

2. Complete the sentences using the past simple tense.

Example:
(a) I <u>was</u> (be) happy as a child.

(b) There______(be) any cars when Grandfather______(be) a child.
(c) Alexander Bell______(invent) the telephone.
(d) Sumitra______(go) to Spain last year.
(e) She______(swim) across the English Channel!
(f) The English______(not win) the Battle of Hastings in 1066.
(g) Queen Victoria______(have) nine children.
(h) 'I______(think) the film was great.' 'Really? I______ (not like) it much.'
(i) I______(lose) my wallet yesterday.
(j) Sophie______(not go) to the party because she______(be) ill.
(k) They______(sing) the National Anthem when the President______(arrive)

3. Make these sentences *negative*.

Example:
(a) The play was very good. <u>The play wasn't very good.</u>

(b) Ian passed all his exams.

____

(c) Indian Railways won the football match.

____

(d) I knew her address.

____

(e) The train stopped in Jaipur.

____

(f) Cars were expensive in the 1960s.

____

(g) After school, Lila went to University.

____

(h) He brought her flowers.

____

(i) She was very friendly.

____

(j) We spoke Greek all evening.

____

(k) I gave up smoking.

____

4. Make *questions* from the following *answers*.

Example:	
(a) John Logie Baird invented the television.	What <u>did John Logie Baird invent?</u>

(b) Priya and Jeet went to Shimla on holiday?	Where______________________?
(c) Chopin and Marie Curie were Polish.	What nationality______________?
(d) Prince Charles married Diana Spencer in 1981.	Who______Prince Charles______?
(e) He bought the car because he likes the colour.	Why ______________________?
(f) Rio de Janeiro was the capital of Brazil in the 1950s.	When ______________________?
(g) Alexander Kwasniewski became president of Poland in 1995.	When ______________________?
(h) Queen Victoria died in 1901.	When ______________________?
(i) He was in Cairo in June.	When ______________________?

5. Correct the mistakes you find.

Example:	
(a) Subbo not watched the football match on tv last night.	***Nick didn't watch the football match on tv last night.***

(b) When died King Henry VIII?
(c) My parents weren't very rich when they were young.
(d) Did you went to the party last night?
(e) 'Did you enjoy the film?' 'Yes, it were great.'
(f) I finished reading that book last night.
(g) Last year on holiday the weather didn't be good.
(h) I didn't gave her a present for her birthday.
(i) Ate you toast for breakfast?

6. Correct any *spelling* mistakes you find.

Example:
(a) I marryed him last year. ***married***

(b) I payed a lot of money for that!
(c) He finally stopped smoking.
(d) John carried Sreya's bags.
(e) We traveled all over Europe.
(f) 'I'm tired' said Maria.
(g) Samir and Hari plaied football yesterday.

Part eight: (Units 26–31) Adding meaning

Answers Page 197

1. Chisako is a Japanese student staying with an Indian family. **Complete the conversation with her Indian host, Mrs Jain.**
Use: *would/can/may/have to/should*

Mrs Jain: 'Hello, dear. Did you have a good day at the college?'
Chisako: 'Yes, thank you.'
Mrs Jain: '(a) Would you like a cup of tea?'
Chisako: 'Yes, please. (b)______I have a sandwich too?'
Mrs Jain: 'Well, we're going to have dinner in half an hour, so you (c)______n't eat too much now. (d)______you like a biscuit?'
Chisako: 'OK. Thank you. I (e)______do some homework before dinner so (f)______I take the tea up to my room?'
Mrs Jain: 'Yes—careful you don't spill it!'

Later...
Mrs Jain: '(g)______you pass the potatoes, please?'
Chisako: 'Here you are. (h)______you like some carrots too?'
Mrs Jain: 'Thank you. You (i)______eat more vegetables, dear—they're good for you.'
Chisako: 'Yes, I know...I (j)______like to go out tonight. (k)______I have a key?'
Mrs Jain: 'OK. where are you going? You (l)______n't stay out late, it isn't safe.'
Chisako: 'To the cinema. My friend will bring me home so I don't (m)______walk in the dark, don't worry.'

TEST YOURSELF

2. Complete the sentences with *may/might/have to/can/could/can't/would.*

(a) 'Where would you like to sit? Near the window?'
(b) '______ you sing?' 'I like singing—but I'm terrible!'
(c) 'Where are you going this weekend?' 'I'm not sure yet. I ______ go to Wales.'
(d) The only problem with my new job is that now I ______ get up really early.
(e) I was a very intelligent child. I ______ read before I went to school.
(f) ______ I read that magazine when you've finished with it?
(g) I want a secretary who______type properly!
(h) Sorry, I______go home now. It's getting very late.
(i) ______ you like to go out this weekend?
(j) ______you lend me some money?
(k) I think she______like him but it's difficult to know.
(l) '______you drive when you were a teenager?' 'No, I learnt when I was 24.'
(m) In England you______wear a seatbelt in the backseat of a car or the police will make you pay a fine.
(n) She______speak three languages now—Portuguese, French and Polish.
(o) I______read that notice—the letters are too small!
(p) ______I use your phone, please?
(q) What______you like for dinner?

3. Complete the horoscopes.
Use: *should or might*

Sagittarius
Work: You (a) <u>should</u> be very careful. Someone (b)______want your job!
Money: You (c)______need to borrow some money if you spend too much this month.
Love: You (d)______think more about your partner's feelings.

Capricorn
Work: You (e)______be working too hard. If you are, take more time off.
Money: You (f)______n't spend so much! You will be very poor at the end of the month.
Love: You (g)______meet the love of your life.

Aquarius
Work: You (h)______get a new job this month—if you're lucky.
Money: You (i)______try to save your money. Next month you (j)______need it!
Love: You (k)______stop thinking about someone you can't have.

4. Choose the correct word.

(a) You *should/might* eat more—you're too thin. <u>should</u>
(b) He's really musical. He *can/may* play four or five instruments.
(c) *Would/Can* you like to sit down?
(d) I *might/can* go swimming this weekend—if the weather's good.
(e) A nurse *would/has* to work very hard.
(f) *Can/Would* I sit here, please?
(g) You *should / can* stop smoking—it's very bad for you.
(h) I *would/can* like to go to Mexico.
(i) You *have to/should* drive on the left in Britain.
(j) I think he *should/would* work harder. He's really lazy.

5. Correct the mistakes you find.

(a) Waiter! I'd likes the menu please. <u>I'd like</u>
(b) Do you can swim?
(c) He haves to work very late.
(d) They should exercise more.
(e) It might rains tomorrow.
(f) May I going out tonight?
(g) English is very difficult. I have work so hard!
(h) What woulds he like?

1. Complete the following sentences using the *past continuous tense.*

(a) I (play) was playing chess.
(b) Nidhi and Rekha (walk)________________in the park.
(c) __________ he __________ (visit) his parents?
(d) You (eat) ____________ breakfast.
(e) Ramesh (not swim) ____________.
(f) '__________ they __________ (listen) to the radio?'
(g) Kavita (not watch) ____________ the television.
(h) We (make) ____________ dinner.
(i) The sun (not shine) ____________.
(j) __________ it __________ (rain)?
(k) Saurav (drive) ____________ to town.

2. Look at the time lines and make sentences using *when.*

(a) I/read the paper — I was reading the paper when the phone rang.

The phone/ring

(b) It/rain ____________________

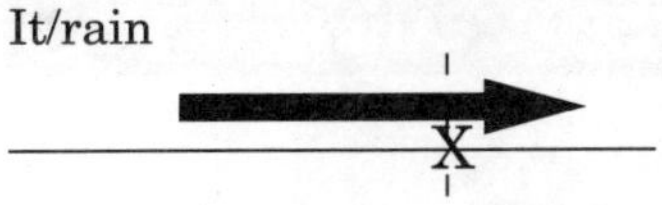

Anjan/arrive

(c) I/drive away ____________________

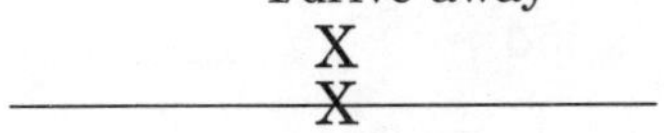

The police/arrive

(d) Sita/visit her uncle ____________________

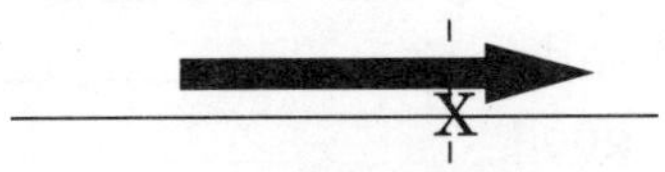

The lights/go out

(e) They/drive home ____________________

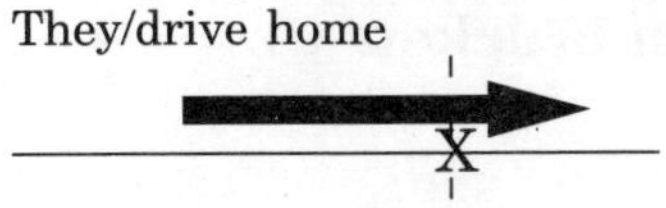

They/see Jane

(f) I/cook dinner ____________________

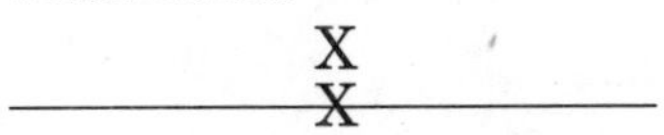

John/get home

(g) Suresh/run in the park ____________________

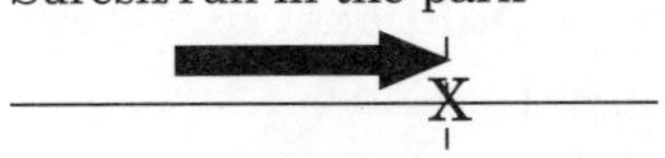

He/fall in the lake

(h) I/write a letter ____________________

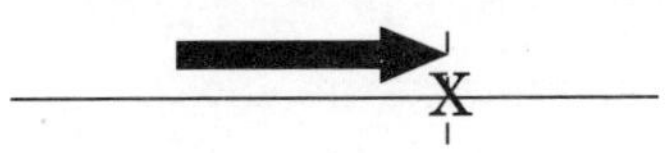

Somebody/knock on the door

(i) Hira/drive to her mother's house ______________________________

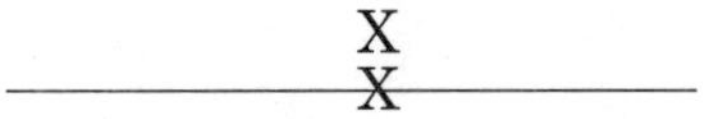

She/hear the news

(j) Shanti/sleep ______________________________

Rima/wake her up

3. Choose *past simple* or *past continuous* to complete the sentences.

(a) While Suman was cooking dinner, I (*was laying/laid)* the table. ***laid***.
(b) As they were dancing, a strange man (*was coming/came*) to talk to them.
(c) Ravi (*slept/was sleeping)* when the storm started.
(d) Sarah was reading when the doorbell (*was ringing/rang*)
(e) Alison and Mina (*walked/were walking*) along the street when they saw an accident.
(f) I (*bought/was buying*) a hamburger while the children were swimming.
(g) Surya (*fell asleep/was falling asleep*) during the film but he woke up at the end.
(h) The sun (*shone/was shining)* when the plane landed.
(i) Ria (*waited/was waiting*) for a train when the rain started.

Part ten: (Units 34–37) Describing

Answers Page 198

1. Write the *comparative form* of these adjectives.

(a) big	bigger	(d) rich	________	(g) intelligent	________
(b) small	________	(e) fat	________	(h) red	________
(c) exciting	________	(f) shy	________	(i) good	________

2. Write the *superlative form* of these adjectives.

(a) quick	***the quickest***	(d) early	________	(g) hungry	________
(b) far	________	(e) hot	________	(h) tall	________
(c) poor	________	(f) lazy	________	(i) good	________

3. *Compare* the two things in each question using the adjectives in brackets ( ).

(a) The Empire State Building/The Eiffel Tower (*high*)

The Empire State Building is higher than the Eiffel Tower.

(b) The Nile/The Thames (*long*) ______________________________
(c) Paris/Warsaw (*expensive*) ______________________________
(d) Mandarin Chinese/Hindi (*difficult*) ______________________________
(e) Tokyo/London (big) ______________________________
(f) A car/a bicycle (*fast)* ______________________________
(g) A trumpet/a flute (*noisy*) ______________________________
(h) An armchair/a stool (*comfortable*) ______________________________

4. Rewrite the sentences so they mean the *opposite*.

(a) He's the most untidy person I know. He's the tidiest person I know.

(b) That football team is the best in the world. ______

(c) It's one of the largest cities in South America. ______

(d) He's the most interesting man I've ever met. ______

(e) Who is the oldest? ______

(f) She must be the ugliest woman in the world! ______

(g) Which is the quietest room? ______

(h) I bought the cheapest ticket. ______

TEST YOURSELF

5. Write the missing *adjective* or *adverb*.

(a) good/***well***

(b) ______/slowly

(c) bad/______

(d) tidy/______

(e) ______/noisily

(f) happy/______

(g) ______/cleverly

(h) ______/quickly

(i) angry/______

6. Choose the correct adjective or adverb to complete the sentences.

(a) He sat down (*heavy / heavily*) heavily.

(b) You cook really (*good / well*)______.

(c) He's a (*terrible / terribly*) teacher!______.

(d) The sea was very (*deep / deeply*)______.

(e) Did you have a (*great / greatly*) holiday?______.

(f) This exercise is quite (*easy / easily*)______.

(g) He drank the water (*thirsty / thirstily*)______.

(h) I feel awful—I slept really (*bad / badly*)______.

(i) He's a very (naughty/naughtily) child______.

(j) I looked for it very (*careful / carefully*)______.

Part eleven: (Units 38–40) Talking about the future

Answers Page 199

1. Choose *be going to* or *will* to complete the following sentences.

(a) Have you got your raincoat? It is going to rain.

(b) Next summer I__________visit my relatives in America. It's all arranged.

(c) 'Oh no! Those cars__________crash!' 'BANG!!!'

(d) A: 'What do you want to do tonight?'
B: 'I don't know. I__________ring you later, OK?'

(e) A: 'My plane gets in at 2.30 am'
B: 'I__________meet you at the airport.'
A: 'Are you sure?'

(f) I'm so happy—I__________have a baby!

(g) You're quite good at maths. I expect you__________pass the exam.

(h) I couldn't answer *any* of the exam questions! I __________fail!

(i) The neighbours__________have a party tonight. Shall we go?

(j) She looks very upset and sad. I think she__________cry.

(k) The weather next week__________ (continue) to be sunny.

(l) When I grow up I__________(be) a marine biologist.

TEST YOURSELF

2. Correct the mistakes in *some* of these dialogues with *going* to and *will*.

(a) A: 'Why are you going into town?'
B: 'I'll buy some food.'
X I'm going to buy some food.

(b) A: 'Is that the phone?'
B: 'I'll get it.'
____

(c) A: 'Can I have some more pudding?'
B: 'You're going to put on weight.'
____

(d) A: 'Why are you saving all your money?'
B: 'I'll buy a car.'
____

(e) A: 'Have you got your suncream?'
B: 'Why? Is it going to be hot today?'
____

(f) A: 'The film starts at 7.00.'
B: 'OK. I'm going to pick you up at 6.30.'
____

(g) A: 'Will you marry me?'
B: 'I'm sorry, I'll marry Julian next month.'
____

3. Choose *present simple* or *present continuous* to complete the following sentences.

(a) The film (start) starts at 7.30.
(b) I (see)__________the doctor tomorrow morning.
(c) What time__________the play__________(end)?
(d) The conference (start)__________on May 22nd.
(e) He (meet)__________Jake later tonight.
(f) What__________you__________(do) tomorrow?
(g) I need to go home now because John (ring)__________me at 8.00.
(h) Suraj and Arjun (come)__________for dinner tomorrow night.
(i) The plane (leave)__________at 9.00 so we need to be at the airport by 7.00.
(j) Can I borrow your new jacket? I (go)__________for a job interview tomorrow.

Part twelve: (Units 41–44) Connecting the past and the present

Answers Page 199

1. Write the *past participle* of these verbs:

(a) think thought
(b) drink ______
(c) see ______
(d) wear ______
(e) write ______
(f) know ______
(g) eat ______
(h) go ______
(i) break ______
(j) have ______
(k) get ______
(l) cut ______

2. Choose the correct verb *form*.

(a) ['*I've never been* / *I never went*] to Brazil. Maybe I'll go next year. I've never been
(b) 'When I was six [*I've broken* / *I broke*] my arm in three places!'
(c) 'How long [*have you lived* / *did you live*] in Surat?' 'Six years. We left there last year.'
(d) '[*Have you paid* / *Did you pay*] the telephone bill yet?' 'Sorry, I'll do it tomorrow.'
(e) 'You're very suntanned—[*have you been* / *did you go*] on holiday?
(f) '[*Have you ever eaten* / *Did you ever eat*] pierogi?' 'What's that?!'
(g) 'It's our wedding anniversary next week. [*We've been married* / *We were married*] for five years.'
(h) 'How are you getting on with your studying?' 'Not bad. [*I've already read* / *I already read*] three books.'
(i) 'When you were in Japan [*have you eaten* / *did you eat*] sushi?'
(j) '[*Have you had* / *Did you have*] your car long?' 'No, it's still almost new.'
(k) ['*Have you written* / *Did you write*] to Auntie Mabel yet?' 'No, not yet.'
(l) 'I didn't recognise you! [*Did you dye* / *Have you dyed*] your hair? It's a different colour.'
(m) 'Oh no! Where's my purse? I think someone [stole/has stolen] it!'

3. Complete the sentences with the verb in the *correct tense*—present perfect or simple past.

(a) 'Where's Pritam?' 'Her tooth was hurting so she has gone (go) to the Dentist.'

(b) 'There's a lot of washing up in the kitchen...' 'I______already______(do) it.'

(c) 'You speak very good Czech. How long______you______(be) in Czech now?'

(d) 'I______(live) in Brazil for two years. It was wonderful.'

(e) 'I______ never ______ (go) in a balloon—but I would love to do it one day.'

(f) 'What______you______(do) to your hair?! It looks terrible!'

(g) 'It was Mita's birthday last week but I am so busy I______(not buy) her a present yet.'

(h) 'Have you ever been to the opera?' 'No, but I______(go) to the ballet last week.'

(i) 'Look! I______(clean) the car. Doesn't it look better?'

(j) 'Oh no! I forgot to write my address on that letter.' 'Sorry, I______already______(post) it.'

4. Complete the dialogues using *present perfect* or *simple past.*

Ritu: 'Hi! How are you, Priya? I (a)______(not see) you for months!'

Priya: 'Fine. You look good. (b)______you______(go) on holiday?'

Ritu 'Yes, I (c)______(go) to the Caribbean for two weeks. It was wonderful.'

Priya '(d)______you ever______(go) to Venezuela? I'm going there next week'.

Priya 'Really? I (e)______(not go) there yet but I'm planning to go next year. Where are you going to stay? (f)______you______(book) a hotel yet?'

Priya 'Yes, we (g)______already______(arrange) everything.'

Mother: 'Are you looking forward to going to the Safari Park, Mark? You (h)______never______ (see) a lion, have you?'

Sanjeev: 'I am looking forward to it but I (i)______(see) a lion in the zoo last year.'

Mother: 'Oh, but that's not the same...Come here, you (j)______(not tie) your shoes up properly.'

Sanjeev: 'Mother! I'm late. I've got to go.'

Mother: 'Wait! You (k)______(forget) your sandwiches!'

Mr Bajaj: 'Well, my wife and I (l)______(be married) for fifty years now and they've all been happy ones.'

Journalist: '(m)______you ever______(argue)?'

Mr Bajaj: 'I don't think we (n)______(have) an argument since yesterday.'

Journalist: 'Yesterday?!'

Further Practice Exercises

Part one: (Units 1–4) Talking about people, places and objects

(Units 1 and 2)

1. Complete these sentences with the *correct form* of the verb 'to be'.

> ***Example:***
> (a) I <u>am</u> an engineer.

(b) My brother______called Raja.

(c) ______she Chinese?

(d) ______we in France?

(e) They______both very intelligent.

(f) It ______a lovely day.

2. Put the words in order to make QUESTIONS, then write true answers.

> ***Example:***
> (a) Student/you/are/a? <u>Are you a student?</u> <u>Yes, I am.</u>

(b) Teacher/your/is/English? ________________________? ________________________

(c) English/easy/is? ________________________? ________________________?

(d) The Eiffel Tower/is/in France? ________________________? ________________________

(e) Your/friend/is/where? ________________________ ? ________________________

(f) Your/name/is/what? ________________________ ? ________________________

FURTHER PRACTICE

This/that/these/those (Unit 3)

3. Use the pictures to *make sentences* using this/that/these/those and the verb 'to be'.

Example:
<u>This is</u> my dog.
<u>That</u> dog <u>is</u> dangerous.

______shoes______too high.__________more comfortable.

What______ ______ called? It's a rose.

What______ ______?!

______ ______my son.

John!______flowers ______dead!

Who______ ____girls?

______ ______my babies.

Singular and plural (Unit 4)

4. Make these sentences singular.

Example:
These are my sisters. This is my sister.

(a) Those people are English. ____________________

(b) The factories are very noisy. ____________________

(c) The buses are always late! ____________________

(d) My keys are on the table. ____________________

(e) These are my children. ____________________

(f) Where are the men? ____________________

5. Write the *plural* of these words (careful with spelling!)

(a) holiday holidays
(b) cat ____________
(c) baby ____________
(d) daughter ____________
(e) church ____________
(f) woman ____________
(g) class ____________
(h) girl ____________
(i) house ____________

Part two: (Units 5–7) Talking about routines and habits

Present simple tense (Unit 5)

1. Complete the text about what Sheila does every day.

Use these verbs: see/get up/have (x 2)/be/arrive/like/leave/help/walk/catch/make/go/live

Sheila______a dentist. She______her work but she______a long way from her surgery so she usually______quite early. She______three children so she______them get dressed and______them breakfast. They______to school, it isn't far. Then she______the house at about 7.30. She______to work by train and then______a bus. She usually______at about 8.30,______a cup of coffee and______her first patient at 9.00.

2. Complete the text about what Manu does every day.

Use these verbs: go/finish/love/watch/stay/start/work

Manu______in a cinema. She ______ work at 3.00 in the afternoon, when the first film is on, and______about 11.00 at night. She ______ her job because she ______ all the new films free! But she______to bed very late. So, in the mornings, she ______ in bed until 10.00 or 11.00.

Present simple auxiliaries (Unit 6)

3. Read about Alfredo's daily routine. Then write questions and short answers.

Alfredo is a disc jockey. He works for a radio station in Milan. He starts work at 7.00 in the morning so he usually goes to bed quite early. He thinks his job is very interesting but he hates getting up so early. He only sees his friends at the weekends but they listen to him on the radio.

Example:
(a) What/Alfredo do?
What does Alfredo do? He's a disc-jockey

(b) He/work in Rome?
________________? ________________

(c) What time/he/start work?
________________? ________________

(d) He/go to bed late?
________________? ________________

(e) He/think his job is interesting?
________________? ________________

(f) He/like getting up early?
________________? ________________

(g) When/his friends/see Alfredo?
________________? ________________

(h) His friends/listen to him on the radio?
________________? ________________

4. Correct these statements about Alfredo with a full sentence.

> ***Example:***
> (a) Alfredo works in Madrid. No, he doesn't work in Madrid.

(b) He starts work at 9.00. ______________________

(c) He goes to bed late. ______________________

(d) He hates his job. ______________________

(e) He likes getting up early. ______________________

(f) His friends see Alfredo every day. ______________________

Adverbs 1: adverbs of frequency (Unit 7)

5. Rewrite these sentences using the adverb in brackets ( )

> ***Example:***
> (a) Alfredo gets up early. (always) Alfredo always gets up early.

(b) Alfredo sees his friends during the week. (never) ______________________

(c) Sheila is late for work. (rarely) ______________________

(d) Manu enjoys her job. (usually) ______________________

(e) Sheila has a cup of coffee in the morning. (always) ______________________

(f) Sheila's children are naughty. (often) ______________________

(g) Alfredo is tired. (usually) ______________________

(h) Manu gets up early. (never) ______________________

(i) Alfredo's friends listen to him on the radio. (often) ______________________

(j) Manu watches new films first. (always) ______________________

Part three: (Units 8–12) Referring to people, places and objects

(Units 8–10)

1. Complete the film review with the correct *pronoun* or *possessive adjective*.

Many people know Shakespeare's play *Romeo and Juliet*, but this film "William Shakespeare's Romeo and Juliet" is something new. The Director sets the story in modern day America. Romeo meets Juliet at a party and **(a)** (*he / him / his*) falls in love with **(b)** (*she / her / hers*) immediately. **(c)** (*She / her / hers*) also loves **(d)** (he/ him/his). But there's a problem. **(e)** (*he / him / his*) family hate **(f)** (*she / her / hers*) and **(g)** (*she / her / hers*) family hate his. Unfortunately **(h)** (*they / their / theirs*) love affair cannot work. Everybody is against **(i)** (*they / them / their*)...

2. Complete the letter with the correct *pronoun* or *possessive* adjective.

Dear Dinesh,

Hi! How are **(a)** (you/your/yours)? **(b)** (*I / me / my*) am very busy at the moment. **(c)** (*We / us / our*) are moving house next week and there is a lot to do. Now we have two children, **(d)** (*we / our ours*) old house is very small and **(e)** (*we / us / our*) need more space. The new house has four bedrooms and **(f)** (*it's / its*) much nicer. The children are very excited because **(g)** (*they / them / their*) will have **(h)** (*they / their / theirs*) own bedrooms. **(i)** (*I / me / my*) hope **(j)** (*they / them / their*) bedrooms will be tidier now since **(k)** (*they / them / their*) have more space.

(Unit 11)

3. Complete the text with *a* or *the*—then solve the puzzle!

(a) ______ policeman is walking past **(b)** ______ house when he hears a shout. 'Rajesh! Don't kill me!' **(c)** ______ policeman rushes into **(d)** ______ house and he sees **(e)** ______ dead body on the floor. There are three people standing near **(f)** ______ body—**(g)** ______ doctor, **(h)** ______ lawyer and **(i)** ______ engineer. **(j)** ______ policeman arrests **(k)** ______ engineer. How does he know who **(l)** ______ murderer is? (*answer: the doctor and lawyer are* ***women***)

(Unit 12)

4. Match the words and the definitions. Then write sentences using *who, which, that* to define these people and things.

(a) Feijoada		1. writes plays.
(b) A baker	is someone ...	2. people eat in some part of northern India for dinner.
(c) A watch		3. works on an aeroplane.
(d) A fork	is something	4. people eat in Brazil.
(e) An air steward		5. people use to eat with.
(f) A playwright		6. tells the time.
(g) Chapati		7. makes bread and cakes.

(a) Feijoada is something which/that people eat in Brazil.

(b) ______________________________

(c) ______________________________

(d) ______________________________

(e) ______________________________

(f) ______________________________

(g) ______________________________

FURTHER PRACTICE

Part four: (Units 13–17) Amounts

(Unit 13)

1. Complete the dialogue using *have/has(n't) got.*

Estate Agent: 'I've got the perfect house for you, sir!'

Customer: '______ it ______ three bedrooms?'

Estate Agent: 'Well, in fact, it ____________ four.'

Customer: 'Is it expensive? I ______ ______ much money.'

Estate Agent: 'No, it's very reasonable. Only Rs 53,000.'

Customer: '______ you ______ the keys? Can I go and see it?'

Estate Agent: 'Certainly. I think I ______ ______ some free time this afternoon, if you like.'

(Unit 14)

2. Write *a* or *some* before these nouns.

(a) ______ milk
(b) ______ paper
(c) ______ newspaper
(d) ______ rain
(e) ______ mushrooms
(f) ______ yoghurt
(g) ______ tomato
(h) ______ bread
(i) ______ money
(j) ______ toast
(k) ______ soap
(l) ______ cup of tea
(m)______ coffee
(n) ______ cheese
(o) ______ chocolate

(Unit 15)

3. Complete the sentences with *some* or *any*.

(a) Have you got ______ orange juice?
(b) There aren't ______ potatoes.
(c) I haven't got ______ money.
(d) There are ______ eggs in the fridge.
(e) I'd like to listen to ______ music.
(f) He usually meets ______ friends at the weekend.
(g) Why doesn't he have ______ friends?
(h) Sorry, we don't have ______ milk today.

(Unit 16)

4. Complete the questions with *much* or *many*.

(a) How ______ does it cost?
(b) How ______ times a week do you go swimming?
(c) How ______ bedrooms has your house got?
(d) How ______ chocolate do you eat in a week?
(e) How ______ cake would you like?
(f) How ______ hours do you work?
(g) How ______ people do you know?
(h) How ______ water is there?
(i) How ______ sandwiches are there?
(j) How ______ bread is there?

(Unit 17)

5. Rewrite these complaints using *too/too much/too many/not enough*.

(a) I don't like this really hot weather. The weather is ____________ hot.
(b) My flat isn't very warm. My flat is ____________ warm ____________.
(c) I work from 8.00 am –7.00 pm. The hours are ____________ long.
(d) It's very noisy in here. There's ____________ noise!
(e) I've eaten a lot of chocolate—I feel sick! I've eaten ____________ chocolate.
(f) It rains all the time here! It's ____________ wet.
(g) There aren't many people at this party—it's boring! There are ____________ people.
(h) I've eaten lunch but I'm still hungry! I have ____________ eaten ____________.

FURTHER PRACTICE

Part Five: (Units 18–19) Talking about now

(Unit 18)

Example:	
(a) It/rain	It's raining.

(b) The children/leave school. ________________

(c) They/wear raincoats. ________________

(d) They/play in the rain. ________________

(e) The sun/shine. ________________

(f) Two children/carry bags. ________________

(Unit 19)

2. Complete the sentences about the pictures with *present simple* or *present continuous*.

Yousuf (be) is a doctor.
He (work) ______ in a hospital.
He (play) ______ football.
He (wear) ______ shorts.
At work he (wear) ______ a white coat.

Jagan (be) ______ 26.
He (drive) ______ his new car.
He (listen) ______ to music.
He (like) ______ rock music.
He (clean) ______ his car every Saturday.

Kumar and Sunita (be) ______ teachers.
They (teach) ______ English.
They (have) ______ dinner.
They often (eat) ______ in restaurants.
They (like) ______ good food!

Jose (be) ______ Spanish.
She (live) ______ in Barcelona.
She (like) ______ Barcelona because the sun always (shine) ______.
Unfortunately, today it (rain) ______.

FURTHER PRACTICE

Part six: (Units 20–22) Prepositions

(Unit 20)

1. Sheila's kitchen is very untidy! She doesn't know where her things are. **Look at the picture and answer the questions to help her find them.**

Use the following words: *in, on, under, near, behind, in front of, opposite, next to.*

(a) Where's the cat? It's under the newspaper.

(b) Where's Sheila's book? ______

(c) Where's the milk? ______

(d) Where's the telephone? ______

(e) Where are the apples? ______

(f) Where's the dog? ______

(g) Where are her keys? ______

(h) Where's the cheese? ______

(i) Where's Sheila's bag? ______

(j) Where are the onions? ______

(k) Where are Sheila's shoes? ______

(l) Where's the shopping list? ______

2. **Look at the picture of Sheila's kitchen again. Are the following statements *true or false?* If they are *false* correct the statement.**

(a) The toy car is under the music system. False - the toy car is on the music system.

(b) The radio is near the telephone. ______

(c) The saucepan is on the cooker. ______

(d) The bananas are on the saucepan. ______

(e) The shoes are in the fridge. ______

(f) The plant is behind the book. ______

(g) The vacuum cleaner is next to the cupboard. ______

(h) The bread is opposite the keys. ______

FURTHER PRACTICE

(Unit 21)

3. Look at Louise' diary and complete the sentences using *in/at/on* or *nothing*.

(a) On Monday morning at 9.00 Louise has got a meeting.

(b) She's got another meeting ______ 3.00 ______ Tuesday.

(c) John's birthday is ______ Wednesday and they're having dinner ______ the evening.

(d) ______ noon ______ 13th April, she's having lunch with the Directors.

(e) ______ the morning ______ Saturday she's playing tennis.

(f) ______ Easter Sunday ______ the afternoon she's visiting her grandmother.

(g) ______ next week is her parents' wedding anniversary.

(h) She isn't working ______ the weekend.

(i) On Friday she finishes her job. ______ the future she won't work so hard!

(Unit 22)

4. Look at the picture and complete the directions with the following words:
across, round, from, to, into, under, on, over, through, down, along, past, out of, up, off.

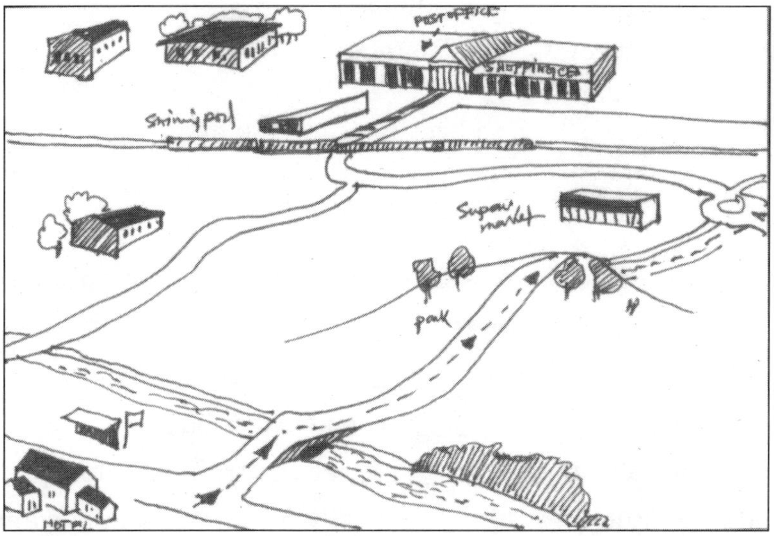

A: 'Excuse me, how do I get to the post office ______ this hotel?'

B: 'Well, go ______ of the hotel, ______ the road, ______ the bridge, ______ the hill, ______ the park, ______the hill, ______the supermarket, ______ the road, ______the roundabout, ______ the railway bridge and ______ the shopping centre. The post office is on the left.'

A: 'That sounds complicated. Is there a bus?'

B: 'Yes, get ______ a number 29 and get ______ next to the swimming pool.'

Part seven: (Units 23–25) Talking about the past I

(Unit 23)

1. Rita has just been on holiday to Prague.
Complete the questions her friend Soma asks her about her holiday. Use *was/were.*

Example:		
(a) Where/the hotel?	In the Old Town	Where was the hotel?
(b) /it nice?	Yes, lovely.	______
(c) /the weather good?	Not bad. It rained a bit.	______
(d) /the museums good?	Yes, very interesting.	______
(e) What/the food like?	Delicious. I ate so much!	______
(f) /you on your own?	No, I went with David.	______

2. Complete these sentences using *wasn't / weren't.*

Example:
(a) The weather wasn't very good.

(b) The Old Town ______ very crowded.
(c) The museums ______ expensive.
(d) I ______ very tired at the end of the day.
(e) David ______ very interested in the museums.
(f) We ______ in Prague for very long—just a week.
(g) The other guests in the hotel ______ very friendly.

FURTHER PRACTICE

(Unit 24)

3. Complete these sentences with the past tense form of the *irregular* verb in brackets ( ).

(a) Seema (make) ______ her own wedding dress.
(b) I (fly) ______ to Paris because it's quicker than the train.
(c) She (sing) ______ really well.
(d) Raja (throw) ______ a stone and (break) ______ the window!
(e) I (write) ______ to her about a week ago.
(f) Last night (I go) ______ to a party and (lose) ______ my umbrella. I think someone (steal) ______ it.
(g) He (drink) ______ six cups of coffee and didn't sleep all night!
(h) I (build) ______ this house myself. It (take) ______ me six years.
(i) She (pay) ______ the bill and (leave) ______.

4. Complete these sentences with the past tense form of the *regular* verb in brackets.
Be careful with spelling!

(a) I really (enjoy) ____________ the film.
(b) He (carry) ____________ the heaviest bag.
(c) The car (stop) ____________ at the traffic lights.
(d) He (study) ____________ really hard to pass his exam.
(e) I (try) ____________ to walk but it was too far.
(f) They (plan) ____________ to go to Buenos Aires but in the end they couldn't.

(Unit 25)

5. In 1996 Stephen lived in Brno, in the Czech Republic. **Complete the questions about his experiences.**

(a) *Why / go / there?*
Why did you go there? I had a job as an English Teacher.

(b) *Where / teach?*
____ ? In a small school in the centre.

(c) *teach children?*
________________________ ______________? Yes, from eight years old to fifteen.

(d) *enjoy it there?*
____ _? Yes, it's a beautiful town.

(e) *learn Czech?*
____ _? No it was very difficult.

(f) *make Czech friends?*
____ ? Yes, people were very friendly.

(g) *What / do in your spare time?*
____ ? I went walking in the countryside.

6. Use the information above to answer these questions with *short answers*.

(a) Did Stephen work in Brno? Yes, he did.

(b) Did he teach in a large school? ____________

(c) Did he teach children? ____________

(d) Did he teach adults? ____________

(e) Did he enjoy it there? ____________

(f) Did he speak good Czech? ____________

(g) Did he make Czech friends? ____________

Part eight: (Units 26–31) Adding meaning

(Unit 26)

1. **Choose *like* or *would like*.**

(a) '*Do you / Would you* like some coffee?' 'No, thanks.' Would you

(b) '*Do you / Would you* like to sit down?' ____________

(c) 'I think *I'd like / I like* a cup of tea—I'm thirsty' ____________

(d) '*He'd like / He likes* listening to very loud music. I hate it!' ____________

(e) 'It's raining. *Do you / Would you* like to borrow my umbrella?' ____________

(f) '*I don't like / wouldn't like* swimming much. It's usually too cold in Norway.' ____________

(g) 'My parents *would like / like* to meet you. Shall I introduce you?' ____________

2. **Complete the dialogues using *would like* (to + infinitive) *or like* (+ ing).**

(a) A: 'Would you like to go (go) to the cinema next week? There's a new thriller on.'
B: 'Well, I ________ (go) to the cinema but I hate thrillers! I __________ (see) comedies better.'

(b) A: 'Do you ____________ (eat) out in restaurants?'
B: 'Yes, I love it! I really ____________ (eat) Indian food.'
A: '____________ you ____________ (go) out for an Indian meal tonight?'
B: 'Yes, please!'

(c) A: 'I ________ you ________ (meet) my friends. Why don't we all go out for dinner next week?'
B: 'Oh, I'm really shy. I don't ____________ (meet) new people.'

(Unit 27)

3. What do you *say*?

(a) You are cold and want to *borrow* some gloves from your friend.
    Can I borrow some gloves, please?

(b) You are in class and haven't got a pen. You want to *borrow* one. ______________________?

(c) You want someone to *close* the door. ______________________?

(d) You are in a shop and you want to *pay by cheque*. ______________________?

(e) You need Re. 1 to make a phone-call. You want a friend to *lend* it to you. ______________________?

(f) You want to *turn on the television* in your friend's house. ______________________?

(g) You want someone to *telephone* you later. ______________________?

4. Complete the dialogues

(a) A: May/Can I use the phone?
    B: Certainly.

(b) A: Are you going to the party?
    B: Well, ______ you give me a lift?

(c) A: My phone number's 27273456.
    B: Wait ... ______ you lend me a pen?

(d) A: ______ I read that magazine when you've finished with it?
    B: Of course.

(e) A: ______ you tell me the time please?
    B: It's exactly 6.00.

(f) A: ______ we sit here?
    B: Sorry, there's only one seat free.

(Unit 28)

5. Look at the picture of Suman's room. **Make six sentences about what she *can* do.**

(a) She can play the guitar.
(b) ______________________
(c) ______________________
(d) ______________________
(e) ______________________
(f) ______________________

6. Suman is eighteen now. Write sentences about what *you think* she *could/couldn't* do when she was twelve?

(a) She could play the guitar.
(b) ______________________
(c) ______________________
(d) ______________________
(e) ______________________
(f) ______________________

FURTHER PRACTICE

(Unit 29)

7. Use the verbs to write about what you *have to do* in different places.

wear a tie *wait in a queue* *be quiet* *buy a ticket*
wait until the light turns green *wear a hat*

(a) In a cinema you have to buy a ticket.
(b) In a library ____________
(c) At the traffic lights ____________
(d) In an expensive restaurant ____________
(e) In many swimming pools ____________
(f) In the bank you often ____________

8. Last year Suresh was still at school. Now he is working in a supermarket. **Write sentences about last year and now using *has to/had to (+)* and *doesn't have to / didn't have to (-)*.**

When Suresh was at school:

(a) He had to do homework. (+)
(c) He ____________ get up very early. (-)
(e) He ____________ work on Saturdays. (-)
(g) He ____________ study French. (+)
(i) He ____________ wear a uniform. (+)

Now he's working in a supermarket:

(b) He doesn't have to do homework. (-)
(d) He ____________ get up at 6.00. (+)
(f) He ____________ work on Saturday mornings. (+)
(h) He ____________ study French. (-)
(j) He *still* ____________ wear a uniform! (+)

(Unit 30)

9. Here are some sentences giving advice about travelling abroad. **Rewrite the sentences using *should/shouldn't*.**

(a) It's a good idea to take out insurance. You should take out insurance.
(b) It's a good idea to write your address on your luggage. ____________
(c) It *isn't* a good idea to take very heavy luggage. ____________
(d) It's a good idea to buy a guidebook. ____________
(e) It *isn't* a good idea to carry too much cash. ____________
(f) It's a good idea to learn to speak a little of the language. ____________

10. Complete the answers to some 'problem page' letters using *should (n't) + one of these verbs:*

eat listen try tell stop make cook walk smoke expect

You (a) ______ to your 'friends'. They are being very cruel. But you (b) ______ to take more exercise.

You (c) ______ to school rather than take the bus and you (d) ______ more fruit and less chocolate.

I think you (e) ______ your friend that she (f) ______ smoking. Obviously it is making her ill. Tell her that if she wants to be healthy and able to run fast she (g) ______ at all.

Your parents (h) ______ you eat meat if you want to be vegetarian but you (i) ______ them to cook two meals every night. You (j) ______ your own dinner.

FURTHER PRACTICE

(Unit 31)

11. Rewrite these sentences using *may (not)* or *might (n't)*.

(a) Perhaps she's on holiday. She might/may be on holiday.
(b) Perhaps he doesn't like me. ______
(c) Perhaps he will pass the exam. ______
(d) Perhaps they live in Sri Lanka. ______
(e) Perhaps I'll go out tonight. ______
(f) Perhaps I'll stay at home. ______
(g) Perhaps he is a doctor. ______
(h) Perhaps they speak Bengali. ______
(i) Perhaps she doesn't speak English. ______
(j) Perhaps they don't live here. ______
(k) Perhaps we are lost. ______

Part nine: (Units 32–33) Talking about the past II

(Unit 32)

1. Elaine and John work for the same company but last week Elaine was on a business trip in Dublin while John was working in the office in London. **Look at the pictures and complete the sentences about what they were doing *last Wednesday*.**

9 am
Elaine/have breakfast
John / drive to work
At 9am Elaine was having breakfast and John was driving to work.

10 am
Elaine/visit an exhibition
John / write letters
______
______

3 pm
Elaine/meet clients
John / do the accounts
______
______

12.30 pm
Elaine/have lunch
John / have a meeting with a Director
______
______

6 pm
Elaine/have dinner with the Director of the Dublin office
John / drive home
______
______

(Unit 33)

2. Elaine didn't have a very good journey home from Dublin. In fact, she had a lot of problems. **Look at the pictures and use *when* and the *past simple* or *past continuous* to describe what happened.**

rain/leave hotel
It was raining when she left the hotel.

drive to the airport/ taxi break down
______
______

stand in the check-in queue/someone steal her handbag
______
______

Talk to the police/ the plane leave without her

______

______

sit on the plane/ spill her drink

______

______

wait for her luggage/someone tell her it was lost

______

______

feel really tired and annoyed/get home

______

______

3. Later Elaine told the story to her husband. **Complete her story using the *past simple* and *past continuous*.**

'The journey home was terrible. First it (rain) <u>was raining</u> when I left the hotel, so I got wet. Then the taxi (break down) ____ on the way to the airport. Then, while I was waiting in the check-in queue someone (steal) ______ my handbag so I had to go to the police. And then I (miss) ______ my plane because I was talking to the police for so long! I was really angry. Then, I finally got on another plane. I (begin) ______ to relax a bit when I spilt my orange juice everywhere! We got to London at last and I (wait) ______ for my luggage when a man came and told me it was lost! 'It might be in Rome.' he said. So you can understand why I (feel) ______ unhappy and tired when I got home!'

Part ten: (Units 34–37) Describing

(Units 35 and 36)

1. Compare the *three* things in each question using a *comparative* and a *superlative*.

(a) 1. The Thames 2. The Amazon 3. The Nile
(*long*) <u>The Amazon is longer than the Thames.</u>
<u>The Nile is the longest.</u>

(b) 1. a bicycle 2. a motorbike 3. a car
(*fast*) ______
______

(c) 1. silver 2. gold 3. platinum
(*precious*) ______
______

(d) 1. a grape 2. an orange 3. a grapefruit
(*big*) ______
______

(e) 1. Norway 2. England 3. Thailand
(*hot*) ______
______

(f) 1. coca-cola 2. fruit juice 3. water
(*healthy*) ______
______

(g) 1. newspaper 2. magazine 3. book
(*expensive*) ______
______

2. *Complete* the quiz questions with *superlatives* and then *match* them with the *answer*.

(a) What are (*new*) <u>the newest</u> states in India?

(b) Which is (*big*) ______ second ______ city in India?

(c) Which restaurant in London is owned by three of (*famous*) ______ American film stars?

(d) What is (*young*) ______ age you can marry in India?

(e) What is India's (*popular*) ______ tourist attraction?

(f) What is India's (*large*) ______ Residence?

(g) Which is India's (*high*) ______ dam?

1. Rashtrapati Bhawan
2. Taj Mahal
3. New Delhi
4. Jharkhand, Uttaranchal, Chhattisgarh (✓)
5. Planet Hollywood
6. 18 for firls, 21 for boys.
7. Bhakhra Dam

FURTHER PRACTICE

(Units 34 and 37)

3. Decide if these words are *adjectives* or *adverbs*.

large adjective poor ______ patiently ______ magic ______ immediately ______

new______ slowly ______ angry ______ comfortable ______ angrily ______

4. Use the adjectives and adverbs *from exercise 3* to complete the story.

Once upon a time there was a very poor fisherman and his wife. One day the fisherman caught a fish which spoke to him. 'Let me go, fisherman.' it said, 'I am a ______ fish.' So the fisherman let him go. He returned home to his wife but when he told her the story she was very ______. 'Why didn't you ask him to give us a ______ house instead of this small hut we live in?' she asked, 'Go back and ask him for a house.' So the fisherman went back to the lake, called the fish and told him what his wife had said. 'Go home', said the fish, 'she has it already'. When the fisherman got home his wife was in a lovely ______ house.

But two weeks later his wife said, 'This house is very small and not very ______ . Go and ask the fish for a castle.' The fisherman didn't want to but he went back to the fish and asked him for a castle. 'Go home,' said the fish, ______ 'she has it already.'

When the fisherman got home, his wife was very happy with her new castle but the next day she said, 'Now I live in a castle I want to be Queen. Go and ask the fish.' The fisherman went to ask the fish. 'Go home', said the fish, 'She is Queen already.'

But when the fisherman got home his wife was watching the sun ______ going down. 'Why can't I do that?' she asked. 'Go back to the fish ______ and tell him I want to be Master of the Universe!' The fisherman went back to the fish and asked him but the fish said ______, 'Go home. Your wife is back in her small hut.'

FURTHER PRACTICE

Part eleven: (Units 38–40) Talking about the future

(Unit 38)

1. Complete the dialogues with *present simple* or *present continuous* to talk about the future.

A: 'When (meet) are you meeting Mr Joshi?

B: 'At lunchtime. We (have) ___________lunch in Quaglino's'.

A: 'Lucky you! (meet) ___________ you ___________ him at the restaurant?'

B: 'No, he (come)___________here. He (give) ___________ me a lift.'

C: 'What time (leave) ___________ the train ___________ ?'

D: 'Twelve o'clock. So hurry up!'

C: 'Where (meet) ___________ we ___________ the others?'

D: 'On the platform.'

E: 'When (go)___________ you ___________ back to University?'

F: 'Well, term (start) ___________ on October 3rd but I (go) ___________ back a few days early.'

E: 'Why?'

F: 'I (move) ___________ in to my new flat on September 30th.'

(Unit 39)

2. Ola works in the office of a language school.

Look at Ola's list of things to do today and write sentences about what she is *going to do*.

To do

type some letters
pay the teachers
telephone the Director
check the registers
check how many students there are in each class

(a) She's going to type some letters.
(b) ______________________________
(c) ______________________________
(d) ______________________________
(e) ______________________________

3. Now complete the dialogues between Ola and the teachers, using *going to* and *will*.

Teacher 1: 'Ola? Are we going to get paid today?'
Ola: 'Yes, I __________ pay you all this afternoon, don't worry.'
Teacher 2: 'Ola? How many students are there in class B501?'
Ola: 'Can I tell you later? I __________ check how many students there are this afternoon. OK?'
Teacher 3: 'Ola? Those plants look almost dead!'
Ola: 'Oh! OK. I __________ give them some water.'
Teacher 4: 'Ola? Is the Director coming here today?'
Ola: 'No, but I __________ ring him later. Do you want me to pass on a message?'
Teacher 5: 'Ola! The phone's ringing. Shall I answer it?'
Ola: 'No, it's OK. I __________ answer it.'
Ola: 'Have you completed your registers properly?'
Teacher 6: 'Er …'
Ola: 'Well, I __________ check them this afternoon.'

(Unit 40)

4. Write a sentence to describe what is *going to* happen in each picture.

(a) They're going to dance.

(b) ______________

(c) ______________

(d) ______________

(e) ______________

(f) ______________

5. Complete the conversation with the gypsy using *will*.

Gypsy: 'You (have) will have a long and happy life.'

Client: 'When (get married) __________ I__________?'

Gypsy: 'Oh, you (not marry) __________ early. You (meet) __________ your husband when you are about thirty.'

Client: 'What (be) __________ his job __________ ?'

Gypsy: 'He (be) __________ a businessman.'

Client: '(have) __________ we __________any children?'

Gypsy: 'Yes, you (have) __________ six children.'

Client: 'Six?!'

Part twelve: (Units 41–44) Connecting the past and the present

(Unit 41)

1. Look at the table and write sentences about what the people *have done/have never done*.

(a) Shankar/climbed Mount Everest — Shankar has climbed Mount Everest.
(b) Sushma/be on television — Sushma has never been on television.
(c) Jaya and Ravi/climb Mount Everest __________
(d) Shankar/write a book __________
(e) Sushma/meet the British Queen __________
(f) Jaya and Ravi/be on television __________
(g) Shankar/have an accident __________
(h) Sushma/write a book __________
(i) Jaya and Ravi/meet the British Queen __________

	Climb Mount Everest	write a book	meet the British Queen	be on television	have an accident
Shankar	✓	×	×	✓	✓
Sushma	×	✓	✓	×	×
Jaya and Ravi	×	×	×	✓	✓

2. Write questions using *ever* and *short answers* using the information in the table.

(a) Shankar/meet the British Queen? Has Shankar ever met the British Queen? No, he hasn't
(b) Sushma/be on television? __________ __________
(c) Jaya and Ravi/write a book? __________ __________
(d) Sushma/have an accident? __________ __________
(e) Shankar/be on television? __________ __________
(f) Jaya and Ravi/have an accident? __________ __________

(Unit 42)

3. *It's now 1997.* **Write sentences about *how long*, using *for* and *since*.**

(a) He got married in 1987 (*be married*).
He's been married for ten years.
He's been married since 1987.

(b) He went to live in Ecuador twelve years ago (*live*).
____
____

(c) They became teachers in 1989 (*be*).
____
____

(d) I bought a computer a year ago (*have*).
____
____

(e) She learnt to play the piano when she was six. Now she's seventeen (*play*).
____
____

(f) I learnt to speak Japanese three years ago (*speak*).
____
____

(g) It started being sunny last week (*be sunny*). ____________________

(h) The shop opened two years ago (*be open*). ____________________

(i) We went to University three years ago (*be at*). ____________________ ____________________

4. Write questions for the situations in *exercise 3* using *How long...?*

(a) How long has he been married?
(b) ____________________
(c) ____________________
(d) ____________________
(e) ____________________
(f) ____________________
(g) ____________________
(h) ____________________
(i) ____________________

(Unit 43)

5. Look at the two pictures of Arjun. **What can you see has *changed* in the second picture? Write sentences using these verbs:**

shave his beard | *grow his hair* | *put on weight*
get older | *start wearing a tie* | *buy some new clothes*
stop wearing an earring | *get married* | *become smarter*

(a) He's shaved his beard.
(b) ____________________
(c) ____________________
(d) ____________________
(e) ____________________
(f) ____________________
(g) ____________________
(h) ____________________
(i) ____________________

6. Write questions and short answers about Arjun in the *second picture*.

(a) cut his hair? Has he cut his hair? No, he hasn't.
(b) grow a moustache? ____________ ____________
(c) put on weight? ____________ ____________
(d) start wearing a tie? ____________ ____________
(e) lose weight? ____________ ____________
(f) get married? ____________ ____________
(g) shave his beard? ____________ ____________

(Unit 44)

7. Raj is in town. He has a list of things to do. Write sentences about what he *has already done* and what he *hasn't done yet*.

- post the letters ✓ (a) He's already posted the letters.
- pay in the cheque ✓ (b) ____________________
- take out some cash ✓ (c) ____________________
- buy some bread and milk ✓ (d) ____________________
- get some petrol for the car (e) ____________________
- take the dog to the vet (f) ____________________
- pay the electricity bill (g) ____________________
- buy some aspirin (h) ____________________

8. Write *questions* and *short answers* about what Raj has done (using 'yet').

(a) Has Raj posted the letters yet? Yes, he has.
(b) ____________________ ____________
(c) ____________________ ____________
(d) ____________________ ____________
(e) ____________________ ____________
(f) ____________________ ____________
(g) ____________________ ____________
(h) ____________________ ____________

Communicative Activities—Part 1

At the end of most Units are 'Practise with a friend' activities, providing the opportunity for communicative oral practice (following on from controlled practice). Reference from the Unit to this Section is given.

The activities in this Section are in Unit sequence. Where an activity requires that friend 'B' is looking at different material to friend 'A' ('information gap' activities), where to find the friend 'B' material is clearly indicated.

Unit 1: am/is/are (Page 2)

Talk to a friend about your family. You could use these words to help you:

my brother, my mother, my parents, my sister, my father	is/are	beautiful, a teacher, quite goodlooking, Italian, very intelligent, from Poland

Unit 4: Singular and plural nouns (Page 8)

A turn to page 133, B turn to page 141

You have two pictures of a street. They are similar but not identical. Find the differences.

> ***Example***
> A: 'In my picture there is a church'.
> B: 'In my picture there are *two* churches'.

Unit 5: Present and simple tense (Page 10)

Use these verbs (and other you know) to talk to your friend about *your* life and where you live. Then listen to your friend carefully.

go live work study play stay finish make
watch have be get up like walk

> ***Example:***
> 'I live in HongKong. It is a very exciting city. I work ...'

Now talk to a different friend and tell him/her about your first friend.

> ***Example:***
> 'Joyce lives in HongKong. She works in a school...'

COMMUNICATION

Unit 7: always/never/sometimes (Page 14)

A: Interview your friend using these questions.

What time do you get up?
What do you have for breakfast?
What time do you start work/school?
What time do you finish work/school?
What do you do at the weekends?
Where do you go on holiday?

B: Answer the questions using *always /sometimes/often/rarely/never.* *(Try to make your answer long—like Julia's)*

Example: 'I often have toast for breakfast but I sometimes have cereal.'

Unit 8: I/me, he/him (Page 16)

Look at these famous singers and groups. Add any other you know.

The Spice Girls ______ Oasis ______ Michael Jackson ______ The Kelly Family ______ Sting ______ Madonna ______

With your friend point and talk about who you *like* and *don't like.* Use him/her/them.

Example:
'I like him. He's a good singer.'
'Really? I hate him!'

Unit 9: Possessive adjectives and 's (Page 18)

Draw your family tree. *Don't* show it to your friend.
Work in pairs and ask questions to find out your friend's family tree. Try to draw it using your answer.

Example : 'What's your mother's name?' 'Lalita'

Unit 10: mine/yours (Page 20)

Who do these things belong to?

Talk with your friend. Make guesses using *his/hers/theirs.*

Example: A: 'I think the gloves are ***his.***'
B: 'I think they're ***hers.*** They're quite small.'

Unit 11: Articles (Page 22)

Talk to your friend for **one minute** about where you live, your town or city. Listen carefully to your friend and try to write down any mistakes they make with **'a', 'an', 'the'** or **'nothing'**.

Unit 12: who/which/that (Page 24)

A: Write the definitions of these *jobs*. (and any others you know)

Example :		
teacher	–	*a person who works in a school*

baker – ______

artist – ______

musician – ______

teacher – ______

______ – ______

______ – ______

______ – ______

Now read your definitions to your friends.
Can they guess the job?

B: Write the definitions of these *animals and birds* (and any others you know)

Example:		
elephant	–	*an animal which (or that) has a long nose*

cat – ______

parrot – ______

donkey – ______

owl – ______

______ – ______

______ – ______

______ – ______

Now read your definitions to your friends.
Can they guess the animal or bird?

Unit 14: Countable and uncountable nouns (Page 28)

Do you know this game?

A: You must choose *uncountable* nouns

B: You must choose *countable nouns*

Unit 19: Present *simple* and present *continuous* (Page 38)

Think about someone in the class. Tell your friend some things that are **generally true** about them and some things that they **are doing now.** Can your friend guess who it is?

Example: **She's got** long hair. **She works** in a shop. **She's looking** out of the window ...

Unit 21: in/at/on (Page 42)

Ask your friend 'When do you.................?' Answer using 'in.../at.../on...'

go to bed eat ice-cream get up have a special meal watch television study English visit friends of family go on holiday get presents have your main meal give presents send cards drink coffee clean the house go for a walk go shopping listen to the radio

Example:	
A: 'When do you go to bed?'	A: 'When do you get presents?'
B: 'Usually **at** midnight.'	B: '**On** my birthday.'

Unit 23: 'to be' (Page 46)

Write down some dates in the past you can remember.

Ask and answer these questions about *you and your family* at those times.

How old / you, your mother, your sisters, etc....?

Where / you, your husband, your children, etc...?

Example :	
A: 'March 1992. How old **were** you?'	A: 'Where **were** you?'
B: 'I **was** 17.'	B: 'I **was** on holiday in Kerala.'

Unit 24: Past simple tense (Page 48)

Look at these holiday photos. Talk with a friend or write sentences about what Mina did on holiday.

Example:
'She **ate** spaghetti.'

Unit 27: can/could/may (Page 54)

You and your friend are going to have a party. There is a lot to do!

Here are some of the things you have to do:

do the washing up ______ ______

clean the bathroom ______ ______

make the sandwiches ______ ______

clean the rooms ______ ______

Think of some more ideas together. Then ask each other to do the things.

Example: A: '**Could** you do the washing up?'
B: 'OK. **Can** you make the sandwiches?'

Unit 28: can/could (Page 56)

Talk with your friend. Ask and answer questions to find:

- three things A *can do* and B *can't*
- three things A *could do when they were ten* that B *couldn't*

* three things B *can do* and A *can't*
* three things B *could do when they were ten* that A *couldn't*

> ***Example:***
> A: '**Can** you play the piano?'
> B: 'Yes, I can. **Can** you play the piano?'
>
> A: 'No, I can't. **Could** you play the piano when you were 10?'
> B: 'No, I couldn't'
>
> A: '**Could** you play any musical instrument?'
> B: 'Well, I could play the recorder!'

Unit 37: Manner (Page 74)

Tell your friend *how* you do some of these things (and other things you can think of):

run talk play tennis speak English drive play music eat pizza study

> ***Example:***
> A : 'I drive **fast**'
> B : 'I eat pizza **noisily**!'

Unit 38: Present tense for future use (Page 76)

What arrangements do you have this week? Tell your friend about *your* arrangements and ask questions: What..? Where..? about *their* arrangements.

Unit 39: Going to/Will—I (Page 78)

Talk together about your plans for next weekend. You could use these verbs.

visit go play cook go shopping relax sleep meet study

> ***Remember*** – if you decided *before* use : going to/ not going to
> – if you decide as *you're speaking* use: will/ won't

Unit 42: time up to now (Page 84)

Ask and ***answer*** questions about your friend's possessions using **How long...?** and **for** and **since.**

> ***Example:*** '**How long** have you had your watch?'
> '**Since** Christmas'.
> '**How long** have you had your car?'
> '**For** a year.'

Unit 45: Questions Rivision (Page 90)

How many correct questions can you make using the words in the box? [You can use other words to complete your questions.]

am	What	are	How	is	How	long	have	has	were
was	Where	you	I	Can	Could	they	she	he	

> ***Example:*** A : '**What are you** doing tomorrow?'
> B : '**Where have you** been in Europe?'

COMMUNICATION

Communicative Activities—Part 2

At the end of most Units are 'Practise with a friend' activities, providing the opportunity for communicative oral practice (following on from controlled practice). Reference from the Unit to this section is given.

The activities in this section are in Unit sequence. Where an activity requires that friend 'B' is looking at different material to friend 'A' ('information gap' activities), where to find the friend 'B' material is clearly indicated.

Unit 3: this/that/these/those (Page 7)

Draw a plan of your room with furniture. Like this:

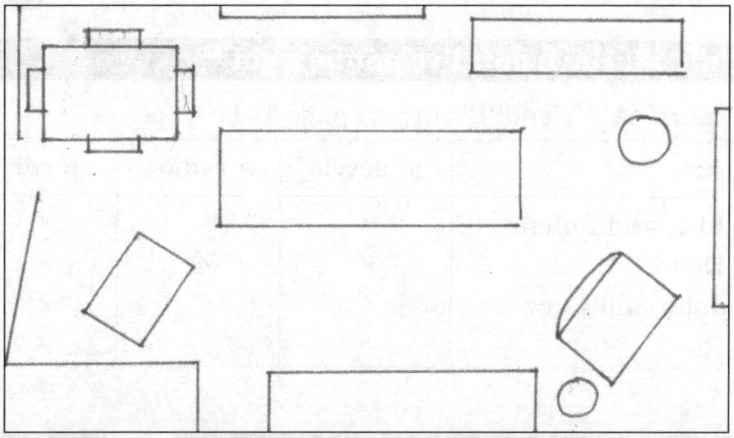

Tell your friend about it and ask questions.

> ***Example:***
> A: '**This** is my TV.'
> B: 'What are **those?**'
> A: 'Armchairs.'
> B: 'Is **that** a lamp?...'

Unit 4: Singular and plural nouns (Page 9)

Friend 'A' picture (friend 'B' picture, see page 141)

Unit 6: Present simple auxiliaries: do/does (Page 13)

Train information: Friend 'A' (friend 'B' turn to page 141)

A: You want to travel to **New Delhi**. Your friend has the information. Ask questions to find out.

What time/it/leave?

When/it/arrive?

How much/it/cost/

/you/need/a reservation?

/it/stop/in Patna?

The train to **Mumbai** leaves at 6.00 in the morning. It arrives at 7.00 in the evening. It stops in Bilaspur and Pune. It costs Rs. 500 second class and Rs. 1000 first class. You need a reservation.

Unit 13: Have got: I've got/he's got (Page 27)

Friend 'A' (friend 'B' turn to page 141)

A:	a bicycle	a radio	a cat	children	a house	a camera
Lisa and Rohan	✓		×		✓	
Dev	✓	✓	×			
John and Lucy			✓	✓		×
Ria	×		×		×	

Unit 15: 'Some' and 'any' (Page 31)

Friend 'A' (Friend 'B' turn to page 142)

Unit 16: Much/many/a lot (Page 33)

Friend 'A' (Friend 'B' turn to page 142)

Unit 17: 'Too' and 'not enough' (Page 35)

Play this game: Throw the two dice and make a sentence about the **picture** using the **word.**

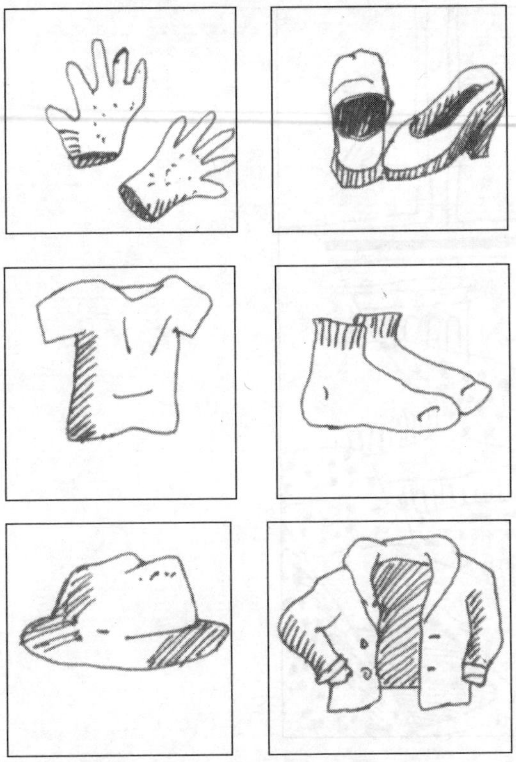

Examples:

Friend A:

 = 1 (gloves)

 = 3 big (enough)

'They aren't big enough'

Friend B:

 = 4 (shoes)

 = 2 expensive (too)

'They are too expensive'

1. small (too)
2. expensive (too)
3. big (enough)
4. big (too)
5. cheap (enough)
6. colourful (enough)

Unit 18: Present continuous tense (Page 37)

Friend 'A' (friend 'B' turn to page 143)

Unit 20: Prepositions of place: in/on/next to (Page 41)

Friend 'A' (friend 'B' turn to page 143)

Unit 22: Prepositions of movement: up/down (Page 45)

How many *logical combinations* can you make with these **places** and these **prepositions?** Who can make the most?

Places				
the river	the school	the stairs	the wall	
the town	the cinema	the hotel	the bridge	
Prepositions				
across	into	down	over	on
along	out of	past	round	

Example:
A: '**Past** the school.'
B: '**Over** the town.'
A: 'That's not logical!'
B: 'Yes, in an aeroplane!'

Unit 25: Past simple auxiliary: did/didn't (Page 51)

Information about Shakespeare: Friend 'A' (Friend 'B' turn to page 144)

A: Read the text and answer your friend's questions.
William Shakespeare was born on (approximately) 23rd April 1564 in Stratford-upon-Avon. His father was a glove-maker. Shakespeare went to school in Stratford, at the local Grammar School. When he was eighteen he married Anne Hathaway. She was twenty-six. They had three children: a daughter, Susannah and twins, Judith and Hamnet. He spent a lot of his life away from his family, working in London. When he died in 1616, he left most of his money to his daughter, Susannah. He left Anne his second-best bed!

Ask your friend these questions about *this* text.

When/Shakespeare/come to London?
What/he/do in London?
How many plays/he/write?
/He/only write plays?
What/he/call his theatre?
What/he/do in 1596?
When/he/return to Stratford?
What day/he/die?

Unit 26: Would like (Page 53)

Ask questions about these things using: *Do you like... ? Would you like... ?*

orange juice   go/going to the theatre   cooking   come to a party   dancing/to dance
play/playing tennis   going on holiday   writing letters   go/going out to dinner

Choose from these answers:					
Yes, please	No, thank you	Yes, I do	No, I don't	Yes, I'd love to	Sorry, I can't

Examples:

A: '**Do you like** orange juice?'
B: 'No, I don't.'

B: '**Do you like** going to the theatre?'
A: 'Yes, I do.'

B: '**Would you like** to go to the theatre on Saturday?'
A: 'Yes, I'd love to.'

Unit 29: Obligation (have to) (Page 59)

Write down five things you *have to do now* that you *didn't have to do* when you were a child.

Example: clean the house ________ ________ ________ ________

Now write down five things you *don't have to* do now that you *had to do* when you were a child.

Example: go to bed very early ________ ________ ________ ________

Now tell your friend about them.

Example:
A: 'Now I have to clean the house. I didn't have to clean the house when I was a child.'
B: 'Oh, I had to clean the house when I was a child—but now my husband does it!'

Unit 30: Advising: should/shouldn't (Page 61)

How often do you do these things? Every day? Sometimes? Never?

exercise   eat chocolate   study English   smoke   eat fruit and vegetables
read in English   drink milk   go for a walk   watch films   relax   speak English

Tell your friend how often you listen to their advice!

Example:

A: 'I never exercise.'
B: 'You **should** exercise more.'

A: 'And I smoke.'
B: 'You **shouldn't** smoke. It's very bad for you.'

A: 'But I eat lots of fruit every day.'
B: 'That's good.'

Unit 31: Possibility (may/might) (Page 63)

You and your friend are going on holiday. Here are some things that **might/may** happen:

rain   get lost   be sunny   run out of money (have no more)   be expensive
be cheap   be dangerous   be fun   meet some interesting people
see some beautiful things   get ill

Talk with your friend. Make sentences about what **might/may** happen on your holiday using these ideas (and your own ideas)

A is very *optimistic*. B is very *pessimistic*.

Example:
A: 'It **may** be fun.'
B: 'We **might** run out of money.'

COMMUNICATION

Unit 32: Past continuous (Page 65)

Ask your friend about what they were doing at these times yesterday:

8.00 am   12.00 pm   4.00 pm   6.00 pm   7.00 pm   10.00 pm

> ***Example:*** A: 'What **were** you **doing** at 8.00?'
> B: 'I **was reading** the newspaper.'

Unit 33: Past continuous and past simple (Page 67)

Friend 'B': turn to page 144.

You each have ten sentence beginnings. Read a sentence *beginning* to your friend. They must *complete* the sentence.

> ***Examples:***
> A: 'As I **was walking** through the park ...' → B: '...**I saw** a boy fall off a bicycle'.
> B: 'She **was wearing** a big hat when...' → A: '...the wind **blew** it off her head'.

A:

1. As I was walking through the park ...
2. While it was raining ...
3. When I was out shopping ...
4. As I was eating dinner ...
5. They were sleeping when ...
6. As he was watching television ...
7. I was walking to work when ...
8. He was out jogging when ...
9. When he was living in Peru ...
10. They were feeling very happy when ...

Unit 34: Adjectives I (Page 69)

Look at the pictures for one minute. Try to remember the objects and *think of an adjective to describe them.* Then *cover* the page and try to remember as many as you can—*with an adjective.* Who can remember more?

> ***Example:***
> A: A black cat, a big watch ...
> B: A fast car ...

Unit 36: Superlatives (Pages 73)

Choose three cities in your country (or countries). Compare them using these adjectives in the **superlative** form.

big polluted exciting beautiful modern expensive interesting
small dangerous relaxing nice hot cold cheap boring noisy

> ***Example:***
> A: 'New Delhi is very old and beautiful.'
> B: 'Kolkata is very interesting and charming.'

Unit 40: Going to/Will - II (Page 81)

Talk together about the picture. Make sentences about what you **can see *is* going to happen** and what you **think *will* happen.**

Unit 41: Present perfect I: experience (Page 83)

Use these verbs (or others you know) to ask questions, using **Have you ever ...**?

be break buy cut drink drive eat fall forget give
have meet read see speak steal take wear

If the answer is '**Yes, I have**', ask another question using **When, Where, Why, What + simple past.**

Examples:	'**Have you ever** eaten sushi?' 'No, I haven't.'	'**Have you ever** worn a fur hat?' 'Yes, I have.' 'Where **did** you wear it?' 'In Shimla! It was very cold.'

COMMUNICATION

Look at the picture and try to find *at least nine things* that you can see that Rohit *has done* in the kitchen today.

Example:
He *has swept* the floor.

Round the world trip: Friend A (friend 'B' turn to page 144)

A: You are on a Round the World Trip. Look at the map below and see where you've **already been** and where you **haven't been yet.** Your friend must try to find out where you are now. They can ask questions: **'Have** you **been** to Bali yet?' and you can tell them some information **'I've already been** to Cape Town.'***But don't tell them where you are now!***

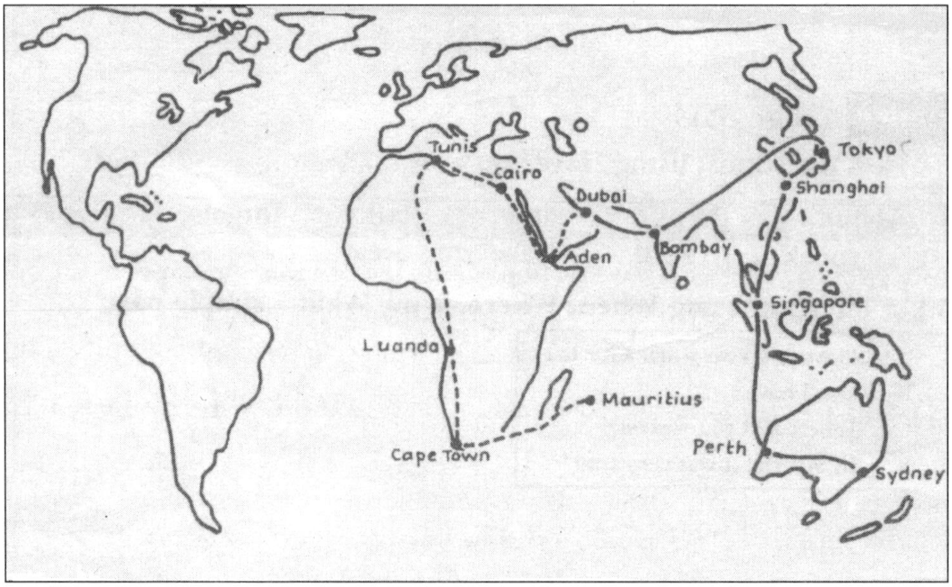

Friend 'B' material

Unit 4: Singular and plural nouns (Page 9)

(Friend 'A' turn to page 133)

Unit 6: Present simple auxiliaries: do/does (Page 13)

Train information friend 'B' (Friend 'A' turn to page 134)

B: You want to travel to **Mumbai**. Your friend has the information. Ask questions to find out.
When/it/leave?
What time/it/arrive?
How much/a first class ticket/cost?
/you/need/a reservation?
/it/stop/in Benares?

The train to **New Delhi** leaves at 8.00 in the evening. It arrives at 6.30 in the morning. It stops in Patna and Allahabad. It costs Rs 375 second class and Rs 800 first class. You need a reservation.

Unit 13: Have got: I've got/he's got (Page 27)

Friend 'B' (friend 'A' turn to page 134)

B:	a bicycle	a radio	a cat	children	a house	a camera
Lisa and Rohan		✓		×		✓
Dev				✓	✓	×
John and Lucy	×	×			✓	
Ria		✓		×		✓

Unit 15: 'Some' and 'any' (Page 31)

Friend 'B' (Friend 'A' turn to page 134)

Unit 16: Much/many/a lot (Page 33)

Friend 'B' (Friend 'A' turn to page 134)

COMMUNICATION

Unit 18: Present continuous tense (Page 37)

Friend 'B' (Friend 'A' turn to page 135)

Unit 20: Prepositions of place: in/on/next to (Page 41)

Friend 'B' (Friend 'A' turn to page 136)

Unit 25: Past simple auxiliary: did/didn't (Page 51)

Information about Shakespeare: Friend 'B' (friend 'A' turn to page 136)

B: Read the text and answer your friend's questions.
No-one knows exactly when Shakespeare came to London but he quickly became a very successful playwright and actor. He wrote at least 37 plays as well as poetry. He and his colleagues built their own theatre, called the Globe. In 1596 he bought the largest house in Stratford, New Place, as a family home. He returned to Stratford a few years before his death and died on the same day he was born, April 23—St George's Day.

Ask your friend these questions about *this* text.

When/Shakespeare/born?
What/his father/do?
Where/Shakespeare/go to school?
When/he/marry Anne Hathaway?
How old/she?
How many children/they/have?
Who/he/leave most of his money to when he died?
What/he/leave his wife?

Unit 33: Past continuous and past simple (Page 67)

Friend 'B' (Friend 'A' turn to page 138)
B

1. She was wearing a big hat when ...
2. While the plane was landing ...
3. They were eating ice-cream when ...
4. As she was crossing the road ...
5. While I was talking to him ...
6. As they were dancing ...
7. I was lying on the beach when ...
8. They were swimming in the sea when ...
9. Were you listening when ...?
10. As I was going to work this morning ...

Unit 44: Present perfect IV; 'yet' and 'already' (Page 89)

Round the world trip: Friend 'B' (friend 'A' turn to page 140)

B: You are on a Round the World Trip. Look at the map below and see where you've **already** been and where you haven't been yet. Your friend must try to find out where you are now. They can ask questions: 'Have you been to Bali yet?' and you can tell them some information 'I've already been to Buenos Aires.'
But don't tell them where you are now!

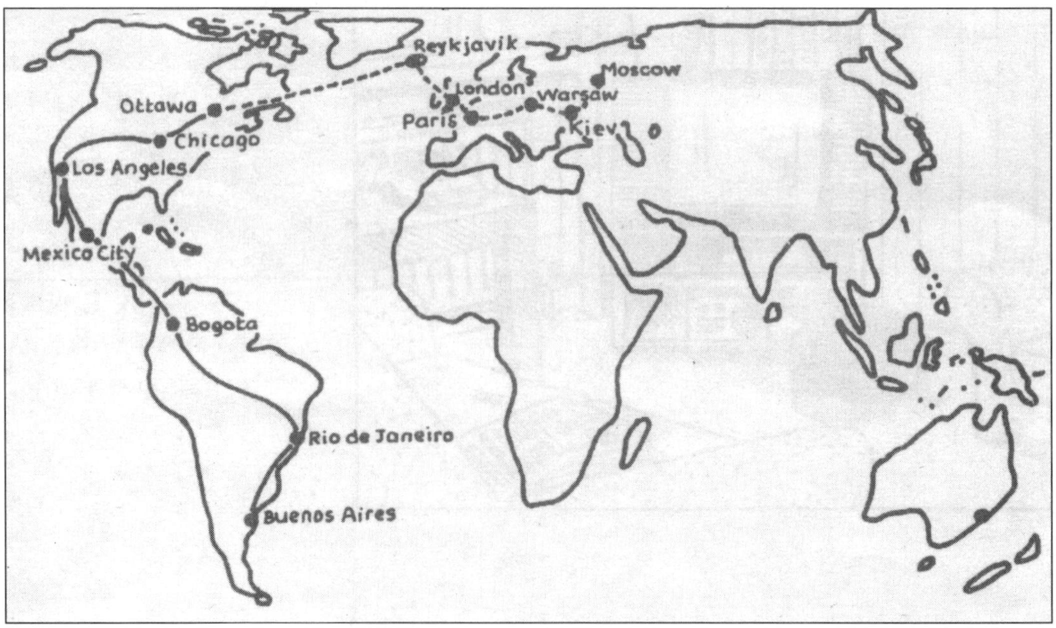

Appendix 1: List of Irregular Verbs

INFINITIVE	PAST SIMPLE	PAST PARTICIPLE
be	was/were	been
beat	beat	beaten
become	became	become
begin	began	begun
bite	bit	bitten
blow	blew	blown
break	broke	broken
bring	brought	brought
build	built	built
burn	burnt (burned)	burnt (burned)
buy	bought	bought
can	could	been able
catch	caught	caught
choose	chose	chosen
come	came	come
cost	cost	cost
cut	cut	cut
do	did	done
draw	drew	drawn
drink	drank	drunk
drive	drove	driven
eat	ate	eaten
fall	fell	fallen
feel	felt	felt
find	found	found
fly	flew	flown
forget	forgot	forgotten
get	got	got (AmEng'gotten')
give	gave	given
go	went	gone (or 'been')*
have	had	had
hear	heard	heard
hold	held	held
hurt	hurt	hurt
keep	kept	kept
know	knew	known
leave	left	left
lend	lent	lent

INFINITIVE	PAST SIMPLE	PAST PARTICIPLE
let	let	let
lose	lost	lost
make	made	made
mean	meant	meant
meet	met	met
must	had to	had to
pay	paid	paid
put	put	put
read/ri:d/	read/red/	read/red/
ride	rode	ridden
ring	rang	rung
rise	rose	risen
run	ran	run
say	said	said
see	saw	seen
sell	sold	sold
send	sent	sent
shine	shone	shone
show	showed	shown
sing	sang	sung
sit	sat	sat
sleep	slept	slept
speak	spoke	spoken
spend	spent	spent
stand	stood	stood
steal	stole	stolen
swim	swam	swum
take	took	taken
teach	taught	taught
tell	told	told
think	thought	thought
throw	threw	thrown
understand	understood	understood
wake	woke	woken
wear	wore	worn
win	won	won
write	wrote	written

**See Unit 41*

APPENDIX

Appendix 2: Answers and Explanations to Unit 'Teaching' Pages

Note: Handscript indicates what is expected to have been filled in

Unit 1: Present tense of the verb 'to be' (is/am/are)

Concept

I am Kavita.
I am from Panaji.

His name is Ravi.
He is from Rajasthan.

You are in Class 2A.

They are from Rome.
They are Italian.

I am John.
My name is Steve.
We are friends.

This is a School.
It is in Kolkata.

This is Sudeshna.
She is a student.

Structure

I'm from London.
You're in my class.
She's from Poland.
He's a student.
It's in London.
We're German.
They're from Denmark.

She's not from Poland.
She isn't from Poland.
We're not German.
We aren't German.

He's not a student.
He isn't a student.
They're not from Denmark.
They aren't from Denmark.

It's not in London.
It isn't in London.
I'm not from London.
(only one possibility here—we DON'T say 'I amn't')

Unit 2: Verb 'to be': questions (Am I?/Are you?/Is he?)

Concept

(a) 'Is he French? - 3 No he isn't
(b) 'Are we friends now?' - 5 No we're not
(c) 'Where are you from ?' - 6 Spain
(d) 'What's your name?' - 4 Keiko
(e) 'Is she from Japan?' - 2 Yes, she is
(f) 'Are you a model?' - 1 No, I'm not

Structure

I/you
'Am I boring?' — 'No, you aren't/you're not'
'Are you tired?' — 'Yes, I am'.
He/She/It
'Is she your sister?' — 'Yes, she is.'
'Is he from Venezuala?' — 'No, he isn't./he's not.'
We
'Are we late?' — 'No, we aren't./we're not.'
They
'Are they married?' — 'Yes, they are.'

Rules

Normally we put the verb 'to be' after the subject, but to make questions with the verb 'to be' we put the verb before the subject.

> ***Example:*** Subject + Verb Verb + Subject
> [You'**re** Polish = **Are** you Polish?]

To make negative short answers we contract but to make positive short answers we do NOT contract.

> ***Example:*** [No, **I'm not.**/Yes, **I am.**]

Negative short answers can contract two different ways (except No, I'm not)*

> ***Example:*** [No, **he's not** or No, **he isn't**.]

*see Unit 1

Question words

1. (a) Is she very rich?
   (b) Why is she very rich?
2. (a) (Is Warsaw in Poland?
   (b) Where is Warsaw?
3. (a) Are they both 16?
   (b) How old are they?
4. (a) Are we late?
   (b) Why are we late?

Unit 3: This/that/these/those

Concept

(a) = (2); (b) = (1); (c) = (1); (d) = (2)

Structure

This is the bathroom.	'This' and 'that' are	These are my children.	'These' and 'those' are
That is the kitchen.	singular	Those are my bags.	plural
This room is beautiful.		These apples are green.	
That bag is mine.		Those chairs are uncomfortable!	

Remember that only '**that's** normally contracts. So we don't write **this's.**

Negative statements and questions

This is your room.	This isn't your room.	It this your room?
That's your daughter.	That isn't your daughter.	Is that your daughter?
These are his keys.	These aren't his keys.	Are these his keys?
Those are our bicycles.	Those aren't our bicycles.	Are those our bicycles?
This room is beautiful.	This room isn't beautiful.	Is this room beautiful?
That room is John's.	That room isn't John's.	Is that room John's?
These curtains are very nice.	These curtains aren't very nice.	Are these curtains very nice?
Those chairs are uncomfortable.	Those chairs aren't uncomfortable.	Are those chairs uncomfortable?

Note: We can use this/that/these/those *next* to a noun—This room is beautiful, or put the noun *after* the verb 'to be'—This is your room.

Unit 4: Singular and plural nouns

Concept

1. In picture (a) there is a dictionary. In picture (b) there are two dictionaries.
2. In picture (a) there is a teacher. In picture (b) there are two teachers.
3. In picture (a) there are two keys. In picture (b) there is a key.
4. In picture (a) there are three desks. In picture (b) there is a desk.
5. In picture (a) there are five people. In picture (b) there are ten people.
6. In picture (a) there is a pen. In picture (b) there are three pens.
7. In picture (a) there is a bus. In picture (b) there are no buses.
8. In picture (a) there are two women. In picture (b) there are four women.
9. In picture (a) there is a man. In picture (b) there are two men.
10. In picture (a) there are two sandwiches. In picture (b) there is a sandwich.
11. In picture (a) there is a book (not the dictionary). In picture (b) there are nine books (not the dictionaries).
12. In picture (a) there are two children. In picture (b) there are four children.

We use the plural form when there is *more than one* [2, 3, 4, 5, 6 …]

Structure

	SINGULAR	PLURAL
(a)	book	books
	desk	desks
	table	tables
	teacher	teachers
	pen	pens

RULE: Most nouns add 's' in the plural.

(b)	bus	buses
	sandwich	sandwiches

RULE: When the last SOUND of the noun is /s/S/tS/dz/ we add 'es' in the plural.

	SINGULAR	PLURAL
(c)	dictionary	dictionaries

RULE: When the noun ends consonant + y the 'y' changes to 'ies'.

(d)	key	keys

RULE: When the noun ends vowel + y the 'y' does NOT change to -ies, we add 's' [Like rule (a)]

(e)	man	men
	woman	women
	person	people
	child	children

RULE: Some nouns (not only these four) are *irregular*. A good dictionary will help you with these.

APPENDIX

Unit 5: Present simple tense

Concept

We use the present simple tense to talk about things that are **generally true.**

Structure

	be	**make**	**work**	**go**	**finish**	**have**	**play**	**study**
I	am	make	work	go	finish	have	play	study
you	are	make	work	go	finish	have	play	study
he/she/it	is	make**s**	work**s**	go**es**	finish**es**	ha**s**	play**s**	stud**ies**
we	are	make	work	go	finish	have	play	study
they	are	make	work	go	finish	have	play	study

After he/she/it we usually add **-s** to the verb.

Spelling

	INFINITIVE	HE/SHE/IT
(a)	work	**works**
	make	makes
	get up	**gets up**
	live	lives

RULE: Most verbs add **'s** after he/she/it.

(b)	**finish**	finishes
	watch	**watches**

RULE: When the last SOUND of the verb is /s/S/tS/dz/ we add **-es** after he/she/it.

(c)	study	**studies**

RULE: *When the verb ends consonant + y the 'y' changes to* **ies.**

(d)	**play**	plays

RULE: When the verb ends vowel + y the 'y' does NOT change to -ies, we add **-s** [Like Rule (a)]

(e)	go	**goes**
	have	has
	be	**is**

RULE: Some verbs (not many) are irregular.

Unit 6: Present simple auxiliaries

Concept

QUESTIONS
What time does the train leave?
Where do I buy a ticket?
When do we arrive in Patna ?
Does this train go to Benares?
Do we stop at Allahabad?

NEGATIVES
Sorry, I don't know.
This train doesn't go to Patna.

SHORT ANSWERS
Yes, we do.

Structure

Look at your examples and complete the rules.

- To make a **question** in the present simple tense with most verbs (go, arrive, etc.) we use:

[QUESTION WORD] + *do* OR *does* + SUBJECT + INFINITIVE
What/When/Why, etc. you/he/I, etc. go/arrive, etc. [NOT goes, arrives]

- To make a **negative** in the present simple tense with most verbs we use:

SUBJECT + *don't* OR *doesn't* + INFINITIVE
I/She/it, etc. go/like/arrive, etc.

- To make a **short answer** in the present simple tense with most verbs we use:

YES/NO + SUBJECT + *do* OR *does* (positive)/*don't* OR *doesn't* (negative)
Yes, I do
No, it doesn't

- When the subject is **I, you, we, they,** we use *do* (positive) or *don't* (negative).
- When the subject is **he, she, it,** we use *does* (positive) or *doesn't* (negative).

Unit 7: Adverbs I: adverbs of frequency

Concept

Mr Joshi is **never** at home in the evenings.
He **always** visits clubs and restaurants.
He **often** goes on holiday.
He **rarely** takes exercise.
He **sometimes** smokes a cigar.

Mr Raj is **always** at home in the evenings.
He **often** runs in the park.
He **never** drives a car.
He **rarely** goes on holiday.
He **sometimes** goes to watch a football match.

ALWAYS 100%	OFTEN	SOMETIMES	RARELY	NEVER 0%

Structure

The VERB in sentence (a) is '**stay**'.
The VERB in sentence (b) is '**is**' (the verb 'to be')

With a verb like stay/go/drink, etc the *frequency adverb* (never, always, etc) **usually*** goes **before** the verb.
With the verb 'to be' (is/are, etc) the *frequency adverb* **usually*** goes **after** the verb.

[*'Usually' because sometimes a different word order is possible but this one is *always correct.*]

Unit 8: Subject and object pronouns

Concept

(a) I = **Ravi**
(b) you = **Harish**
(c) you = **Harish**
(d) you = **Harish**
(e) me = **Ravi**
(f) I = **Harish**
(g) I = **Harish**
(h) my = **Harish**
(i) you = **Harish**
(j) you = **Harish**
(k) I = **Harish**
(l) he = **Harish's father**
(m) we = **Ravi and Harish**
(n) you = **Ravi**
(o) I = **Ravi**
(p) him = **Ravi's father**
(q) He = **Ravi's father**
(r) me = **Ravi**
(s) I = **Harish**
(t) my = **Harish**

Structure

(a) I = **subject**
(b) you = **object**
(c) you = **object**
(d) you = **subject**
(e) me = **object**
(f) I = **subject**
(g) I = **subject**
(h) my = **object**
(i) you = **subject**
(j) you = **object**
(k) I = **subject**
(l) he = **object**
(m) we = **subject**
(n) you = **object**
(o) I = **subject**
(p) him = **object**
(q) He = **subject**
(r) me = **object**
(s) I = **subject**
(t) my = **object**

Notice *that 'you'* and *'it'* can be both subject *and* object pronouns

SUBJECT PRONOUNS	OBJECT PRONOUNS
I	**me**
you	you
he	**him**
she	her
it	**it**
we	us
you	**you**
they	them

APPENDIX

Unit 9: Possessive adjectives and 's

Concept

Possessive adjective		**...'s**
(a) my	=	*Ritu's*
(b) your	=	*Debesh's*
(c) his	=	*Great-grandfather's*
(d) her	=	*Hari's wife's/Mita's*
(e) their	=	*Hari and Mita's*
(f) its	=	*the dog's*
(g) our	=	*Ritu and Debesh's*

(a) *is*
(b) *is*
(c) *possession*
(d) *is*
(e) *possession*
(f) *is*
(g) *possession*
(h) *is*

Structure

I	*my*
you	*your*
he	*his*
she	*her*
it	*its*
we	*our*
they	*their*

Notice that 'her' has the same form as the object pronoun (Unit 8).

Unit 10: Possession pronouns

Concept

Whose is this? I think it is *hers.*

Is this *his?*

These are *ours.*

Richard? Is this *yours?*

I think these are *theirs.*

Look! *Mini's* is here now.

This isn't *mine.*

Where are *yours?*

Structure

Possessive adjective + noun	**Possessive pronoun**
my suitcase(s)	*mine*
your bag(s)	*yours*
his suitcase(s)	his
her bag(s)	*hers*
our bag(s)	ours
their suitcase(s)	*theirs*

's + noun	**'s**
Mini's bag(s)	*Mini's*

Unit 11: Articles

Concept

Rajesh lives in *o* London. It is **the** capital of *o* Britain. It is **an** expensive city but Rajesh has **a** good job. He is **a** lawyer. He has **a** big house near **the** Thames. **The** house was very expensive but it is beautiful.

1. London and Britain are places. **So, we generally use** *nothing* **with places.**
2. The Thames is a river. **So, we use 'the' with the names of rivers.**
3. Lawyer is a job. **So, we use 'a' [or 'an'] with jobs.**
4. There is only one capital of Britain. **So, we use 'the' when there is only one.**
5. There are **many** big cities in Britain.
   There **many** expensive cities.
   There are **many** good jobs.
   There are **many** big houses. **So, we use 'a' when we talk about** ***one of many.***
6. The first time the text talked about Rajesh's house it was one of many [He has a big house], but the second time [The house was very expensive] you knew *which* house.
   So, when we know ***which*** **thing we mean we use 'the'.**

Structure and Pronunciation

We use **an** when the first SOUND of the next word is a vowel sound [ae/e/i/i:/au, etc].
We use **a** when the first SOUND of the next word is a consonant [b/d/f/t//g/h, etc].

Remember it is the first **sound** and maybe not the first **letter.**

Sometimes the letter '**u**' is pronounced /ju:/so we DON'T use 'an' [Example: university].
Sometimes the letter '**h**' is silent so we DO use 'an' [Example: hour].

Unit 12: Relative pronouns (who/which/that)

Concept

A person **who** has children is *a parent.*
An animal **that** has a very long nose is *an elephant.*
A house **which** only has one floor is *a bungalow.*
A man **who** is married is *a husband.*
An animal **which** eats grass is *a cow.*
A person **that** can play the piano is *a pianist.*

- We can use **who** to define (a) - people.
- We can use **which** to define (b) - things.
- We can use **that** * to define (c) - people and things.

(*It is possible to use 'that' for people but we usually prefer 'who'.)

So, to say more about **what sort of** *person* it is we use who or sometimes that.
To say more about **what sort of** *thing* it is we use which or that.

Structure

1. A parent is a person. (What sort of person?)—He/She has children.
   A parent is a person who has children.
   What happens to 'he/she'? We replace 'he/she' with who.
2. A dictionary is a book (What sort of book?)—Students use it.
   A dictionary is a book that students use.
   What happens to 'it'? We replace 'it' with that.

A wife is a woman who has a husband.
A mechanic is a person who repairs cars.
A Maruti 800 is a car which (or 'that') has four wheels.
Concorde is a plane which (or 'that') goes very fast.

APPENDIX

Unit 13: Have got

Structure

Positive sentences	Negative sentences	Questions	Short answers
I have got.	I have not got.	Have I got?	Yes, I have/No, I have not.
You have got.	You have not got.	Have you got?	Yes, you have/No, you have not.
He/She/It has got.	He/She/It has not got.	Has he/she/it got?	Yes, he/she/it has. No, he/she/it has not.
We have got.	We have not got.	Have we got?	Yes, we have/No, we have not.
They have got.	They have not got.	Have they got?	Yes, they have/No, they havenot.

Remember: We can use 'have' with 'got' or as a normal present simple verb (see unit 5).

How many has he got? = How many does he have?
He has not got it = He does not have it.
I have got 625,000 = I have 625,000.

Have you got a big collection?	Yes, I have.
Does he have all the cards he wants?	No, he does not.
Has he got more than 100,000 cards?	Yes, he has.
Do you have a complete set?	No, I do not.

Notice how the answer *matches* the question.

Unit 14: Countable and uncountable nouns

Concept

What can you **count**? Write the noun and the letter.

Eggs (b) *Cakes(e)* *Chocolates (g)* *Bananas (i)* *Rupees (k)*

THESE ARE **COUNTABLE** NOUNS.

What **can't** you **count**? Write the noun and the number.

Milk (a) *Flour (c)* *Cake (d)* *Chocolate (f)* *Bread (h)* *Money (j)*

THESE ARE **UNCOUNTABLE** NOUNS.

What can you **sometimes count** and **sometimes not count**—with a ***different meaning***?
Write the noun and the letter.

Chocolate (f) *Chocolates (g)* *Cake (d)* *Cakes (e)*

SOME NOUNS CAN BE COUNTABLE **AND** UNCOUNTABLE *WITH A DIFFERENT MEANING.*

Structure

'Banana' is countable.
Yes, we **can use a/an** with countable nouns.
Yes, we **can use a number** with countable nouns.
Yes, we **can make countable nouns plural.**

'Milk' is uncountable.
No, we **can't use a/an** with uncountable nouns.
No, we **can't use a number** with uncountable nouns.
No, we **can't make uncountable nouns plural.**

Unit 15: 'Some' and 'any'

Concept

Bob and Marcia can make **Shepherd's Pie** for dinner.

When we say 'some' or 'any' we DON'T know exactly how many potatoes, peppers and onions there are.
Potatoes, peppers and *onions* are **countable.**
We use **are** with plural countable nouns.

When we say 'some' or 'any' we DON'T know exactly how much rice, pasta and meat there is.
Rice, pasta and *meat* are **uncountable.**
We use **is with uncountable nouns.**

We usually* use **some** with *positive* sentences.
We usually* use **any** with *negative* sentences.
We usually* use **any** with *questions.*

[*'usually' because, *with a different meaning,* we can use 'some' in questions and 'any' in positive sentences.
For example:
Would you like **some** tea?
Anything you can do, I can do better.]

Structure

Complete the table with **is/are** **some/any/a**

	COUNTABLE NOUNS	UNCOUNTABLE NOUNS
Positive	*Singular* There **is a** pepper. *Plural* There **are some** peppers.	There **is some** rice.
Negative	*Singular* There **isn't a** pepper. *Plural* There **aren't any** peppers.	There **isn't any** rice.
Questions	*Singular* **Is** there **a** pepper? *Plural* **Are** there **any** peppers?	**Is** there **any** rice?

Unit 16: Much/many/a lot

Concept

Cigarettes are **countable.** (We can say *a* cigarette, *three* cigarettes.)
Cigars are **countable.**
With countable nouns the question is **How many...?**
For more information on countable/uncountable see Unit 14.

Wine is **uncountable.** (We say *some* wine.)
Perfume is **uncountable.**
With uncountable nouns the question is **How much...?**

Structure

COUNTABLE

positive	**negative**
a lot of cigarettes	**not a lot of** cigarettes *or* **not many** cigarettes

UNCOUNTABLE

positive	**negative**
a lot of perfume	**not a lot of** perfume *or* **not much** perfume

APPENDIX

Unit 17: 'Too' and 'not enough'

Concept

Is the size of the class (number of students) OK? — No.
Is it more than is good or less than is good? — More than is good.
So, the class is *too* big.

Is the size of the room OK? — No.
Is it more than is good or less than is good? — Less than is good.
So, the room is *not* big *enough*.

Is the number of students OK? — No.
Is it more than is good or less than is good? — More than is good.
So, there are *too* many students.

Is the amount of noise OK? — No.
Is it more than is good or less than is good? — More than is good.
So, there is *too* much noise.

Is the number of chairs OK? — No.
Is it more than is good or less than is good? — Less than is good.
So, there is *not enough* chairs.

Is the amount of light OK? — No.
Is it more than is good or less than is good? — Less than is good.
So, there is *not enough* light.

When there is *more* than is good we use **too**.
When there is *less* than is good we use **not enough**.

Structure

With adjectives:

The class is *too* big. The room is not big *enough*.

TOO

'Too' comes **before** the adjective.

ENOUGH

'Enough' comes **before** the adjective.

We use '**much**' and '**many**'—with 'too'.

Unit 18: Present continuous tense

Concept

Does she speak French?	**Yes** [generally]	Is she speaking Polish?	**No** [not at the moment]
Is she speaking French?	**No** [not at the moment]	Does she speak Chinese?	**Yes** [generally]
Does she speak Polish?	**Yes** [generally]	Is she speaking Chinese?	**Yes** [at **this** moment]

'She speaks French' means **(b)**—generally, around now but maybe not at this exact moment.
'She is speaking Chinese' means **(a)**—now, at this *exact* moment.

Structure

Present continuous sentences:

I/eat/dinner = **I am eating dinner.**
You/look/well = **You are looking well.**
She/speak/Chinese = **She is speaking Chinese.**
He/drink/coffee = **He is drinking coffee.**
It/rain = **It is raining.**
We/sit/down = **We are sitting down.**
They/feel/ill = **They are feeling ill.**

The present continuous is formed: I am eating dinner
Subject + **verb 'to be'** + **verb+ing**

Spelling

Remember that we usually add *-ing* to the infinitive of the verb. *But sometimes the spelling changes.*

A. bite-biting
smoke-smoking [**We take away the 'e'**]
write-writing

B. lie-lying
die-dying [**The 'ie' becomes 'y'**]

C. run-running
hit-hitting
swim-swimming [When we have consonant (bcdfgh, etc) + vowel (aeiou) + consonant at the end of the word **we double the last consonant.**]

APPENDIX

Unit 19: Present simple and present continuous

Concept

Paul is a doctor.
He works in a hospital.
He is giving an injection.

John is a journalist.
He writes for a national newspaper.
He is interviewing someone.

Ram is a teacher.
He teaches small children.
He is thinking about going home.

All these sentences are about the present but sentences (b), (d) and (f) emphasize NOW.
These sentences are present continuous.

Sentences (a), (c), (e), (g), (h) and (i) are about the present *in general.*

These sentences are present simple.

Unit 20: Prepositions of place: in/on/next to

Concept

It is in front of the fire.
It is next to a box.
It is on a cushion.

It is under the table.
It is opposite the dog.
It is near my feet.

It is next to my feet.
It is behind the chair.
It is opposite the television.

It is in front of the television.
It is near the bowl.
It is in a box.

Structure

Which preposition is this? next to
Which preposition is this? in front of
Can we say opposite to? No, we usually say 'It is opposite the bank'.

Unit 21: Prepositions of time: in/at/on

Concept and Structure

AT
We use **at** for:
the time of day: at 6.00, at midnight, at noon
festivals of more than one day: at Christmas, at Dussehara*
mealtimes: at tea time
and three more you need to remember: at the weekend*, at night, at the moment
*In American English you can say on the weekend.

IN
We use **in** for:
years, or groups of years: in 1966, in the 1980s, in the 20th century
periods of the day: in the evening, in the afternoon
seasons: in (the) summer
months: in April
and two more you need to remember: in the future, in the past

ON
We use **on** for:
days: on Saturday, on Friday evening
special days: on Republic Day, on my birthday
dates: on 16th August*
* We **write** 'on 16th August' but we **say** 'On *the* 16th *of August*'

APPENDIX

NO PREPOSITION

When there is an *adjective* (this/next, etc) we *don't* use a preposition: **next week, last night.**

AT
at Christmas
at **the** moment
at 11.00
at midnight
at **the** weekend
(possible with and without *the*)

IN
in **the** future*
in April
in **the** 15th Century
in **the** morning
in (**the**) winter

ON
on Friday
on Tuesday morning
on 15th December (but we *say* the)
on Republic Day
on Saturdays

* We can also say 'In future...' when we mean 'From this moment on...'
Example: 'You are late again. In future, please come on time.'

Unit 22: Prepositions of movement

Concept

out of the barracks
up the hill
past the post-office
and jump **off** the box—20 times!

from the barracks **to** the river
down the hill
across/over the road
Then you can go **into** the barracks and rest.

across/over the bridge
through the park
under the railway bridge

along the river-bank
round the statue
Then jump **on** this box.

Unit 23: Past simple tense of verb 'to be': was/were

Structure

SIMPLE PRESENT			SIMPLE PAST		
Positive	**Negative**	**Question**	**Positive**	**Negative**	**Question**
I am	I am not	Am I...?	I **was**	I **was not**	**Was** I...?
You are	You are not	Are you...?	You **were**	You **were not**	**Were** you...?
He is	He is not	Is he...?	He **was**	He **was not**	**Was** he...?
She is	She is not	Is she...?	She **was**	She **was not**	**Was** she...?
It is	It is not	Is it...?	It **was**	It **was not**	**Was** it...?
We are	We are not	Are we...?	We **were**	We **were not**	**Were** we...?
They are	They are not	Are they...?	They **were**	They **were not**	**Were** they...?

Unit 24: Past simple tense

Concept

was **-be**
made **-make**
decorated **-decorate**
got **-get**

lit **- light**
rose **-rise**
were **-be**

built **-build**
stayed **-stay**
flew **-fly**

Structure

'Decorate' and 'stay' are regular verbs. So, to form the past tense of regular verbs we add *-ed* to the infinitive.
Example: stay - stay**ed**
Notice that if there is already an 'e' on the end of the word we do NOT add *another* 'e'.
Example: decorate - decorate**d**

The irregular verbs:

Infinitive	Past Simple	Infinitive	Past Simple
begin	began		
break	broke	buy	bought
can	could	do	did
drink	drank	go	went
have	had	say	said
see	saw	take	took
write	wrote		

Spelling

(a) ied
(b) d
(c) consonant

Unit 25: Past simple auxiliary: did/didn't

Concept

1. When **did** the Alexander the Great invade India?
2. When **did** Queen Victoria *die*?
3. **Did** Mughal Emperor Babur speak Hindi?
4. What **did** Thomas Alva Edison invent?
5. **Did** Queen Victoria have nine children?
6. Why **did** Nicholas II, the Czar of Russia give up the throne?
7. **Did** the Italians ever kill their leader?

(a) The electric bulb. (4)
(b) No, **he didn't** (only Persian) (3)
(c) In 326 BC (1)
(d) Yes, **she did** (5)
(e) Because of the Bolshevik Revolution (6)
(f) In 1901 (2)
(g) Yes, they **did** (Benito Mussolini) (7)

Henry the Eighth **didn't have** six wives.	FALSE
Sikandar Lodhi didn't build the Taj Mahal at Agra.	TRUE
The Duke of Wellington **didn't win** the Battle of Waterloo.	FALSE
Subhash Chandra Bose **didn't** form the 'Azad Hind Fauj'.	FALSE
The American people **didn't like** President George Washington.	FALSE

Structure

QUESTIONS

	[Question word] +	did +	subject +	infinitive +......
1.	When	did	Alexander the Great	invade India?
2.	When	did	Queen Victoria	die?
3.		Did	Mughal Emperor Babur	speak Hindi?
4.	What	did	Thomas Alva Edison	invent?
5.		Did	Queen Victoria	have nine children?
6.	Why	did	Nicholas II, the Czar of Russia	give up his throne?
7.		Did	the Italians	ever kill their leader?

NEGATIVES

Subject +	didn't +	infinitive
Henry VIII	didn't	have six wives
Sikandar Lodhi	didn't	build the Taj Mahal at Agra.
The Duke of Wellington	didn't	win the battle of Waterloo
Subhash Chandra Bose	didn't	form the 'Azad Hind Fauj.'
The American people	didn't	like President George Washington.

SHORT ANSWERS

Yes/No, +	subject +	did/didn't
No,	he	didn't
Yes,	she	did
Yes,	they	did

Unit 26: Would like

Concept

Does Kishan like chocolate?	Yes	Does Kishan want chocolate **now**?	No,—because he's on a diet.
Does Kishan like apples?	Yes, probably	Does Kishan want an apple **now**?	Yes

When Rita asks '**Do you like** chocolate?' she is talking about **in general**.
When Rita asks '**Would you like** some chocolate?' she is talking about **now**.
Which question **means the same** as 'Do you want...? (a) or (b) b

Does Sreya like going to the theatre? Yes
Does she want to go with Ravi on Friday? No
Which question **means the same** as 'Do you want...? (c) or (d) d

Structure

I would like	I'd like	You would like	Would you like?
You would like	You'd like	He would like	Would he like?
He would like	He'd like	She would like	Would she like?
She would like	She'd like	We would like	Would we like?
We would like	We'd like	They would like	Would they like?
They would like	They'd like		

I like *cooking**
I would like *to cook* dinner tonight.

She likes *going to* the cinema.
She would like *to go* and see a film tonight.

He likes *watching* television.
He would like *to watch* the football this afternoon.

We like *playing* tennis.
We would like *to play* tennis this afternoon.

*In American English it is often possible to say like + to + infinitive 'I like to cook.'

APPENDIX

Unit 27: Requests and permissions: can/could/may

Concept

Sentence a [**'Can** you give me a lift?'] is *asking someone to do something.*
Sentence b [**'Can I** have some more dessert, please?'] *is asking permission.*

Two words for asking someone to do something: can and could.
Could is more formal/polite.
Raj is more polite in the second dialogue because Rs. 5 is a bigger favour than salt.

Two words for *asking permission:* can and may.
May is more formal/polite.
The child is more polite in the second dialogue because permission to go to a party is a bigger favour than permission to watch tv.

Structure

Requests (asking for something)
'Can/Could you help me?' is correct.

Permission
'Can/May I smoke?' is correct.
So, after could/can/may we use the **infinitive.**

Unit 28: Ability (can/could)

Concept

a secretary can type
a waiter can add up a bill
a cook can make a cake
a translator can speak two or more languages
a journalist can write

We use **can/can't** to talk about the present.
We use **could/couldn't** to talk about the past.

Structure

	PRESENT	**PAST**
Question	How many languages can you speak?	Could you speak Hindi well then?
Positive	I can speak French, German and Hindi.	I could speak Hindi when I was a child.
Positive Short Answer	Yes, I can.	Yes, I could.
Negative	I can't speak any other languages.	I couldn't speak German until I went to live in Germany.
Negative Short Answer	No, I can't.	No, I couldn't.

The ***present tense*** form of **can** for I/you/he/she/it/we/they (all persons) is can.
The ***past tense*** form of **can** for I/you/he/she/it/we/they (all persons) is could.

Unit 29: Obligation (have to)

Concept

Is it necessary/obligatory for Suresh to wear a uniform? Yes
So, Suresh **has to** wear a uniform.

Is it necessary/obligatory for Suresh to study Latin? No
So, Suresh ***doesn't have*** to study Latin.

Is it necessary/obligatory for Suresh's father to wear a hat *now?* No
Was it necessary/obligatory for Suresh's father to wear a hat when he was at school? Yes
So, Suresh's father **had to** wear a hat when he was at school.

Is it necessary/obligatory for Suresh's father to eat school dinners now? No
Was it necessary/obligatory for Suresh's father to eat school dinners when he was at school? No
So, Suresh's father **didn't have to** eat school dinners when he was at school.

Structure

Use the examples above to help you complete the table.

	PRESENT	**PAST**
NECESSARY		
I	have to study French	had to study Latin
You	have to study French	had to study Latin
He/She	has to study French	had to study Latin
We	have to wear a uniform	had to wear a hat
They	have to wear a uniform	had to wear a hat
NOT NECESSARY		
I	don't have to study Latin	didn't have to study French
You	don't have to study Latin	didn't have to study French
He/She	doesn't have to study Latin	didn't have to study French
We	don't have to wear a hat	didn't have to eat school dinners
They	don't have to wear a hat	didn't have to eat school dinners

Questions and short answers.

He has to study French.	Does he have to study French?	Yes, he does/No, he doesn't.
They have to wear a uniform.	Do they have to wear a uniform?	Yes, they do/No, they don't.
He had to wear a hat.	Did he have to wear a hat?	Yes, he did/No, he didn't.
They had to study Latin.	Did they have to study Latin?	Yes, they did/No, they didn/t.

Unit 30: Advising (should/shouldn't)

Concept

- smoke ×
- eat less fat ✓
- eat fruit ✓
- exercise three times a week ✓
- eat a big meal before you go to bed ×
- walk up the stairs rather than take the lift ✓
- drive everywhere ×
- stay awake all night ×

- You should eat fruit.
- You should exercise three times a week.
- You shouldn't eat a big meal before you go to bed.
- You should walk up the stairs.
- You shouldn't drive everywhere.
- You shouldn't stay awake all night.

It **isn't** a good idea to smoke if you want to be healthy.
So, if you want to be healthy you **shouldn't (should not)** smoke.

It **is** a good idea to eat less fat if you want to be healthy.
So, if you want to be healthy, you **should** eat less fat.

Structure

The present tense form for **should/shouldn't** with I/you/he/she/it/we/they (all persons) is **should.**

- **I shouldn't smoke** is *correct.* [after **should** we use the *infinitive]*

Unit 31: Possibility (may/might)

Concept

Positive

Is the Princess definitely going to marry Prince Humphrey? No
Is she definitely NOT going to marry him? No
What word does she use to show she is not sure? might

Is the Princess definitely going to marry Prince Alfred? No
Is she definitely NOT going to marry him? No
What word does she use to show she is not sure? may

Do *may* and *might* have the same meaning when talking about possibility? Yes—(though some people think **might** is *less* possible than **may**)

Negative

Is the Princess definitely NOT going to marry either of the princes? No
What word does she use to show she is not sure? might not

Is the Princess definitely NOT going to marry anyone? No
What word(s) does she use to show she is not sure? may not

Do *may not* and *might not* have the same meaning when talking about negative possibility? Yes—(though some people think **might not** is *less* possible than **may not**)

Structure

The form of **might/mightn't (might not)** for *I/you/he/she/it/we/they* (all persons) is might/mightn't.

The form of **may/may not** for *I/you/he/she/it/we/they* (all persons) is may/may not.
It is not possible to write **mayn't.**

Unit 32: Past continuous

Concept

What time did Bill start playing the piano? 5.00
What time did he finish playing the piano? 7.00

What time did Tom and Tina start visiting? 4.00
What time did they finish visiting? 6.30

Sentence (**a**) and (**b**) are past continuous.
Sentence (***c***) is past simple.

Structure

SUBJECT +	VERB TO BE (past) +	VERB+ing
I	was	reading
You	were	speaking
He/She/It	was	eating
We	were	playing
They	were	working

Was I reading?	I wasn't reading.
Were you speaking?	You weren't speaking.
Was he eating?	He wasn't eating.
Were we playing?	We weren't playing.
Were they working?	They weren't working.

Unit 33: Past continuous and past simple

Concept

(a) I was feeling really tired. = (1)

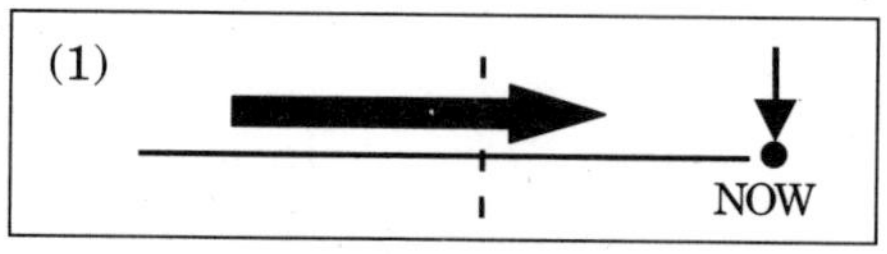

(b) I finally arrived home. = (2)

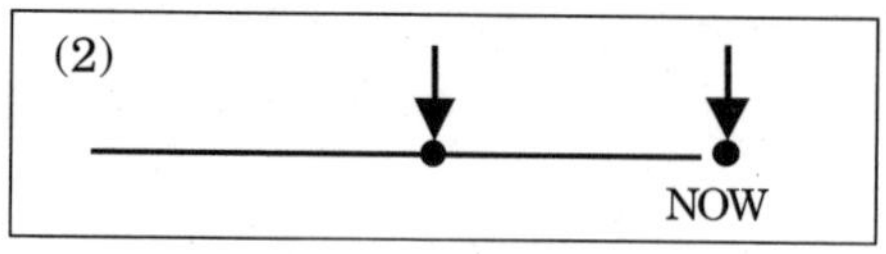

Was he feeling tired before the train arrived in New Delhi? **Yes**
Did he *continue* feeling tired after the train arrived in New Delhi? **Yes**
Sentence **a** describes the *background situation.*
Sentence **a** is **past continuous.**
Sentence **b** describes an *action* that happened *during* the background situation.
Sentence **b** is **past simple.**

(c) The car-park attendent was sleeping. = (1)

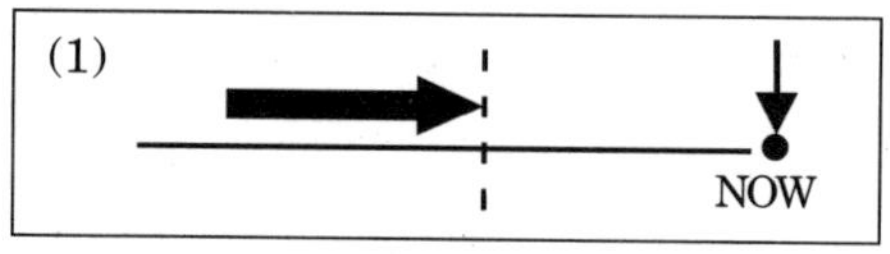

(d) I woke him up. = (2)

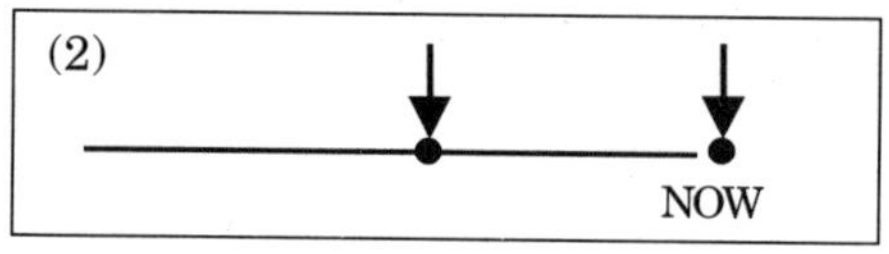

Was the car-park attendent sleeping before the man found him? **Yes**
Did he *continue* sleeping after the man found him? **No**
Sentence **c** describes the *background situation.*
Sentence **c** is **past continuous.**
Sentence **d** describes an *action* that happened *after* the background situation.
Sentence **d** is **past simple.**

Structure

Note:-
We use **when, as** and **while** to *join* past simple and past continuous in one sentence.
Look at these examples:

I *was walking* across the car-park **when** I *saw a* yellow clamp.
When I *was walking* across the car-park I *saw* a yellow clamp.
As I *was walking* across the car-park, I *saw a* yellow clamp.
While I *was walking* across the carpark, I *saw a* yellow clamp.

We normally use **when** with *both* past simple and past continuous.
We normally* use **as** with past continuous.
We normally* use **while** with past continuous.

*But it *is* possible to use **as** and **while** with past simple.

Unit 34: Adjectives I

Concept

A **black** cat. An **old** house. He is **happy.**
A **white** cat. A **new** house. He is **sad.**
A **fat** man. A **young** woman. We are **tall.**
A **thin** man. An **old** woman. We are **short.**

Structure

The adjective goes **before** the noun.
'**a big house**' is correct.

he's thin
they're rich
it's cold
I'm hungry

'**big houses**' is the correct plural

Unit 35: Comparatives

Structure

APPENDIX

One syllable adjectives

clean cleaner
cheap cheaper
small smaller
near nearer

Rule: To make a comparative from adjectives with *one* syllable we add **-er.**

-y adjectives

ugly uglier
dirty dirtier

Rule: To make a comparative from adjectives with two syllables that **end in y** we change the 'y' to i and add er.

irregular adjectives

good better
bad worse
far further

(there aren't many irregular adjectives but you need to learn them)

Spelling

big bigger **We double the last letter of the adjective.**
hot hotter **We double the last letter of the adjective.**
safe safer **We don't need two 'e's.**

two or more syllable adjectives

beautiful more beautiful
dangerous more dangerous
boring more boring

Rule: To make a comparative from adjectives with two syllables that **DON'T end in y** we use the word more before the adjective.

We often use *'than'* with comparatives. Look at these examples.

Rio is a much better place to live *than* **Brasilia.**
It's not true that **Brasilia** is uglier or more boring *than* **Rio.**
The beaches in Rio are dirtier *than* **ours.**

Unit 36: Superlatives

Concept

Which sentence (a, b or c) compares one rollercoaster to a second rollercoaster? b
Write the comparative adjective* in the sentence. faster

Which sentence compares one rollercoaster to all the other rollercoasters? c
Write the superlative adjective in the sentence. the fastest

Which sentence just describes one rollercoaster? a
Write the adjective** in the sentence. fast

* see Unit 35
**see Unit 34

(a) Bolton Towers is Rs. 12.
(b) Courtney Park is Rs. 8.
(c) Wondsworth Safari Park is Rs.6.

Which is **the most expensive**? Bolton Towers
Which is **the cheapest**? Wondsworth Safari Park
Is Courtney Park **more expensive** than Wondsworth Safari Park? Yes

Structure

ADJECTIVE	COMPARATIVE ADJECTIVE	SUPERLATIVE ADJECTIVE
One syllable adjectives		
fast	faster	the fastest
cheap	cheaper	the cheapest
big	bigger	the biggest
near	nearer	the nearest
long	longer	the longest

To make a superlative adjective from an adjective with one syllable we add the........-est.

Two syllables or more		
exciting	more exciting	the most exciting
expensive	more expensive	the most expensive
educational	more educational	the most educational
comfortable	more comfortable	the most comfortable

To make a superlative adjective from an adjective with two syllables or more we add the most......... .

APPENDIX

Irregular

good	better	the best
bad	worse	the worst
far	further	the furthest

[*For spelling rules—see Unit 35.*]

Unit 37: Adverbs II: Manner

Concept

night	noun	climbed	verb	Mrs Kumar	noun
blew	verb	house	noun	run	verb
		candle	noun	went out	verb
		voice	noun	screamed	verb
		said	verb		

cold	night	(It was a *cold* night.)	blew	noisily	(The wind blew *noisily* around the house.)
dark	house	(The house was *dark*.)	climbed	slowly	(Mrs Kumar climbed the stairs *slowly*.)
long	candle	(She was holding a *long* candle.)	said	quietly	('Welcome' it said, *quietly*.)
strange	voice	(She heard a *strange* voice.)	run	quickly	(She started to run *quickly* down the stairs.)
frightened	Mrs Kumar	(Mrs Kumar was really *frightened*.)	went out	suddenly	(*Suddenly* the candle went out.)
			screamed	loudly	(Mrs Kumar screamed *loudly*.)

Structure

'quick' is an adjective.
'quickly' is an adverb.
We usually add ly to an adjective to make an adverb.

What happens to the *spelling* when the adjective ends in -y? 'y' changes to 'i'.

ADJECTIVE	IRREGULAR ADVERB
I am a **good** tennis player.	I play tennis well.
This is a **fast** car.	Don't drive so fast.
This unit is quite **hard**.	You need to work hard to learn English!
I am always **late**.	He arrived late again.

An **adjective** usually goes before the **noun**.
An **adverb** usually goes after the **verb**.

Unit 38: Present tenses for future use

Concept

The two TENSES underlined are present simple and present continuous.
In these examples they are talking about future TIME.

Sentences a, c, d, e, f, h are talking about *an arrangement between people.*
They are present continuous.

Sentences b, g, i are talking about *an event happening at a specific time/on a specific date.*
They are present simple.

Unit 39: Going to/will—I

Concept

Sentences *a, b, c, d* show what Ravi decided **about the future** *before* the conversation with Jay.
He uses going to.

Sentences *e, f* show what Ravi decided **about the future** *during* the conversation with Jay.
He uses will.

Structure

Going to

To make the *going to* future we use SUBJECT (I/you/he, etc) + VERB 'TO BE'+ GOING TO + INFINITIVE

They're going to take the children.	Are they going to take the children?
He's going to lie on the beach.	Is he going to lie on the beach?
We're going to visit Disneyland.	Are we going to visit Disneyland?

Will

The form of will for I/you/he/she/it/we/they (all persons)* is will.
The **negative** form of will is won't.

Contractions

I will	I'll	You will	You'll	It will	It'll
		He will	He'll	We will	We'll
		She will	She'll	They will	They'll

I think I'll go to the cinema is the **only** correct sentence.

Unit 40: Going to/will—II

Concept

Does the gipsy *know* for certain the man will get a good job? No
Does the gipsy *know* for certain the man will have a happy and prosperous life? No
Does the man *know* for certain that the crystal ball is going to fall? Yes
How does the man know? What can he *see*? The ball is nearly falling/on the edge.

In the first picture does she *know* for certain that they will have to get some more petrol? No
In the second picture does she *know* for certain that they are going to have to get some more petrol? Yes
How does she know? What can she *see*? The petrol gauge shows 'Empty'.

We use will when we are *guessing or predicting* about the future.
We use going to when we can see *now* that something is *certain* to happen in the future.

APPENDIX

Unit 41: Present perfect I: experience

Concept

Do you know *when* she went to these places? No
What *tense* is 'She has been'? Present Perfect
'*Been*' is the *past participle** of the verb 'to go'*

*There are *two* possible past participles for the verb 'to go'—**been** and **gone.**
'She has *been* to Paris' means she has **gone and come back.**
'She has *gone* to Paris' means she **is there now**.

'I**'ve been** there five or six times.'—Do you know *when*? No
What **tense** does she use? Present Perfect or Simple Past? Present Perfect
'I first **went** there in 1985'—Do you know *when*? Yes
What tense does she use? Present Perfect *or* Simple Past? Simple Past

Did you visit the Winter Palace when you were in St Petersburg?
Is the interviewer talking about **a definite time** in the past? Yes

Have you **been** to Seoul?
Is the interviewer talking about **a definite time** in the past? No

Structure

The **positive** form of Present Perfect Simple is	subject + has or have + past participle (been/visited/eaten, etc)
The **negative** form of Present Perfect Simple is	subject + has or have + not + past participle
The **question** form of Present Perfect Simple is	have or has + subject + past participle
The **short answer** form of Present Perfect Simple is	Yes, + subject + has or have
	No, + subject + hasn't or haven't

Note:
Ever and never

I have *never* been to Moscow.
Have you *ever* been to Paris?

We often use 'ever' and 'never' with *this meaning* of Present Perfect Simple.
They **don't** change the meaning but **add emphasis**.

Unit 42: Present perfect II: time up to now

Concept

Jeetu *lives* in Venezuela—This is talking about now.
Jeetu *came* to Venezuela **in 1991**— this is talking about the past.
Jeetu *has lived* in Venezuela **for six years**—This is talking about now and the past.

Jeetu *is married*—This is talking about now.
Jeetu *got married* **in 1993**—This is talking about the past.
Jeetu *has been married* **since 1993**—This is talking about now and the past.

(a) I have been married since 1993 = 2 (a **point** of time)
(b) I have been married for four years = 1 (a **period** of time)

since	**for**
last February	a long time
1989	two months
a week ago	a couple of hours
I was born	three years
yesterday	
9.00	

APPENDIX

Unit 43: Present perfect III: present result

Concept

When did he break his leg? **Last weekend.**
This is talking about the **past.**

Is his leg still broken now? **Yes.**
This is talking about the **present.**

He **has broken** his leg—This is talking about **a past action with a present result.**
This is **the present perfect tense**.

When did he cut his head? **Last weekend.**
This is talking about the **past.**

Is his head still cut now? **Yes.**
This is talking about the **present.**

He **has cut** his head—This is talking about **a past action with a present result.**
This is **the present perfect tense**.

Unit 44: Present perfect IV: 'yet' and 'already'

Concept

Already means something has happened before now.
Yet means something has *not* happened before now, but it is going to happen.

ALREADY DONE
walked along Unter den Linden
visited Checkpoint Charlie
seen Krakow
been skiing in Zakopane
crossed the Charles Bridge in Prague
drunk Czech beverage

NOT DONE **YET**
visited Bratislava
eaten goulash
visited the Thermal Baths in Budapest

Structure

'I have **already** been to Czech.'
We usually use **already** in *positive sentences*.
'Have you been to Poland **yet**?'
'I have not been to Hungary **yet**.'
We usually use **yet** in *questions* and *negative sentences*.

SUBJECT + have/has + already + PAST PARTICIPLE

Have/Has + SUBJECT + PAST PARTICIPLE + yet?
Subject + HAVE NOT / HAS NOT + past participle + yet

ALREADY DONE
She's already walked along Unter den Linden.
She's already visited Checkpoint Charlie.
She's already seen Krakow.
She's already been skiing in Zakopane.
She's already crossed the Charles Bridge in Prague.
She's already drunk Czech beverage.

NOT DONE **YET**
She hasn't visited Bratislava yet.
She hasn't eaten goulash yet.
She hasn't visited the Thermal Baths yet.

APPENDIX

Unit 45: Questions Revision 1

Concept

Find two questions asking about someone's plans or arrangements. d e [Units 38 and 39]
Find one question making a request. f [Unit 27]
Find one question asking for permission. g [Unit 27]
Find one question asking politely if someone wants something. i [Unit 26]
Find one question asking about a non-definite time in the past. c [Unit 41]
Find one question asking about NOW, this moment. b [Unit 18]
Find one question asking about ability. a [Unit 28]
Find three questions asking about the past. c, h, j [Unit 23, 32 and 41]

Structure

[QUESTION WORD] +	AUXILIARY VERB +	SUBJECT +	MAIN VERB	
	Can	you	play	the piano?
What	are	you	doing	with that gun?
	Have	you	been	to Paris?
What	are	you	going to do	next?
	Are	you	meeting	Ravi tomorrow?
	Can	I	borrow	Rs 500?
	May	I	go	now?
Where	were	you		yesterday?
	Would	you	like	some tea?
What	were	you	doing?	

Unit 46: Questions Revision 2

Concept and Structure

A

1. Do elephants eat leaves?
2. Where does he come from?
3. Where did you go?
4. Did she give up smoking?
5. Do they like strong coffee?
6. How many children do you have?

B.

1. Can tigers run very fast?
2. Where are the Galapagos Islands?
3. What have you forgotten?
4. Is she going to give up smoking?
5. Would they like some tea?
6. Has he got three cars?

What **three words** do we use to **make questions** in column A? do, does, did

1. Can 2. are 3. have 4. is 5. would 6. has

[Any problems? See Unit 45]

We use did to talk about the past.
We use does with *he, she, it* to talk about the present.
We use do with *I, you, we, they* to talk about the present.

Appendix 3: Key to Unit 'Practice' Pages

Unit 1: Present Tense of the verb 'to be' (is/am are)

1. A. This **is** my brother. He**'s** very tall and thin. He**'s** a teacher too.
   B. My mother and father **are** quite young. They **are** both photographers. At the moment they **aren't** in India, they **are** on holiday in Africa.
   C. My house **is** in Allahabad. It**'s** quite old, but it **isn't** very big.

2. Nita and Ria are my friends.
   They're very intelligent.
   They aren't (they're not) very rich.

   My father's name's Rohit.
   He's a photographer.
   He's from Allahabad.

   My mother's called Shanti.
   She's a photographer.
   She's 49 years old.

3. (a) They**'re** from England.
   (b) My house **is** quite old.
   (c) Correct
   (d) Correct
   (e) I'm not a student, **I'm** a teacher.
   (f) Correct
   (g) Correct
   (h) His name**'s** Peter.

Unit 2: Verb 'to be': Questions (Am I? Are you?/Is he?)

1. (a) Is Rosa a teacher? — No, she isn't.
   (b) Is the International School of English in France? — No, it isn't.
   (c) Where is Rosa a doctor? — In Brazil.
   (d) Is Rosa forty years old? — No, she isn't.
   (e) How old is Rosa? — Thirty two.
   (f) Is Rosa married? — Yes, she is.
   (g) Is Juliana six year old? — Yes, she is.
   (h) Is Pedro six year old ? — No, he isn't.
   (i) How old are the children? — Six and three.
   (j) What's her husband's name? — Paulo.
   (k) Is Paulo in London now? — No, he isn't.
   (l) Where are Paulo and the children? — At school/In Brazil.

2. Hari: Pleased to meet you. My name's Hari.
   Mita: Sorry, are you my brother's friend?
   Hari: No, **I'm not**. I'm Ria's friend.
   Mita: **Are you** a doctor?
   Hari: No, **I'm not**.
   Mita: Sorry!

   Ria: Who is that over there?
   Jay: That is Kishore. He**'s** very famous.
   Ria: Why **is he** famous?
   Jay: He is a singer.

   Ramesh: Mita's my sister.
   Sita: What**'s** her boyfriend's name?
   Ramesh: Tony. He's a teacher too.
   Sita: **Are they** married?
   Ramesh: No, not yet.

   Mita: **Where are** Ria and Jay?
   Ramesh: In the kitchen.
   Mita: Are they hungry?

APPENDIX

Unit 3: This/that/these/those

1. 'This is Rina.'
   'What are these in English? Crisps or chips?'
   'Is this your recipe?'
   'These flowers are beautiful.'
   'This coffee is excellent!'
   'That's Robert Saunders.'
   'Who are those people?'
   'That cake is delicious.'
   'Who are those children in the garden?'
   'Is that your husband?'

2. R: This is the new REM CD.
   A: Is that you new favourite band?
   R: Yes, it is.
   A: Is that their best CD?
   R: No, it is not. This is.
   A: That is very expensive.

3. R: This is a good shop.
   These shoes are lovely.
   A: Well, I think these are better.
   R: But these are brown. This shirt is the same colour.
   A: OK. Try them on.
   R: Ahh. These are uncomfortable.
   A: So, these are better! And this is a lovely colour.

4. How much are those?
   That's the last one!
   Why is that so expensive?
   This isn't very good.
   These are very fashionable.
   These aren't good for you.
   This is very cheap!
   Is this the new REM CD?
   Those aren't English newspapers.
   How much are these?
   That isn't fresh!
   A: These shoes are lovely.
   R: No, I think those are nicer.

Unit 4: Singular and plural nouns

1. (a) There are ten children.
   (b) There is a teacher.
   (c) There are two balls.
   (d) There is a dog.
   (e) There is a sandwich.
   (f) There is a bus.
   (g) There are two houses.
   (h) There are five girls.
   (i) There is a book.
   (j) There are two pens.

2. There are 1,02,70,15,247 people.
   There are 495.7 million women.
   There are 531.3 million men.
   There are 742 million persons in village.
   There are 285 million persons in towns and cities.
   There are 339,969,048 literate males.
   There are 226,745,947 literate females.
   There are 56 important national highways.
   There are 7 international airports.
   There are 11 major ports.
   There are 7,100 railway stations.
   There are 16,125 telephones exchanges.
   There are 1,54,551 post offices.

3. (a) There **are** approximately 495.7 million women in India.
   (b) Correct
   (c) In Mumbai, the bus**es** are red.
   (d) Correct
   (e) There is an old **man** in the shop.
   (f) There are 56 important national highways in India.
   (g) This is my **house**.

4. (a) Are the child**ren** happy?
   (b) The sandwich**es** are fresh.
   (c) Why are the bus**es** late?
   (d) The teacher**s** are tired.
   (e) There are five church**es** in the town.
   (f) Indian Railways has 7,000 locomotive**s**.
   (g) There are 10 boy**s** and 12 girls in the class.

Unit 5: Present simple tense

1. Devon **is** in the southwest of Britain. The countryside **is** very beautiful and many tourists **go** there in the summer. They **swim** in the sea, **lie** on the beach and **walk** in the hills.
Mr Swinnon **lives** in Torquay. He **works** in a hotel. In the morning he **gets** up early, **goes** for a walk on the beach and then he **cooks** breakfast for the visitors.
'I **love** Devon. We **have** lots of tourists because the sun **shines** all summer.'

2. Portugal **is** in the southwest of Europe. It **has** many kilometres of beaches so the Portuguese **eat** a lot of fish. They **make** very good wine too.
Jorge **comes** from Angola but he **lives** in Lisbon, the capital of Portugal. He **studies** medicine at the university. At the weekend he **goes** to the beach and **plays** volleyball. When it **rains** he watches football on the television.
'I **think** about Angola a lot but I **like** Lisbon. I **have** lots of friends here and we **enjoy** life.'

3. St Petersburg is in Russia, near the Baltic Sea. It is a beautiful old city, on forty-four small islands. It snow**s** a lot in the winter and night comes very early, but in the summer the sun never go**es** down.
Irena works as a tourist guide. She take**s** visitors to the *Hermitage* Museum of Art. She gets up early and has breakfast—tea and bread and jam. Then she goes to work and meets the first group of tourists at 9.30 am. She works hard and she walks a lot—the *Hermitage* is very big—20 kilometres to see everything!
'I **finish** work at 6.00 pm and I always feel very tired, so in the evenings I read a book or **listen** to music.'

4. (a) Irena finish**es** work at 6.00.
(b) Jorge pla**ys** volleyball.
(c) Yuko stud**ies** hard.
(d) Mr Koshurs **works** for Toyota.
(e) Irena go**es** to work at 9.00.
(f) Jorge **has** a lot of friends in Lisbon.
(g) Jorge watch**es** football on the television.

Unit 6: Present simple auxiliaries

1. (a) **When does the train to Kolkata leave?**
(b) **How much does it cost?**
(c) **When does it arrive?**
(d) **How many states does it go through?**
(e) **Where do you need to buy your food?**
(f) **Where else do they sell food?**

2. (a) **Yes, it does.**
(b) **Yes, it does.**
(c) **No, it doesn't.**
(d) **Yes, we do.**
(e) **Yes, it does.**
(f) **Yes, they do.**
(g) **Yes, it does.**

3. 'When **do** we **arrive** in Patna?' — 'Six o'clock.'
'**Do** you often **go** to Kolkata?' — 'Yes, I **do**.'
'**Do** you **like** travelling?' — 'I love it!'
'**Does** the train **stop** in Benares ?' — 'No, it **doesn't**.'
'How much **does** it **cost** to travel 1st class?' — 'I **Don't know**'
'Oh no! I **don't have** a reservation.' — 'Thirty-three hours is a long time to stand up!'
'Where **do** you **get** your food?' — 'At the pantry.'

4. 'Do you have a ticket?' — 'Yes, I **do**.'
'Where does the train **stop**?' — 'In Mughalsarai, Allahabad and Patna.'
'When **do** we arrive in Patna?' — 'I **don't** know.'
'Does the ticket inspector check the tickets?' — 'Yes, he **does**!'
'I don't speak Hindi.' — 'I do.'
'We don't stop in Benares.' — 'Yes, I **know**.'

Unit 7: Adverbs 1: adverbs of frequency

1. (a) **Sunita always gets up at 7.30.**
   (b) **She never eats breakfast.**
   (c) **She often has a cup of coffee.**
   (d) **She always drives to work.**
   (e) **She is sometimes late.**
   (f) **The traffic is always bad.**
   (g) (In the evenings) **Suraj often watches old films on the television.**
   (h) **He always gets up late.**
   (i) **He never goes to bed before 2.00 am.**

2. (a) Shyam **always goes** running.
   (b) He **often goes** swimming.
   (c) He **never eats** meat.
   (d) He **is always** very healthy.
   (e) Suresh **always gets up** at 5.00.
   (f) He **is always** tired.

3. Interviewer: 'What time do you finish work, Mina?'
   Mina: 'Well, I **often finish** about 6.00 am, but it is sometimes later. **I often** don't get home until 8.00 am—then **I always** go straight to bed!'
   Interviewer: 'What time do you get up?'
   Mina: '**I usually** get up at about 3.00 pm to do some shopping and cooking. I **rarely** get up later than 4.00 pm because the children always come home from school then. **I am always** busy in the evening but my husband often helps me to cook the dinner and **he sometimes** puts the children to bed.'

Unit 8: Subject and object pronouns

1. (a) 'Ravi likes Harish because he is **his** good friend.'
   (b) 'It is a good movie and both of them want to see **it**.'
   (c) 'Ravi thinks Harish's family likes **him**.'
   (d) 'We are Harish's family—why doesn't Ravi often visit **us**?'
   (e) 'Harish's family is very good. I like **them** very much.'
   (f) 'I like to accompany **you**. Why don't you come with **me**?'

2. Harish: 'Ravi wants **me** to accompany **him**. What do you think?'
   Harish's father: 'Do you like **him**?'
   Harish: 'I *like* **him.** Do you like him?'
   Harish's father: 'Well, **he** seldom visits **us** ... and his family is not very cordial—**they** do not welcome an unfamiliar face.'

   Ravi: 'Harish's father doesn't want him to accompany **me**.'
   Jay: 'Good! I don't like **him**. **He** is boring.'
   Ravi: 'But, Jay, **he** is very good and **I** like **him**!'
   Jay: 'Maybe, but there are lots of good boys ... look at **them**!'

3. Ravi likes Harish but Jay doesn't like **him. He** wants Harish to accompany him to the cinema, but Harish has to ask his family. Ravi thinks Harish's family is strange. **He** never visits **them** and he thinks **they** don't like him. May be **he's** right.

4. (a) Jay thinks Harish is boring. He doesn't like **him.**
   (b) Jay likes the other boys in the class. He thinks **they** are friendly and he wants to speak to **them.**
   (c) Correct
   (d) Ravi likes Harish and **he** thinks he is friendly.
   (e) 'I like you, do you like **me**?'
   (f) Harish is unhappy because Jay doesn't like **him**.

Unit 9: Possessive adjective and 's

1. (a) Kusum's **Shankar** and **Sunetra's** daughter.
   (b) Kishori**'s** **Kaveri's** sister.
   (c) Ramesh**'s** **Kishori** and **Kaveri's** cousin.
   (d) Ravi's **Mira** and **Kusum's** brother.
   (e) Sudhangshu's **Mira's** husband.
   (f) Kishori and Kusum **are Ravi** and **Kavita's** daughters.
   (g) Sunetra*'s* **Shankar's** wife.
   (h) Kusum*'s* **Ravi** and **Mira's** sister.

2. (a) Kaveri's (**is**) Kishori's (**possession**) sister.
   (b) Mira's (**is**) Sudhangshu's (**possession**) wife.
   (c) Ravi's (**is**) a journalist.
   (d) Kavita's (**is**) Kaveri and Kishori's (**possession**) mother.
   (e) Sunita's (**possession**) sister's (**possession**) name's (**is**) Katha.
   (f) Shankar's (**possession**) son's (**is**) a journalist.

3. Kavita and **her** husband live near Ahmedabad. They have two children. **Their** names are Kishori and Kaveri. The have a cat. **Its** name is Ruby.
   Sudhangshu has three children. **His** son's name's Ramesh and **his** daughter's names are Sunita and Katha. **Their** cousins' names are Kishori and Kaveri.
   Shankar and Sunetra live near Indore. **Their** house is very old.

4. Let me tell you about my family. My father**'s** name**'s** Ravi and my mother**'s** Kavita. My father**'s** a journalist. I have one sister, her name**'s** Kishori. She**'s** OK but I like our cat better. Its name**'s** Ruby ...

5. (a) Who**'s** Kishori's sister?
   (b) Kaveri likes **her** sister Kishori.
   (c) Ruby's Kaveri and Kishori**'s** cat.
   (d) Kishori and Kaveri are sister**s**.
   (e) Correct
   (f) Sudhangshu lives with **his** wife, Mira.
   (g) Correct
   (h) Where's Shankar and Sunetra**'s** house?
   (i) 'My name's Katha. What's **your** name?'

Unit 10: Possessive pronouns

1. (a) Is this **yours?**
   (b) No, I think it's **his.**
   (c) This isn't **mine.**
   (d) Is it **yours?**
   (e) No, it isn't **mine.**
   (f) Perhaps it's **theirs.**
   (g) Have you got **ours?**
   (h) No, I have got but I do not know where.
   (i) **ours** are.
   (j) This isn't **mine.**
   (k) No, it's **theirs.**

2. (a) This isn't my bag. **Mine** is bigger.
   (b) Are these **your** glasses?
   (c) Have you got **our** bags?
   (d) It's **mine**!
   (e) I think **my** bag is lost!
   (f) Can you help me carry **my** bags?
   (g) Is that **hers**?
   (h) **Their** bags are heavy.

3. (a) **Give me her bag.**
   (b) **Is that his?**
   (c) **Their bag is red.**
   (d) **Are those theirs?**
   (e) **Hers is over there.**
   (f) **Are those his gloves?**
   (g) **Her umbrella is green.**
   (h) **His is blue.**

4. (a) This isn't **mine**.
   (b) Correct
   (c) **My** parents are retired.
   (d) Correct
   (e) Correct
   (f) They know our family but we don't know their**s**.
   (g) Correct
   (h) Your camera is better than **mine**.
   (i) Is that **her** coat?

APPENDIX

APPENDIX

Unit 11: Articles

1. an artist a doctor an electrician a politician a teacher a university professor*
   a dentist a secretary a manager a housewife a shop assistant
   *Remember that it is the first SOUND that is important /ju:niversiti/

2. (a) O London is (b) a big city. (c) The centre is very busy. (d) O Oxford Street is (e) a good place for shopping. You can also go to (f) a department store, like 'Harrods', (g) a very famous shop.
   If (h) the weather is nice, you can go in (i) a boat on (j) the Thames, or walk in (k) a park. It is difficult to find (l) a cheap hotel in (m) O London but, if you are rich you can stay in (n) an expensive hotel like the Park Lane Hilton—with (o) a restaurant on (p) the top floor of (q) the hotel.

3. **1.** (a), (d), (m) — We generally use *nothing* with places.
   2. (j) — We use 'the' with the names of rivers.
   4. (h), (p) — We use 'the' when there is only *one*.
   5. (b), (e), (f), (g), (i), (k), (l), (n), (o) — We use 'a' when we talk about *one of many*.
   6. (c) — [We know it's the centre of *London*.]
   (q) — [We know it's the top floor of *the Park Lane Hotel*.]
   When we know *which* thing we mean we use 'the'.

4. How are you? I'm fine. I'm living in O [Rule 1] Warsaw now. I have a [Rule 5] small flat in the [Rule 6] centre. It is very nice. I also have a new job. I'm a [Rule 3] secretary now in a big company. The [Rule 6] company sells computers. I am an [vowel] expert now about computers!
   The [Rule 4] weather is very nice now in O [Rule 1] Poland. It's sunny and warm ...

Unit 12: Relative pronouns

1. (a) I don't like people who are unfriendly.
   (b) An express is a train that goes fast.
   (c) I know someone that can play the violin really well.
   (d) I like children who don't make too much noise!
   (e) Do you know the woman that lives upstairs?
   (f) I like films which have a happy ending.
   (g) This book is about a man who went to Antarctica.
   (h) He has a bicycle that costs Rs 500!

2. (a) A giraffe is an animal that/which has a very long neck.
   (b) The man who/that works in that office isn't very friendly.
   (c) Is this the train which/that is always late?
   (d) Can you write a sentence which/that uses a relative pronoun?
   (e) Do you know the children who/that live in that house?
   (f) A suitcase is a big bag which/that you take on holiday.
   (g) Perfume is something which/that makes you smell nice.
   (h) A briefcase is a bag which/that business people use.

3. (a) Chips are potatoes that/which are cut and fried.
   (b) Football is a game that/which has eleven players.
   (c) A typewriter is a machine that/which writes.
   (d) A waiter is a person that who works in a cafe.
   (e) Tea is a drink that/which people drink in India.
   (f) A watch is a thing that/which tells the time.
   (g) A husband is a man that/who is married.

APPENDIX

Unit 13: Have got

1. (a) How many sisters have you got?
   (b) I have not got any.
   (c) Has he got a car?
   (d) No, he hasn't.
   (e) I've got a big house in the country.
   (f) How many bedrooms has it got?
   (g) Have you got any pets?
   (h) Yes, I've got a dog.
   (i) They've got three children.
   (j) Have they got any grandchildren?
   (k) Yes, They have.

2. (a) Vinay and Kiran **have got** a car.
   (b) Nidhi **has got** children.
   (c) Shama and Kedar **haven't got** a television.
   (d) Subodh **hasn't got** a house.
   (e) Vinay and Kiran **have got** a dog.
   (f) Nidhi **hasn't got** a flat.
   (g) Shama and Kedar **haven't got a car.**
   (h) Nidhi **hasn't got** a car.
   (i) Subodh **hasn't got** a dog.
   (j) Vinay and Kiran **have got** a house.

3. (a) **Has** Nidhi **got** a house? **Yes, she has.**
   (b) **Has** Subodh **got** a dog? **No, he hasn't.**
   (c) **Have** Kedar and Shama **got** children? **No, they haven't.**
   (d) **Has** Nidhi **got** a car? **No, she hasn't.**
   (e) **Have** Vinay and Kiran **got** a television? **No, they haven't.**
   (f) **Have** Kedar and Shama **got** a flat? **Yes, they have.**
   (g) **Has** Subodh **got** children? **Yes, he has.**

Unit 14: Countable and uncountable nouns

1.

COUNTABLE	UNCOUNTABLE
Eggs	Chocolate
Potatoes	Orange Juice
Apples	Bread
Oranges	Sugar
Cakes	Tomato Sauce
Chocolates	Mineral Water

2.

an apple	a potato
O mineral water	O sugar
an orange	O orange juice
O bread	an egg

3.

(a)	rice	not possible
(b)	egg	eggs
(c)	banana	bananas
(d)	bread	not possible
(e)	milk	not possible
(f)	potato	potatoes
(g)	apple	apples
(h)	money	not possible
(i)	orange	oranges
(i)	orange juice	not possible
(k)	flour	not possible
(l)	salt	not possible
(m)	sugar	not possible
(n)	rupee	rupees

In this context it is not possible to say orange juices/milks. BUT, sometimes when you ask for drinks in a cafe you can say for example 'Three orange juices, please'. This is different because you mean 'Three *glasses* of orange juice.' Also with 'sugar' you can say 'Two sugars, please.' when you mean 'Two *spoons* of sugar (in your coffee)'.

Unit 15: 'Some' and 'any'

1. (a) There are some grapefruits.
   (b) Are there any eggs?
   (c) Do you have any lemons?
   (d) There aren't any peppers in the fridge.
   (e) Give me some apples.
   (f) Aren't there any oranges on the table?
   (g) We need some onions.

2. (a) There are some onions but there aren't any potatoes.
   (b) There is some milk and some water.
   (c) There aren't any peppers.
   (d) There is an egg.
   (e) There are some apples.
   (f) There isn't a grapefruit.
   (g) There is some rice but there isn't any pasta.
   (h) There isn't any cheese or any bread.

3. (a) Is there a banana?
   No, there isn't.
   (b) Are there any peppers?
   No, there aren't.
   (c) Are there any apples?
   Yes, there are.
   (d) Is there any milk?
   Yes, there is.
   (e) Is there any pasta?
   No, there isn't.
   (f) Are there any potatoes?
   No, there aren't.
   (g) Is there a grapefruit?
   No, there isn't.
   (h) Is there any cheese?
   No, there isn't.
   (i) Are there any onions?
   Yes, there are.
   (j) Is there an egg?
   Yes, there is.

Unit 16: Much/many/a lot

1. (a) How much shampoo have you got?
   (b) How many t-shirts have you got?
   (c) How many books have you got?
   (d) How much money have you got?
   (e) How many cassettes have you got?

2. (a) shampoo? A lot
   (b) t-shirts? Not a lot or not many
   (c) books? Not a lot or not many
   (d) money? A lot
   (e) cassettes? Not a lot or not many

3. (a) There is a lot of shampoo.
   (b) There aren't many/a lot of cassettes.
   (c) There is a lot of money.
   (d) There aren't many/a lot of books.
   (e) There aren't many/a lot of t-shirts.

4. (a) There aren't many books.
   (b) Correct
   (c) Correct
   (d) Correct
   (e) Correct
   (f) How many books are there?

Unit 17: 'Too' and 'Enough'

1. (a) The class isn't small enough.
   (b) The room is too dark.
   (c) The teacher isn't experienced enough.
   (d) The lessons aren't difficult enough.
   (e) The course is too expensive.
   (f) My hostel is too far.
   (g) The school isn't clean enough.
   (h) The lessons are too short.

2. (a) There **isn't enough** homework.
   (b) There **is too much** homework.
   (c) There **aren't enough** books.
   (d) There **are too many** breaks.
   (e) There **aren't enough** breaks.
   (f) There **aren't enough** desks.
   (g) There **isn't enough** listening practice.
   (h) There **is too much** writing practice.

3. Suman: 'I don't like Mumbai. It's **too** dirty. There is **too much** pollution'.
   Ritu: 'But it is very exciting—there are lots of shops.'
   Suman: 'Well, yes, but the shops are **too** expensive for me. I don't have **enough** money and there are **too many** people. It is so crowded!'
   Ritu: 'What about transport? Don't you like the red buses?'
   Suman: 'They look nice, but they are not cheap **enough**. It costs me Rs.30 a week to go to work! My house is **too** far from the centre.'
   Ritu: 'Do you have a nice house?'
   Suman: 'No, it is not big **enough**. I live with four students and they have parties every weekend. It is **too** noisy for me.'
   Ritu: 'So why don't you go out at the weekend? There is so much to do in Mumbai! There are lots of theatres and cinemas.'
   Suman: 'Yes, but there are **too many** theatres and cinemas—I cannot decide where to go!'

Unit 18: Present continuous tense

1. (a) The dog is running.
   (b) The children are swimming.
   (c) Grandmother is sleeping.
   (d) Father is lying down.
   (e) The birds are singing.
   (f) Mother and Father are talking.
   (g) Grandfather's eating.
   (h) The sun is shining.
   (i) The baby is crying.
   (j) The tree is dying.

2. (a) Q: Who's smoking? A: Father is
   (b) Q: Who's sleeping? A: Grandmother is
   (c) Q: Who's crying? A: The baby is
   (d) Q: Who's eating? A: Grandfather is
   (e) Q: Who's swimming?(*) A: The children are
   (f) Q: What's dying? A: The tree is
   (g) Q: Who's wearing shorts? A: Father is
   (h) Q: What are singing? A: The birds are

   Remember (*) In this case 'Who' is followed by 'is' even if the answer is plural.

3. (a) Q: Is Grandmother talking? A: No, she isn't.
   (b) Q: Where are the children swimming? A: In the lake.
   (c) Q: Are the birds singing? A: Yes, they are.
   (d) Q: What is Grandfather eating? A: An icecream.
   (e) Q: Is the sun shining? A: Yes, it is.
   (f) Q: Is the dog sleeping? A: No, it isn't.
   (g) Q: Who's Mother talking to? A: Father.
   (h) Q: Is Father writing a letter? A: No, he isn't.

   [*Sometimes people call their dog 'he' or 'she'.]
   If you have problems with these questions look at Unit 2—Question with the verb 'to be'.

4. (a) 'Help! The dog is **biting** me!
   (b) Correct
   (c) 'You are **running** too fast for me.'
   (d) 'Mary is **swimming** really well.'
   (e) Correct
   (f) 'Mother is **talking** to Father.'
   (g) 'I love **sleeping** in the afternoon.'

Unit 19: Present simple versus continuous

1. Satyam is a mechanic.
He mends cars.
He is having lunch.

Rekha is a secretary.
She types letters.
She is answering the phone.

Suresh is a postman.
He delivers letters.
He's running away from a dog!

Rita is a pilot.
She flies planes.
She's going home.

Vikram is a writer.
He writes books.
He's reading a book.

John is a painter.
He paints houses.
He's having a cup of tea.

2. (a) Japan is in the Pacific Ocean.
(b) Ria has ten cups of tea every day.
(c) We cannot go out—it's raining.
(d) I cannot hear you because I am listening to music.
(e) Where is Julia? She's reading a book.
(f) I usually get up early.
(g) I never eat chocolate—it makes you fat!

3. (a) What does Sally do?
(b) What are you doing?
(c) What languages do you speak?
(d) Where do you usually go on holiday?
(e) How many sisters do you have?
(f) Where are you going now?
(g) What are you eating?

Unit 20: Prepositions of place (in/on/next to)

1. (a) The box is **in front of** the plant.
(b) The chair is **opposite** the table.
(c) The saucer is **under** the cup.
(d) The book is **on** the table.
(e) The plant is **behind** the television.
(f) The cup is **on** the saucer.
(g) The picture is **next to** the mirror.
(h) The cushion is **on** the sofa.
(i) The glass is **near** the apples.

2. (a) The lamp is **on** the television.
(b) **True**
(c) **True**
(d) The videos are **under** the television.
(e) The curtains are **behind** the television.
(f) The apples are **in front of** the calendar.
(g) **True**
(h) The cat is **under** the table.
(i) **True**

3. (a) The glasses are **next to** the bottle.
(b) The apples are **in** the bowl.
(c) The radio is **on** the table.
(d) The photograph is **next to** the lamp.
(e) The shoes are **on** the floor.
(f) The calendar is **behind** the apples.
(g) The table is **opposite** the sofa.
(h) the remote control is **on** the sofa.

APPENDIX

Unit 21: Prepositions of time: in/at/on

1. (a) Teacher's Day is **on** 5th September.
   (b) Flag Day is **in** December.
   (c) Indians celebrate Gandhi Jayanti **on** 2nd October.
   (d) National Youth Day is celebrated **on** 12th January.
   (e) Childeren's Day is celebrated **on** 14th November, birthday of Pt Jawaharlal Nehru.
   (f) Some people go to church **at** midnight **on** Christmas Eve.
   (g) There is usually a ten day holiday **at** Dussehara.
   (h) Most people don't work **at** the weekends.

2. (a) **On** Monday morning **at** 9.00 Ruby's going to the Dentist.
   (b) She is meeting Rita **at** on Tuesday.
   (c) **In** the evening **on** 14th March she is going out for dinner.
   (d) She has a meeting **at** 3.00 **in** the afternoon **on** Thursday.
   (e) **On** 16th March she has a meeting **at** noon.
   (f) She's having a party **on** her birthday.
   (g) She isn't working **at** the weekend.
   (h) **On** Sunday she's visiting Ritu's parens.
   (i) Shiela's birthday is **next week** **on** 21st March.
   (j) Ruby is very busy **at** the moment.

3. (a) I was born **in** the 1970s.
   (b) Correct.
   (c) I can't sleep **at** night.
   (d) Are you going on holiday **at** Christmas?
   (e) Correct.
   (f) Do you think life will be very different **in** the future?
   (g) Life was different **in** the past.
   (h) Correct
   (i) Is it cold in Shimla **in** (the) winter?
   (j) I'm learning Urdu **at** the moment.
   (k) The telephone rang **at** midnight.
   (l) I'm going **on** holiday next week.

Unit 22: Prepositions of movement: up/down

1. (a) **Map B**
   (b) **Map A**
   (c) **Map C**
   (d) **Map D**

2. (a) Go **across** the road.
   (b) How do I get **from** the post office **to** the bank?
   (c) Go **into** the hotel.
   (d) Get **on** the bus.
   (e) Go **down** the hill.
   (f) Go **along** the road.
   (g) Go **through** the shopping centre.
   (h) Go **past** the supermarket.
   (i) Go **under** the subway.

3. A: 'How do I get **from** the school **to** the post office?'
   B: 'Go **out of** the school, **along** the road, **round** the roundabout, then turn left. Go **across/over** the bridge and it is the building on your left.'
   A: 'Is it a long way?'
   B: 'About half an hour. You could get **on** a number 9 bus outside the school and get **off** next to the bridge.'

Unit 23: Past simple tense of verb 'to be'

1. (a) He **was** a policeman.
   (b) We **were** very happy.
   (c) **Were** you busy?
   (d) They **were not** interested in it.
   (e) I **was** at school.
   (f) It **was not** expensive.
   (g) **Was** she your teacher?

2. Interviewer: 'What **was** it like during the First World War, Bill?'
   Bill: 'It **was** a terrible time. I **was** a young man, so I **was** in the army. We **were** in France.'
   Interviewer: 'Where **were** your wife and children?'
   Bill: 'They **were** in London. That **was** dangerous too. There **were** bombs and there **was not** a lot of food. The children **were** very young and they **were** very frightened.'

3. (a) **False - Bill was not an old man during the First World War.**
   (b) **True**
   (c) **True**
   (d) **False - Bill's wife and children weren't in France .**
   (e) **True**
   (f) **False - There wasn't a lot of food in London.**
   (g) **False - The children weren't very old.**
   (h) **True**

4. (a) **How old was Bill during the First World War?**
   (b) **Was Bill in the army?**
   (c) **Where was Bill?**
   (d) **Where were Bill's wife and children?**
   (e) **Was it dangerous in London?**
   (f) **Were there bombs?**
   (g) **Was there a lot of food?**
   (h) **How old were the children?**
   (i) **Were the children frightened?**

Unit 24: Past simple tense

Down			**Across**		
1.	Bring	**brought**	3.	Take	**took**
2.	Rise	**rose**	5.	Sing	**sang**
4.	Drink	**drank**	6.	Begin	**began**
6.	Blow	**blew**	7.	Know	**knew**
8.	Write	**wrote**	9.	Steal	**stole**
9.	Stand	**stood**	10.	Be	**was**
11.	Swim	**swam**	13.	See	**saw**
12.	Hate	**hated**	14.	Think	**thought**
15.	Give	**gave**	16.	Make	**made**
17.	Eat	**ate**	18.	Ride	**rode**

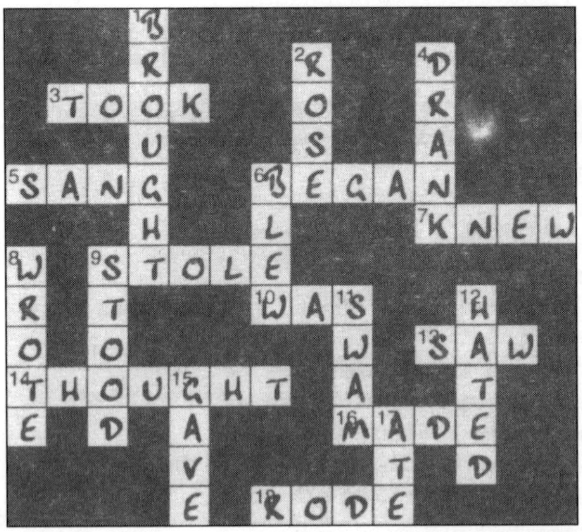

2. Carl Benz (invent) **invented** the petrol engine. Another German, Daimler, **designed** a car with an engine. This **was** the start of the modern car. At first, there **weren't** many cars. In England, a man **had** to walk in front of every car with a red flag. Then, in America, Henry Ford **built** a cheaper car, **called** the Model T Ford, which ordinary people **could** buy.

3. George Stephenson **invented** the first steam train, **called** "Locomotion". Steam engines **burnt/burned*** coal and **heated** water. The hot water **produced** steam and the steam **made** the wheels go round. Railways **became** very popular. Trains **travelled** faster. They **carried** passengers, parcels, letters and food.

*Some irregular verbs have *two* possible forms. Another example is 'dream' = 'dreamt' or 'dreamed'.

Unit 25: Past simple auxiliary

1. (a) Did Victoria have any brothers or sisters? No, she didn't.
   (b) Did she go to school? No, she didn't.
   (c) Did she speak French and German? Yes, she did.
   (d) Did William IV die in 1837? Yes, he did.
   (e) Did Victoria and Albert get married in 1840? Yes, they did.
   (f) Did she love her husband? Yes, she did.
   (g) Did they have ten children? No, they didn't.
   (h) Did she die in 1861? No, she didn't.

2. (a) Where did Victoria study? At home.
   (b) When did she have lessons? Every day from 9.30–5.00.
   (c) What did she collect? Dolls.
   (d) How many dolls did she have? 132.
   (e) When did William IV die? When Victoria was 18.
   (f) When did Victoria become Queen? In 1837.
   (g) When did she marry Albert? In 1840.
   (h) How many children did they have? Nine.
   (i) When did Albert die? In 1861.

3. (a) True
   (b) Victoria didn't go to school.
   (c) True
   (d) Victoria didn't speak Chinese.
   (e) Victoria didn't have 200 dolls.
   (f) Victoria didn't become Queen when she was twelve.
   (g) Victoria and Albert didn't get married in 1845.
   (h) True
   (i) Victoria and Albert didn't have five sons.
   (j) True
   (k) Victoria didn't die in 1861.

Unit 26: Would like

1. (a) Do you like tea? 4. Yes, I do/No, I do not.
   (b) Would you like a cup of tea? 2. Yes, please/No, thanks.
   (c) Do you like going to the cinema? 1. Yes, I do/No, I do not.
   (d) Would you like to go to the cinema? 3. Yes, I would love to/Sorry, I cannot.

2. (a) **Would you** like a coffee? Yes, please.
   (b) **I would** like to go and see the new film at the Roxy Cinema this weekend.
   (c) What **would you** like to do tonight?
   (d) **Do you** like getting up early? No, I hate it!
   (e) **I** like getting up late on Saturdays.
   (f) **Do you** like London? It is OK, but it rains all the time!
   (g) When he is older, **he would** like to be a doctor.
   (h) Why are you a teacher? Because **I** like teaching!
   (i) **Would you** like to go out to dinner? Yes, I would love to.

3. (a) Would you like (go) **to go** to the beach?
   (b) Do you like **playing** tennis?
   (c) What do you like **doing** on holiday?
   (d) I really like **lying** on the beach and **doing** nothing! My wife likes **sightseeing**.
   (e) I like **cooking** but I don't like **doing** the washing up.
   (f) I'd like **to see** "Macbeth" tonight. I really like **going** to the theatre.
   (g) Would you like **to dance**? No, sorry, I don't like **dancing**.

4. A: 'What **would** you **like to do** today?'
   B: 'Well, I think **I would like to go swimming** in the sea. It's a lovely day. So, what **would you like to do** today, then?'
   A: '**I would like to visit** the Castle.'
   B: 'But it's so hot! Why don't we go to the castle later?'

   A: 'Do you **like playing** tennis?'
   B: 'No, not much.'
   A: 'What sports do you **like?'**
   B: '**I like running.**'
   A: 'Oh, good! Would you **like to go** running with me this evening?'
   B: 'Sorry, I can't. I'm going to the cinema.'

Unit 27: Requests and permission: can/could/may

1. (a) Can you tell me the time, please?
   (b) Could you spell that, please?
   (c) Can I sit here?
   (d) May I smoke?
   (e) Can I borrow your pen, please?
   (f) Could you give me a lift, please?
   (g) Can you pass me the salt?
   (h) May I go to the disco, Mother?/ Mother, may I go to the disco?

2.

REQUESTS	ASKING FOR PERMISSION
Can you tell me the time, please?	Can I sit here?
Could you spell that, please?	May I smoke?
Could you give me a lift, please?	Can I borrow your pen, please?
Can you pass the salt?	May I go to the disco, Mother?

3. (a) Could you/Can you open the window, please?
   (b) Can I sit here, please?
   (c) Could you/Can you say that again, please?
   (d) Could you/Can you spell that, please?
   (e) Can I/May I leave early, please?
   (f) Can you/Could you help me, please?

4. Manuel: 'Can I/May I use the kitchen?'
   Mr Kumar : 'Yes, you can.'
   Manuel: 'May I/Can I invite my friends round?'
   Mr Kumar: 'Yes, of course, but can/could you ask us first?'
   Manuel: 'Can/Could you give me a key to the house?'
   Mr Kumar: 'Yes, but can/could you be quiet if you come in late?'
   Manuel: 'May I/Can I smoke in my room?'
   Mr Kumar: 'No, I am sorry. This is a non-smoking house.'

Unit 28: Ability (can/could)

1. (a) A teacher can write on the board.
   (b) A teacher can explain grammar.
   (c) A teacher can help students.
   (d) A politician can make a speech.
   (e) A politician can understand politics.
   (f) A waiter can take orders.
   (g) A waiter can serve food.
   (h) A waiter can add up a bill.
   (i) A secretary can type fast.
   (j) A secretary can answer the phone.
   (k) A secretary can take dictation.

2. (a) Can Sarah take dictation? Yes, she can.
   (b) Can John answer the phone? Yes, he can.
   (c) Can Sarah use a computer? Yes, she can.
   (d) Can John type 100 words a minute? Yes, he can.
   (e) Can Sarah answer the phone? Yes, she can.
   (f) Can John write shorthand? Yes, he can.
   (g) Can Sarah type 100 words a minute? No, she cannot.
   (h) Can John take dictation? Yes, he can.
   (i) Can Sarah take dictation? Yes, she can.
   (j) Can John use a computer? No, he cannot.

   Who do you think should get the job?—Perhaps John - he can do more than Sarah.

APPENDIX

Unit 29: Obligation (have to)

1. (a) The teacher has to be friendly.
   (b) The students have to work hard.
   (c) The teacher has to give some homework.
   (d) The students have to do their homework.
   (e) The teacher has to help the students.
   (f) The students have to be on time.
   (g) The teacher has to speak clearly.
   (h) The students have to speak English in class.

2. When Reena **was** a secretary
   (a) She **had to** type letters (+).
   (c) She **did not have to** travel a lot (-).
   (e) She **did not have to** work at the weekend (-).
   (f) She **had to** work from 9.00–5.00 (+).
   (h) She **had to** work hard (+).

   Now Reena is a salesperson
   (b) She **does not have to** type letters (-).
   (d) She **has to** travel a lot (+).
   (e) She **has to** work at the weekend (+).
   (g) She **does not have to** work from 9.00–5.00 (-).
   (i) She still **has to** work hard (+).

3. I am a teacher. I work in the centre of London but I live in the Southeast, quite a long way from the school. So every morning I **have to** get up at 7.00. There are no buses so I **have to** walk to the train station. I get a train to Victoria Station and then I usually go on the Underground. The school is quite near so I **do not have to** go on the Underground—if the weather is good, I sometimes walk. I **have to** be at work at 8.45 because classes start at 9.00.

   Yesterday was terrible because there was a train strike, so there were no trains to Victoria. I **had to** get up at 6.00 and walk a long way to catch a bus. When I got to the bus stop the buses were all full so I **had to** wait a long time. Luckily a friend gave me a lift home at the end of the day so I **did not have to** walk or wait for a bus again.

4. (a) What time does she have to get up? 7.00.
   (b) Why does she have to walk to the train station? There are no buses.
   (c) Does she have to go on the Underground? No, she does not.
   (d) What time does she have to be at work? 8.45.
   (e) What time did she have to get up yesterday? 6.00.
   (f) Why did she have to wait a long time? The buses were all full.
   (g) Did she have to walk at the end of the day? No, she did not.

Unit 30: Advising (should/shouldn't)

1. (a) You should read in English.
   (b) You should write vocabulary in a notebook.
   (c) You should not try and translate every word you read.
   (d) You should listen to the radio in English.
   (e) You should not speak your own language in your English class.
   (f) You should not forget to do your homework.
   (g) You should watch English films.
   (h) You should study hard!

2. Suraj: 'I'm really worried about my exam, Raj.'
   Raj: 'You should not worry. You'll be OK.'
   Suraj: 'Yes, but I have got too much work to do!'
   Raj: 'You should plan your time.'
   Suraj: 'I know, but I do not have much time. I am going to a party on Saturday.'
   Raj: 'Well, you should not go to the party.'
   Suraj: 'But I need to relax sometimes.'
   Raj: 'Yes, well, you should not work all the time. You can work on Sunday.'
   Suraj: 'I'm going swimming on Sunday.'
   Raj: ' I think you should work harder."

3. He should give up smoking.
   They should speak English in class.
   They should not drink so much.
   He should buy a new car.
   She should exercise more.
   She should spend less money.
   He should not eat so much chocolate.
   She should be careful!

APPENDIX

Unit 31: Possibility (may/might)

1. (a) The Princess may not make a decision.
   (b) The Princess may not want to be rich.
   (c) The Princess might not like Prince Humphrey better.
   (d) Her father may not like Prince Alfred better.
   (e) Prince Alfred may not love someone else.
   (f) Prince Humphrey might not love someone else.

2. (a) I might marry Prince Humphrey or I might marry Prince Alfred.
   (b) I might decide this week or I might decide next year.
   (c) I might travel the world or I might write a book.
   (d) I might live here or I might live abroad.

3. (a) The Princess may marry me.
   (b) We may live in my castle.
   (c) She may not like that.
   (d) We may live with her father.
   (e) Her father may not like me.
   (f) I may build a new castle in her country.
   (g) They may not like that.
   (h) She may not marry me.

4. (a) The Princess might dance with Prince Humphrey.
   (b) Prince Humphrey might ask the Princess to marry him.
   (c) The Princess might say 'No'.
   (d) Prince Humphrey might be sad.
   (e) Prince Alfred might be successful.
   (f) Then Prince Humphrey might be angry.
   (g) Prince Humphrey might hit Prince Alfred.
   (h) The Princess might be very angry.
   (i) She might not marry either of them.
   (j) She might not get married at all.

Unit 32: Past continuous

1. At 8.00am in Britain
   Sunita was having breakfast.
   But, in Australia
   Rajiv was leaving work.

   At 12.00 pm in Britain
   Sunita was having lunch.
   But in Australia
   Rajiv was having a coke.

   At 10.00pm in Britain
   Sunita was going to bed.
   But in Australia
   Rajiv was getting up.

   At 11.00pm in Britain
   Sunita was reading in bed.
   But in Australia
   Rajiv was going to work.

2. Rajiv: 'Hi, Sunita?'
   Sunita: 'Rajiv! I tried to telephone you yesterday but you were never at home. What were you doing?'
   Rajiv: 'What time did you ring?'
   Sunita: 'Well, first I rang at 8.00am—that is 5.30pm in Australia.'
   Rajiv: 'I was leaving work.'
   Sunita: 'Then I rang at 12.00pm—that is 9.30pm in Australia.'
   Rajiv: 'I was having a coke with my friends.'
   Sunita: 'Then I rang at 5.00pm—oh dear, that is 2.30am in Australia!'
   Rajiv: 'Yes, I was sleeping—or I was *trying* to sleep!'

3. (a) Tim was talking to Lisa.
   (b) John and Jay were having an argument.
   (c) Jane was having a hamburger.
   (d) Mary and Louisa were dancing.
   (e) Peter was drinking a coke.
   (f) Tim and Jay were having pizza.
   (g) Tim and Lisa were sitting on a bench.
   (h) Rajiv's friends were having a good time.

4. (a) Was Tim talking to Louisa? No, he wasn't.
   (b) Was Jane drinking a coke? No, she wasn't.
   (c) Were Mary and Louisa dancing? Yes, they were.
   (d) Were Tim and Lisa eating? No, they weren't.
   (e) Was Tim sitting? Yes, he was.
   (f) Was Lisa standing up? No, she wasn't.
   (g) Were Rajiv's friends having a good time? Yes, they were.

APPENDIX

Unit 33: Past simple and continuous

1. ... I explained that I was twenty four hours late because there was a railway strike.
'Sorry,' sir, he said, 'Rules are rules - Rs. 40 please.'

I was so angry that while **he was writing** the ticket for the fine **I went** to my car and **took out** my steering wheel lock and **locked** his steering wheel. 'Right,' I said. 'Now I can't move my car and you can't move your van!'

'I'll call the police!' he said. 'No, I will.' I replied and so we both called them.

But while we were waiting for the police to arrive **he said**, 'OK, you win.' and **he took** the clamp off my car. So I took off the steering wheel lock. I got in my car but as I was leaving **the police arrived** and I had to stop and explain the whole story. They couldn't stop laughing. I don't know what they thought was so funny!

2. Last night I **was feeling tired**. I **was sleeping** when this man **woke me up**. He was really angry because his car had been clamped. While he **was shouting** at me I tried to tell him he had to pay a fine of Rs. 40. As I **was writing** the ticket he **went** to his car and came back with a steering wheel lock and he locked my steering wheel! I could not believe it! I called the police—and so did he. While we **were waiting** for the police he got angrier and angrier. I felt quite scared so I decided to let him go. He **was driving** away when the police **arrived** but he stopped to talk to them. For some reason the policemen thought the story was really funny.

3. (a) He drove away when the police arrived.
(b) He was driving away when the police arrived.
Sentence **b** means he started driving *before* the police arrived.
Sentence **a** means he started driving *at the same time* as the police arrived.

(c) I was feeling really tired and annoyed when I arrived home.
(d) I felt really tired and annoyed when I arrived home.
Sentence **c** means he started feeling tired and annoyed *before* he arrived home.
Sentence **d** means he started feeling tired and annoyed *at the same time* as he arrived home.

4. **I was driving home when I saw an accident.**
We were dancing when the electricity went out.
It was raining when I arrived.
They were robbing a bank when the police arrived.
I was reading when the phone rang.
She was shopping when she met him.

Unit 34: Prepositions of place (in/on/next to)

1. (a) quiet **noisy**
(b) expensive **cheap**
(c) rich **poor**
(d) boring **exciting**
(e) cold **hot**
(f) good **bad**
(g) difficult **easy**
(h) slow **fast**
(i) short **tall***
(j) happy **sad**
(k) old (people) **young**
(l) old (things) **new**

*The opposite of short for *people* is tall, for things (eg a film) the opposite is long.

2 & 3.
(a) The children are very **noisy** today. **(2)**
(b) He bought a **new** car. It was very **expensive**. **(1 & 2)**
(c) The weather was **cold** today. **(2)**
(d) I love **hot** weather! **(1)**
(e) This TV programme is really **exciting**. **(2)**
(f) This is a **difficult** exercise. **(1)**
(g) My aunt is really **young**. **(2)**
(h) He wrote a really **good** essay. **(1)**
(i) The train is really **fast**. **(2)**
(j) My brother is quite **short**. **(2)**
(k) He bought me a **small** present. **(1)**

4. The weather **is really beautiful**.
Brighton **is an exciting town**
but it **is quite expensive**.
Yesterday I went to see **a great play** at the theatre.
The actors **were very good**.
Today I am going shopping. There are some **wonderful shops**.
I want to buy **a new dress**.
Then tomorrow we are going on a boat-trip—if **the sea is calm**.

Unit 35: Comparatives

1.

-er	-ier	more...	irregular
old	easy	important	good
nice	sunny	exciting	bad
cheap	noisy	expensive	far
warm	lucky	comfortable	
quiet	heavy		
tall			
fast			

2. (a) Rio is **hotter** than Brasilia.
   (b) Brasilia is **smaller** than Rio.
   (c) Correct
   (d) Brasilia is **sunnier** than Rio.
   (e) Correct
   (f) Correct
   (g) Rio is **nicer** than Brasilia.
   (h) Brasilia is **drier** than Rio.

3. (a) Manchester is **bigger** than York.
   (b) Manchester is **nearer** London than York.
   (c) The train ticket from York to London is **more expensive** than from Manchester to London.
   (d) Manchester is **dirtier** than York. (look at the picture!)
   (e) York is **smaller** than Manchester.
   (f) York is **further** from London than Manchester.
   (g) The train ticket from Manchester to London is **cheaper** than from York to London.
   (h) York is **cleaner** than Manchester. (look at the picture!)

4. (a) (big) **Oporto is bigger than Faro.**
   (b) (small) **Faro is smaller than Oporto.**
   (c) (sunny) **Faro is sunnier than Oporto.**
   (d) (cloudy) **Oporto is cloudier than Faro.**
   (e) (hot) **Faro is hotter than Oporto.**
   (f) (cool) **Oporto is cooler than Faro.**
   (g) (rainy) **Oporto is rainier than Faro.**
   (h) (dry) **Faro is drier than Oporto.**

Unit 36: Superlatives

1. (a) beautiful **the most beautiful**
   (b) delicious **the most delicious**
   (c) cheap **the cheapest**
   (d) safe **the safest**
   (e) dangerous **the most dangerous**
   (f) hot **the hottest**
   (g) boring **the most boring**
   (h) good **the best**
   (i) large **the largest**
   (j) small **the smallest**
   (k) relaxing **the most relaxing**
   (l) expensive **the most expensive**
   (m) clean **the cleanest**
   (n) bad **the worst**
   (o) near **the nearest**

2. (a) Recife is (expensive) **the most expensive** holiday.
   (b) Hotel Boa Viagem is **the nearest** to the Beach.
   (c) Recife is **the longest** holiday.
   (d) Hotel Thai is **the furthest** from the beach.
   (e) Hotel Thai is **the biggest** hotel.
   (f) Phuket is **the shortest** holiday.
   (g) Key West is **the cheapest** holiday.
   (h) Palm Hotel is **the smallest** hotel.

3. Suresh: 'Well, I think (a) (good) **the best** place to go is Thailand. It is certainly (b) **the cheapest** country and it has got (c) **the most beautiful** beaches. The weather is wonderful—Bangkok is (d) **the hottest** city in the world.'
   Shweta : 'But Brazil has beautiful beaches too and I think it is (e) **the most relaxing** place.'
   Suresh: 'Relaxing!! It is (f) **the most dangerous**! We'll probably get shot!'
   Shweta: 'Rubbish! The United States is (g) **the worst**. Florida is really dangerous for tourists.'
   Suresh: 'So, let us go to Thailand. Its (h) **the safest**. It is (i) **the most interesting** place too—a completely different culture. And the food is (j) **the most delicious** in the world.'
   Shweta: 'Well, yes, American food is probably (k) **the most boring**—all hamburgers and steaks and it is (l) **the most expensive** place to go too.'

4. (a) Brazil is **the furthest** place.
   (b) French food is the **best** in the world.
   (c) **Correct**
   (d) Madame Tussauds is the **most interesting** thing to see in London.
   (e) Are you the **oldest** in your family?
   (f) I sat in **the most comfortable** chair.

5. (a) Tokyo is the **biggest** city in Japan.
   (b) Jonny is the **noisiest** student in the class!
   (c) **Correct**
   (d) The **fastest** car won the race.
   (e) Jane and Sue are both thin but Mary is the **thinnest**.
   (f) Who is the **busiest** person in the office?

Unit 37: Adverb II: manner

1. (a) bad **badly**
   (b) good **well**
   (c) easy **easily**
   (d) careful **carefully**
   (e) angry **angrily**
   (f) quiet **quietly**
   (g) noisy **noisily**
   (h) slow **slowly**
   (i) silent **silently**
   (j) violent **violently**

2. 'I am really looking forward to our holiday.' she said, **happily.**
   'Er, do you think we have enough money to go on holiday, darling?' he asked, **nervously.**
   'Of course we do!' she said, **confidently.**
   'But, have you forgotten we have got to pay for the new car?' he asked, **quietly.**
   'I thought you did that last month!' she shouted, **angrily.**
   'No, we had to pay for your new clothes last month – Rs. 500!' he replied, **crossly.**
   'Oh, well, no holiday, then' she said **sadly.**

3. (a) He did it **accidentally.**
   (b) He laughed **wickedly.**
   (c) He speaks English **fluently.**
   (d) She behaves **politely.**
   (e) They dress **differently.**
   (f) He sings **well.**
   (g) He won **easily.**
   (h) She laughed **happily.**

4. Driving in Kolkata is not (a) **easy.** The traffic moves very (b) **slowly** in central Kolkata, about 12 km per hour. You also need to drive (c) **carefully** because some drivers are very (d) **impatient** and drive (e) **dangerously.** Another problem is finding a place to park. Car-parks are very (f) **expensive.** It is often better to leave your car outside the city centre and then you can (g) **easily** travel into the centre on public transport. The buses and the metro railway are very (h) **good.**
   There are lots of (i) **excellent** restaurants in Kolkata and—if you have the money—you can eat very (j) **well.** In Kolkata you can eat Indian, Thai, French, Chinese food … everything!

Unit 38: Present tenses for future tense

1. (a) The plane (leave) **leaves** at 8.00 on 16th June.
   (b) Mr Joshi **is meeting** Mr Kuhato at 3.00 pm on 17th June.
   (c) He **is having** lunch with the Directors at 1.00 on 18th June.
   (d) On 19th June he **is visiting** a textile factory.
   (e) On 20th June he **is going** to a concert.
   (f) The concert **starts** at 8.00pm.
   (g) On the 21st June he **is having** dinner with Jane Fairfax.
   (h) On the 22nd June he **is playing** golf with Mr Kuhato.
   (i) The plane back to London **leaves** at 20.20 on the 23rd June.

2. (a) **What time does the plane leave London?**
   (b) **Who is he meeting on 17th June?**
   (c) **What is he doing on 18th June?**
   (d) **Where is he visiting on 19th June?**
   (e) **What time does the concert start?**
   (f) **When is he having dinner with Jane Fairfax?**
   (g) **What is he doing on 22nd June?**
   (h) **What time does the plane back to London leave?**

3. (a) **leaves**
   (b) **am staying**
   (c) **Correct**
   (d) **am meeting**
   (e) **Are you visiting**
   (f) **Correct**
   (g) **Correct**
   (h) **lands**

APPENDIX

Unit 39: Going to/Will - I

1. (a) She is going to lie on the beach.
   (b) She is not going to take her mobile phone.
   (c) She is going to sleep late every day.
   (d) She is not going to take her lap-top computer.
   (e) She is not going to telephone her office every day.
   (f) She is going to eat delicious healthy food.
   (g) She is going to go scuba diving.
   (h) She is going to have a really good time.

2. (a) 'I feel hungry.' 'I will have something to eat.'
   (b) 'The sun is really hot.' 'I will go in the shade.'
   (c) 'I feel thirsty.' 'I will have something to drink.'
   (d) 'I think I am burning.' 'I will put on some suncream.'
   (e) 'The sea looks wonderful.' 'I will go for a swim.'
   (f) 'I am bored.' 'I will read a book.'

3. Minu: 'What are you going to do next week Fatima?'
   Fatima: 'Did not I tell you? I am going [to go] on holiday.'
   Minu: 'You lucky thing! Where are you going [to go]?'
   Fatima: 'Sri Lanka. Are you going [to go] anywhere this year?'
   Minu: 'I do not know yet. Maybe we will visit friends in Wales.'
   Fatima: 'Well, I will send you a postcard!'
   Minu: 'Thanks!'

4. Dear Minu,
   Having a lovely time in Sri Lanka. Tomorrow I am going to visit an old palace in the jungle but today it is really hot so I think I will just lie on the beach. It is so relaxing! I will ring you when I get back, OK?
   Love, Fatima

   Dear Mother and Father,
   I am really enjoying my holiday in Sri Lanka. I am going to stay here three weeks and really relax. Next week I am going (to go) on a trip into the jungle—Do not worry! I will be very careful!
   Love, Fatima

Unit 40: Going to/Will - II

1.

(a)	the train/come	The train is going to come.
	the hero/rescue her	The hero will rescue her.
(b)	they/fight	They're (they are) going to fight.
	one of them die	One of them will die.
(c)	they/fall in love	They are going to fall in love.
	they get married	They'll (they will) get married.
(d)	he/fall	He's going to fall.
	he/die	He'll die.
(e)	he/ask her to marry him	He's going to ask her to marry him.
	she/say 'Yes'	She'll say 'Yes'.
(f)	he/give her flowers	He's going to give her flowers.
	she/be happy	She'll be happy.

2. (a) Is the train going to come?
   Will the hero rescue her?
   (b) Are they going to fight?
   Will one of them die?
   (c) Are they going to fall in love?
   Will they get married?
   (d) Is he going to fall?
   Will he die?
   (e) Is he going to ask her to marry him?
   Will she say 'Yes'?
   (f) Is he going to give her flowers?
   Will she be happy?

3. Director: 'OK, in this scene the villain (kidnap) is going to kidnap the heroine and he is going to tie her to the train tracks. She is going to scream very loudly and, before the train comes, the hero is going to hear her screaming and rescue her.'
   Actor: 'Are they going to fall in love?
   Director: 'Yes, but first the hero and the villain are going to fight.'
   Actor: 'Is the hero going to win?'
   Director: 'Of course!'

4. (a) The hero will kill the villain.
   (b) The villain will apologise and the hero won't kill him.
   (c) The heroine will be very happy.
   (d) The hero and heroine will get married.
   (e) They'll live happily ever after.
   (f) They'll have two children.

Unit 41: Present perfect I: experience

1. (a) be - **been** (b) break - **broken** (c) buy - **bought** (d) come - **come** (e) cut - **cut** (f) drink - **drunk**
(g) drive - **driven** (h) eat - **eaten** (i) fall - **fallen** (j) forget - **forgotten** (k) get - **got*** (l) give - **given**
(m) go - **been** or **gone** (n) have - **had** (o) know - **known** (p) make - **made** (q) meet - **met** (r) read - **read**
(s) see - **seen** (t) speak - **spoken** (u) steal - **stolen** (v) take - **taken** (w) think - **thought** (x) write - **written**

*American English 'gotten'.

2. (a) **Has** Samir ever **eaten** snails?
Yes, he has.
(b) **Has** Katha ever **read** Shakespeare?
No, she hasn't.
(c) **Have** Rohit and Jaya ever **met** the President?
Yes, they have.
(d) **Has** Samir **driven** a lorry?
Yes, he has.
(e) **Has** Katha **been** to Australia?
Yes, she has.
(f) **Have** Rohit and Jaya **eaten** snails?
No, they haven't.

3.

(a)	You/eat/snails?	**Have you (ever) eaten snails?**	Yes, I have.
(b)	Where/you/eat them?	**Where did you eat them?**	In France.
(c)	Rohit and Jaya/meet the President?	**Have Rohit and Jaya met the President?**	Yes, they have.
(d)	When/they/meet him?	**When did they meet him?**	Last year.
(e)	Samir/read/Shakespeare?	**Has Samir read Shakespeare?**	Yes, he has.
(f)	What/he/read?	**What did he read?/has he read?**	Hamlet.
(g)	Katha/drive/a lorry?	**Has Katha driven a lorry?**	Yes, she has.
(h)	When/she/drive it?	**When did she drive it?**	A few years ago.
(i)	You/meet the President?	**Have you met the President?**	Yes, I have
(j)	Where/you/meet him?	**Where did you meet him?**	At Rashtrapati Bhavan.

4. (a) Have you **been** to China? (b) I **went** there last year. (c) I have never **eaten** sushi.
(d) **Has** she been to France? (e) They **have** travelled all over the world.

Unit 42: Present perfect II: time up to now

1. (a) Ravi **has been** in England **since** March.
Ravi **has been** in England **for** three months.
(b) Deepak and Sumitra **have known** Peter **since** 1995.
Deepak and Sumitra **have known** Peter **for** two years.
(c) I **have had** a cat **for** a year.
I **have had** a cat since last year.
(d) She **has lived** in Maldives **since** 1993.
She **has lived** in Maldives **for** four years.
(e) Shyam **has been** 21 **for** two weeks.
Shyam **has been** 21 **since** 16th November.
(f) We **have worked** in Chennai **since** January.
We **have worked** in Chennai **for** three months.

2. (a) **How long has Ravi been in England?**
(b) **How long have Deepak and Sumitra known Peter?**
(c) **How long have you had a cat?**
(d) **How long has Sheila lived in Maldives?**
(e) **How long has Shyam been 21?**
(f) **How long have you worked in Chennai?**

3. (a) **He has not been married long.**
(b) **We have not lived in England long.**
(c) **They have not worked here long.**
(d) **I have not been a teacher long.**
(e) **She has not had a car long.**
(f) **He has not known her long.**
(g) **You have not been married long.**

4. Jan **has been** a teacher for ten years. She **became** a teacher when she left university in 1987. She likes travelling and **has been** all over the world. Last year she **went** to China.

My wife and I **got married** in 1976, so we **have been married** for more than twenty years now. When we got married we **lived** with my wife's mother but we **bought** this house fifteen years ago and since then we **have lived** here.

APPENDIX

Unit 43: Present perfect III: present result

1. (a) hurt hurt
   (b) break broken
   (c) burn burnt/burned
   (d) drink drunk
   (e) sprain sprained
   (f) catch (measles) caught
   (g) watch watched
   (h) cut cut
   (i) bump bumped

2. (a) He has bumped his head.
   (b) He has watched too much television!
   (c) He has drunk poison by accident.
   (d) They have caught measles.
   (e) He has sprained his ankle.
   (f) He has sprained his arm.
   (g) He has cut his leg.
   (h) She has burnt her finger.
   (i) She has hurt her back.

3. (a) I have lost my keys—I cannot get into my house!
   (b) I have broken my leg, but it is OK again now.
   (c) I have eaten too much. I feel sick.
   (d) He has fallen over—help him to stand up!
   (e) I have won. Shall we play again?
   (f) Duncan arrived early but he has gone now.
   (g) Why are you wet? Have you been swimming?

4. (a) 'Have you eaten enough?'
   'Yes, thanks. It was delicious.'
   (b) 'Why is the dog barking?'
   'Because the post has arrived.'
   (c) 'Oh no! It is raining and I have forgotten my umbrella!'
   (d) 'She dyed her hair purple but her mother did not like it so she has dyed it brown again now.'
   (e) 'She missed the train so she caught a bus instead.'
   (f) 'Your shoes look new. Have you cleaned them?'
   (g) 'I felt terrible this morning but now my headache has gone.'

Unit 44: Present perfect IV: 'yet' and 'already'

1. (a) She has already seen the Old Town.
   (b) She has already had lunch at Ariel's.
   (c) She has already gone shopping.
   (d) She has already visited the Sukiennice.
   (e) She has already heard the Chopin Concert.
   (f) She has not eaten at Staropolska Restaurant yet.
   (g) She has not visited Wawel Castle yet.
   (h) She has not had lunch at the Cafe Jama Michalika yet.
   (i) She has not been on a trip to Wieliczka Salt Mines yet.

2. (a) Has she seen the Old Town yet? Yes, she has.
   (b) Has she been shopping yet? Yes, she has.
   (c) Has she visited Wieliczka yet? No, she has not.
   (d) Has she seen the Wawel Castle yet? No, she has not.
   (e) Has she heard the Chopin Concert yet? Yes, she has.
   (f) Has she had dinner at the Staropolska yet? No, she has not.

3. (a) I have already seen the museum.
   (b) Have you been to Prague yet?
   (c) She has not eaten pierogi yet?
   (d) I have already taken lots of photos.
   (e) I have not spent much money yet.
   (f) I have already been to the Castle.
   (g) She has not crossed the bridge yet.
   (h) Has Dia visited Bratislava yet?

APPENDIX

Unit 45: Questions Revision 1

1. (a) Is he a Portuguese builder?
   (b) Are they dancing?
   (c) Were you late?
   (d) Can Ali dance really well?
   (e) Are they going to the seaside?
   (f) Was your computer very expensive?
   (g) Would you like to go?
   (h) Is he coming home by train?
   (i) Could she swim?
   (j) Are you feeling better?

2. (a) How long have you lived here?
   (b) Can you pass the salt?
   (c) Was he happy?
   (d) What will you do?
   (e) Where is he going?
   (f) Can I help you?
   (g) Who are you going to marry?
   (h) Has long was the film?
   (i) Where is your bag?
   (j) Where were they going?

3. (a) Where **are** you from?
   (b) **Can/May** I use the phone?
   (c) Where **are you going** on holiday?
   (d) What **would you** like to eat?
   (e) How old **were** you in 1975?
   (f) **Have** you ever **eaten** crab?
   (g) Where **are** you going?
   (h) **Have** you finished yet?

Unit 46: Questions Revision 2

1. (a) Where did the poor woman and her children live?
   (b) What colour of hair did Snow White have?
   (c) When did the Bear knock on the door?
   (d) What did he say?
   (e) What did they give the Bear?
   (f) Who did they see in the forest?
   (g) What did the Dwarf find in the tree?

2. (a) What did Snow White take out?
   (b) What did she cut off?
   (c) What did he pick up?
   (d) When did they see him again?
   (e) What did he say?
   (f) What did the Bear explain?
   (g) Who did Rose Red marry?

3. (a) Did the Bear kill the Dwarf?
   (b) Did the Bear hit the Dwarf?
   (c) Did they try to help him?
   (d) Did the Bear fall asleep by the fire?
   (e) Did he come back every day?
   (f) Did he walk off?
   (g) Did the Dwarf steal the treasure?

4. (a) Does Snow White have some scissors?
   (b) Where do the family live?
   (c) Does the Bear eat people?
   (d) Does the Dwarf steal the Prince's gold?
   (e) Does the Dwarf like fishing?
   (f) Do Snow White and Rose Red love their husbands?

Appendix 4: 'Test Yourself' Answers and Study/Revision Guide

Answers to Test Yourself Exercises (see page 94)

Part one: (Units 1–4) Talking about people, places and objects

		Answer	Study/revise Unit 1	2	3	4
1	(a)	What is (What's) this?	•	•		
	(b)	Are these expensive?	•	•		
	(c)	Is this the Post Office?			•	
	(d)	Are we late?	•	•		
	(e)	Is that your sister?			•	
	(f)	Are they German?	•	•		
	(g)	Are these her shoes?			•	
2.	(a)	Are	•	•		
	(b)	this			•	
	(c)	isn't	•	•		
	(d)	that			•	
	(e)	is	•	•		
3.	(a)	Those children are very intelligent.			•	•
	(b)	Are these your bags?			•	•
	(c)	These are English dictionaries.			•	•
	(d)	Are these cheese sandwiches?			•	•
	(e)	The buses are red.				•
	(f)	These are your keys.			•	
4.	(a)	Correct	•	•		
	(b)	I like **children.**				•
	(c)	I **am** an artist.	•	•		
	(d)	Are **those** your sisters?			•	
	(e)	Correct	•			
	(f)	Correct			•	•
	(g)	We aren't very happy. (**no '?'**)	•	•		
	(h)	Correct			•	
	(i)	**He's/He is** my friend.	•	•		
	(j)	Correct			•	•
	(k)	Correct			•	•
	(l)	Is **this your** husband?	•	•	•	
5.	(a)	We **are** French.	•	•		
	(b)	**These** are my parents.			•	
	(c)	What **is** your name?	•	•		
	(d)	The people **are** happy.				•
	(e)	Yes, it **is.**	•	•		
	(f)	The men **are** in the field.				•
	(g)	Are you a student? No, **I'm** not.	•	•		
	(h)	What's **that**?			•	

Part two: (Units 5–7) Talking about routines and habits

		Answer	Study/revise Unit 5	6	7
1.	(b)	The Japanese **make** very good cars.	•		
	(c)	**I live** in Devon.	•		
	(d)	Yuko **wants** to go to England.	•		
	(e)	In the winter he **goes** skiing.	•		
	(f)	Sita and Ria **have** breakfast at 8am.	•		
	(g)	Gita **finishes** work at 6pm	•		
	(h)	She **studies** French in the evening	•		
	(i)	Priya **gets up** at 6am every day.	•		
2.	(b)	Tony and Vicky **don't live** in Italy.		•	
	(c)	We **don't get up** early on Sundays.		•	
	(d)	Rina **doesn't study** medicine at University.		•	
	(e)	**I don't stay** late at the office in the evenings.		•	
	(f)	Priya **doesn't like** going shopping.		•	
3.	(b)	How much does a ticket cost?		•	
	(c)	Do you like living in Bhopal?		•	
	(d)	Does she work for Toyota?		•	
	(e)	Where do Mina and Raj study?		•	
	(f)	When does the plane arrive in New Delhi?		•	
4.	(b)	Sarah sometimes gets up early.			•
	(c)	Sheila **never** drives.			•
	(d)	They are **always** happy.			•
	(e)	Emma **rarely travels.**			•
	(f)	**I often** go running.			•
5.	(b)	Jo never drinks tea.			•
	(c)	Ravi sometimes goes to watch a football match.			•
	(d)	I often go swimming.			•
	(e)	Debbie rarely goes to the cinema.			•
	(f)	Jim is always hungry.			•
6.	(b)	Jean and Brian **always go** to Spain on holiday.			•
	(c)	The buses **are never** late.			•
	(d)	When the sun **shines,** I go swimming in the sea.	•		
	(e)	Correct.		•	
	(f)	What time **does** Mr Kumar **get up?**		•	
	(g)	Ram **finishes** work at 5.30.	•		
	(h)	What **does** Shiv do at the weekend?		•	
	(i)	He **plays** football.	•		
	(j)	Minu never **goes** to the cinema.			•

Part three: (Units 8–12) Referring to people, places and objects

			Study/revise Unit 8	9	10	11	12
1.	(b)	No, but I like **her**.	•				
	(c)	**We** don't live in **our** old house now.	•	•			
	(d)	Is that car **yours**?			•		
	(e)	No, it's **hers**.			•		
	(f)	**Their** daughter is a doctor.		•			
	(g)	Where does **she** live?	•				
	(h)	Where is **her** house?		•			
	(i)	Please write to **me** soon.	•				
	(j)	That book isn't **mine**.			•		
	(k)	I don't think that house is **theirs**.			•		
2	(b)	What floor is **his** flat on?		•			
	(c)	**They** are **her** friends.	•	•			
	(d)	**Her** flat is near **theirs**.		•	•		
	(e)	Is that **hers?**			•		
	(f)	No, it's **his**.			•		
3.	(b)	is		•			
	(c)	possession		•			
	(d)	is		•			
	(e)	is		•			
	(f)	possession		•			
4.	(b)	**He's** a doctor.	•				
	(c)	**Their** house is in London.		•			
	(d)	**She's** interested in tennis.	•				
	(e)	**She's** one of the richest women in the world.	•				
	(f)	**Their** wedding anniversary's in June.		•			
5.	(b)	**The** house has only one garage.					
	(c)	**a** Maruti 800				•	
	(d)	**a** Fiat Padmini.				•	
	(e)	**The** Maruti 800 is quite new				•	
	(f)	**the** Fiat Padmini is older.				•	
	(g)	**the** Maruti 800				•	
	(h)	**the** garage.				•	
	(i)	**a** businessman.				•	
	(j)	(**nothing**) London				•	
	(k)	(**nothing**) Henley				•	
	(l)	**the** River Thames.				•	
	(m)	**a** teacher				•	
	(n)	**a** school				•	
	(o)	(**nothing**) Henley				•	
	(p)	**an** eight year old son				•	

			Study/revise Unit 8	9	10	11	12
6.	(b)	Oh no, it's raining. Can you lend me **an** umbrella?				•	
	(c)	He often gives **her** flowers.		•			
	(d)	Is that **her** house?		•			
	(e)	**Correct**	•	•			
	(f)	A pet is an animal **which** lives in your house.					•
	(g)	**The** River Nile is the longest in the world.				•	
	(h)	**Correct**	•	•			
	(i)	**Correct**				•	
	(j)	He travels all over **the** world.				•	
	(k)	The Prime Minister is the person **who** governs India.					•
	(l)	I'd love to meet **the** President of India.			•		
	(m)	**Correct**	•	•			
	(n)	That's **my** car, over there.			•		
7.	(b)	I like food **which** tastes good.					•
	(c)	A wife is a woman **who** is married.					•
	(d)	That's the man **who** works in my office.					•
	(e)	She's the woman **who** lives next door.					•
	(f)	A tram is a type of bus **which** uses electricity.					•
	(g)	A fountain pen is a pen **which** uses liquid ink.					•
	(h)	**Which** is your favourite book?					•

APPENDIX

Part four: (Units 13–17) Amounts

		Answer	Study/revise Unit 13	14	15	16	17
1.	(a)	Has	•				
	(b)	got	•				
	(c)	much				•	
	(d)	too					•
	(e)	some			•		
	(f)	many				•	
	(g)	have	•				
	(h)	any			•		
	(i)	some			•		
	(j)	much				•	
	(k)	enough					•
	(l)	many				•	
	(m)	got				•	
	(n)	any			•		
	(o)	too					•
	(p)	any			•		
	(q)	some			•		
2.	(a)	are		•		•	
	(b)	are		•			
	(c)	is		•			
	(d)	is		•			
	(e)	are		•			
	(f)	is		•			
	(g)	is		•		•	
	(h)	are		•			
	(i)	is		•			
3.	(a)	too much					•
	(b)	much				•	
	(c)	enough					•
	(d)	too					•
	(e)	much				•	
	(f)	enough					•
	(g)	enough					•
	(h)	many				•	
4.	(a)	has	•				
	(b)	has	•				
	(c)	a lot of				•	
	(d)	hasn't	•				
	(e)	many				•	
	(f)	hasn't	•				
	(g)	any			•		
	(h)	haven't	•				
	(i)	much				•	

Part five: (Units 18–19) Talking about now

		Answer	Study/revise Unit 18	19
1.	(b)	Grandmother's sitting on the sofa.	•	
	(c)	The dog and cat are eating.	•	
	(d)	The baby's crying.	•	
	(e)	Grandfather's lying down.	•	
	(f)	Father's reading a book.	•	
	(g)	The children are playing.	•	
	(h)	Grandfather's sleeping.	•	
	(i)	Mother's writing a letter.		
2.	(b)	Who's reading a book?	•	
	(c)	What's Father reading?	•	
	(d)	Who's sitting on the sofa?	•	
	(e)	Are the children playing?	•	
	(f)	What's Mother writing?	•	
	(g)	Is Father reading a newspaper?	•	
	(h)	Is Grandfather sleeping?	•	
3.	(b)	No, she isn't.	•	
	(c)	Yes, it is.	•	
	(d)	No, they aren't.	•	
	(e)	No, he isn't.	•	
	(f)	Yes, they are.	•	
4.	(b)	What are the children doing?	•	
	(c)	What does Raj do?	•	
	(d)	How many CDs do you have?	•	
	(e)	What are you drinking?	•	
	(f)	What time do you usually get up?		
	(g)	What are you listening to?		

		Study/revise Unit 18	19
5. (b)	'Shyam runs in the park every day.'		•
(c)	'I can't answer the door, I'm talking on the phone?'		•
(d)	'Sshh! Quiet! The baby is sleeping.'		•
(e)	'Where are you going this afternoon?' 'Shopping. Do you want anything?'		•
(f)	'Where's Grandmother?' 'She is sitting on the sofa.'		•
(g)	'What are you eating?' 'Pizza. Do you want some?'		•
(h)	'What does Ratan do?' 'He's a teacher.'		•

		Study/revise Unit 18	19
6. (b)	lying	•	
(c)	Correct	•	
(d)	swimming	•	
(e)	shining	•	
(f)	Correct	•	
(g)	telephoning	•	

APPENDIX

Part six: (Units 20–22) Prepositions

		Study/revise Unit 20	21	22
1. (b)	True	•		
(c)	False - the cup is **near** the oranges	•		
(d)	True			
(e)	False - the bus is in **front of** the car	•		
(f)	True			
(g)	False - the clock is **next to** the picture			
(h)	False - the dog is **behind** the chair	•		
(i)	True	•		
2. (b)	through			•
(c)	past			•
(d)	over			•
(e)	into			•
(f)	along			•
(g)	down			•
(h)	under			•
(i)	up			•
(j)	round			•
(k)	into			•
3. (b)	to			•
(c)	along			•
(d)	round			•
(e)	under			•
(f)	past			•
(g)	on			•
(h)	off			•

		Study/revise Unit 20	21	22
4. (b)	at		•	
(c)	nothing		•	
(d)	in		•	
(e)	nothing		•	
(f)	at		•	
(g)	on		•	
(h)	in		•	
5. (b)	I usually get home from work **at** 6.00.		•	
(c)	Correct		•	
(d)	Sue's going to visit her grandmother **at** the weekend.		•	
(e)	Rina is coming to England **next month**.		•	
(f)	Correct		•	
(g)	It's very cold **at** night now.		•	
(h)	**In** the past not many people had telephones.		•	
6. (b)	**On NewYear's Day**, Sheila got four cards!		•	
(c)	**At midnight** it started raining.		•	
(d)	I'm studying English at **the** moment.		•	
(e)	**On Saturdays** I stay in bed late.		•	

APPENDIX

Part seven: (Units 23–25) Talking about the past I

		Study/revise Unit 23	24	25
1. (b)	I rang Justin and Sue but they **were** away on holiday.	•		
(c)	The bank **was** in the main square.	•		
(d)	**Were** you at home last night?	•		
(e)	No, **I was** out.	•		
(f)	We **were** really excited about going on holiday.	•		
2. (b)	There **weren't** any cars when Grandfather **was** a child.	•		
(c)	Alexander Bell **invented** the telephone.		•	
(d)	Sumitra **went** to Spain last year.		•	
(e)	She **swam** across the English Channel!		•	
(f)	The English **didn't win** the Battle of Hastings in 1066.			•
(g)	Queen Victoria **had** nine children.		•	
(h)	'I **thought** the film was great.' 'Really? I **didn't like** it much.'		•	•
(i)	I **lost** my wallet yesterday.		•	
(j)	Sophie **didn't go** to the party because she **was** ill.	•		
(k)	They **sang** the National Anthem when the President **arrived**.		•	
3. (b)	Ian didn't pass all his exams.			•
(c)	Indian Railways didn't win the football match.			•
(d)	I didn't know her address.			•
(e)	The train didn't stop in Jaipur.			•
(f)	Cars weren't expensive in the 1960s.	•		
(g)	After school, Lila didn't go to University.	•		
(h)	He didn't bring her flowers.			•
(i)	She wasn't very friendly.	•		
(j)	We didn't speak Greek all evening.			•
(k)	I didn't give up smoking.			•
4. (b)	Where did Priya and Jeet go on holiday?			•
(c)	What nationality were Chopin and Marie Curie?	•		
(d)	Who did Prince Charles marry in 1981?			•
(e)	Why did he buy the car?			•
(f)	When was Rio de Janeiro the capital of Brazil?	•		
(g)	When did Alexander Kwasniewski become the president of Poland?			•
(h)	When did Queen Victoria die?			•
(i)	When was he in Cairo?	•		
5. (b)	When **did** King Henry VIII **die?**			•
(c)	Correct	•		
(d)	Did you **go** to the party last night?			•
(e)	'Did you enjoy the film?' 'Yes, it **was** great.'	•		
(f)	Correct		•	
(g)	Last year on holiday the weather **wasn't** good.	•		
(h)	I didn't **give** her a present for her birthday.			•
(i)	**Did** you **eat** toast for breakfast?			•
6. (b)	I **paid** a lot of money for that!		•	
(c)	Correct		•	
(d)	Correct		•	
(e)	We **travelled** all over Europe.		•	
(f)	Correct		•	
(g)	Samir and Hari **played** football yesterday.		•	

Part eight: (Units 26–31) Adding meaning

		Study/revise Unit 26	27	28	29	30	31
1. (b)	Can/Could/May		•				
(c)	should					•	
(d)	Would	•					
(e)	have to				•		
(f)	can/could/may		•				
(g)	Can/Could		•				
(h)	Would	•					
(i)	should					•	
(j)	would	•					
(k)	Can/Could/May		•				
(l)	should					•	
(m)	have to				•		

		Study/revise Unit 26	27	28	29	30	31
2 (b)	Can			•			
(c)	might						•
(d)	have to				•		
(e)	could			•			
(f)	Can/May		•				
(g)	can			•			
(h)	have to				•		
(i)	Would	•					
(j)	Can/Could		•				
(k)	might						•
(l)	Could			•			
(m)	have to				•		
(n)	can			•			
(o)	can't			•			
(p)	Can		•				
(q)	would	•					

		Study/revise Unit 26	27	28	29	30	31
3. (b)	might						•
(c)	might						•
(d)	should					•	
(e)	might						•
(f)	should					•	
(g)	might						•
(h)	might						•
(i)	should					•	
(j)	might						•
(k)	should					•	
4. (b)	can			•			
(c)	Would	•					
(d)	might						•
(e)	has to				•		
(f)	Can		•				
(g)	should					•	
(h)	would	•					
(i)	have to				•		
(j)	should					•	
5. (b)	**Can** you swim?			•			
(c)	He **has** to work very late				•		
(d)	Correct					•	
(e)	It might **rain** tomorrow.						•
(f)	May I **go** out tonight?		•				
(g)	English is very difficult. I have **to** work so hard!			•			
(h)	What **would** he like?	•					

APPENDIX

Part nine: (Units 32–33) Talking about the past II

		Study/revise Unit 32	33
1. (b)	Nidhi and Rekha **were walking** in the park.		•
(c)	**Was** he **visiting** his parents?		•
(d)	You **were eating** breakfast.		•
(e)	Ramesh **wasn't** swimming.		•
(f)	**Were** they **listening** to the radio?		•
(g)	Kavita **wasn't watching** the television.		•
(h)	We **were making** dinner.		•
(i)	The sun **wasn't shining.**		•
(j)	**Was** it **raining**?		•
(k)	Saurav **was driving** to town.		•

		Study/revise Unit 32	33
2. (b)	It **was raining** when Anjan **arrived**.		•
(c)	**I drove away** when the police **arrived.**		•
(d)	Sita **was visiting** her uncle when the lights **went out.**		•
(e)	They **were driving** home when they **saw** Jane.		•
(f)	I **cooked** dinner when John **got** home.		•
(g)	Suresh **was running** in the park when he **fell** in the lake.		•
(h)	**I was writing** a letter when somebody **knocked** on the door.		•
(i)	Hira **drove** to her mother's house when she **heard** the news.		•
(j)	Shanti **was sleeping when Rima** woke her up.		•

		Study/revise Unit 32	33
3.	(b) As they were dancing, a strange man **came** to talk to them.		•
	(c) Ravi **was sleeping** when the storm started.		•
	(d) Sarah was reading when the doorbell **rang.**		•
	(e) Alison and Mina **were walking** along the street when they saw an accident.		•
	(f) I **bought** a hamburger while the children were swimming.		•
	(g) Surya **fell asleep** during the film but he woke up at the end.		•
	(h) The sun **was shining** when the plane landed.		•
	(i) Ria **was waiting** for a train when the rain started.		•

Part ten: (Units 34–37) Describing

		Study/revise Unit 34	35	36	37
1.	(b) smaller		•		
	(c) more exciting		•		
	(d) richer		•		
	(e) fatter		•		
	(f) shyer		•		
	(g) more intelligent		•		
	(h) redder		•		
	(i) better		•		
2	(b) the furthest			•	
	(c) the poorest			•	
	(d) the earliest			•	
	(e) the hottest			•	
	(f) the laziest			•	
	(g) the hungriest			•	
	(h) the tallest			•	
	(i) the best			•	
3.	(b) The Nile is **longer** than the Thames.		•		
	(c) Paris is **more expensive** than Warsaw.		•		
	(d) Mandarin Chinese is **more difficult** than Hindi.		•		
	(e) Tokyo is **bigger** than London.		•		
	(f) A car is **faster** than a bicycle.		•		
	(g) A trumpet is **noisier** than a flute.		•		
	(h) An armchair is **more comfortable** than a stool.		•		

		Study/revise Unit 32	33
4.	(b) That football team is the **worst** in the world.	•	
	(c) It's one of the **smallest** cities in South America.	•	
	(d) He's the most **boring/ uninteresting** man I've ever met.	•	
	(e) Who is the **youngest**?	•	
	(f) She must be the **most beautiful** woman in the world.	•	
	(g) Which is the **noisiest** room?	•	
	(h) I bought the **most expensive** ticket.	•	
5.	(b) **slow**/slowly	•	
	(c) bad/**badly**		•
	(d) tidy/**tidily**		•
	(e) **noisy**/noisily	•	
	(f) happy/**happily**		•
	(g) **clever**/cleverly	•	
	(h) **quick**/quickly	•	
	(i) angry/**angrily**		•
6.	(b) You cook really **well**.	•	•
	(c) He's a **terrible** teacher!	•	•
	(d) The sea was very **deep**.	•	•
	(e) Did you have a **great** holiday?	•	•
	(f) This exercise is quite **easy**.	•	•
	(g) He drank the water **thirstily**.	•	•
	(h) I feel awful – I slept really **badly**.	•	•
	(i) He's a very **naughty** child.	•	•
	(j) I looked for it very **carefully**.	•	•

Part eleven: (Units 38–40) Talking about the future

		Answer	Study/revise Unit 38	39	40
1.	(b)	Next summer **I'm going to** visit my relatives in America. It's all arranged.		•	
	(c)	'Oh no! Those cars **are going to** crash!' 'Bang!!!'			•
	(d)	A: 'What do you want to do tonight?' B: 'I don't know. **I'll** ring you later, OK?'		•	
	(e)	A: 'My plane gets in at 2.30 am.' B: '**I'll** meet you at the airport.' A: 'Are you sure?'		•	
	(f)	I'm so happy – **I'm going to** have a baby!			•
	(g)	You're quite good at maths. I expect you**'ll** pass the exam.			•
	(h)	I couldn't answer any of the exam questions! **I'm going to** fail!			•
	(i)	The neighbours **are going to** have a party tonight. Shall we go?		•	
	(j)	She looks very upset and sad. I think she's **going to** cry.			•
	(k)	The weather next week **will continue** to be sunny.			•
	(l)	When I grow up **I'm going to be** a marine biologist.		•	
2.	(b)	Correct		•	
	(c)	You'll put on weight.			•
	(d)	I'm going to buy a car.		•	
	(e)	Correct			•
	(f)	I'll pick you up.		•	
	(g)	I'm going to marry Julian.		•	
3.	(b)	**I'm seeing** the doctor tomorrow morning.	•		
	(c)	What time **does** the play **end**?	•		
	(d)	The conference **starts** on May 22nd.	•		
	(e)	He **is meeting** Jake later tonight.	•		
	(f)	What **are** you **doing** tomorrow?	•		
	(g)	I need to go home now because John **is ringing** me at 8.00.	•		
	(h)	Suraj and Arjun **are coming** for dinner tomorrow night	•		
	(i)	The plane **leaves** at 9.00 so we need to be at the airport by 7.00.	•		
	(j)	Can I borrow your new jacket? **I'm going** for a job interview tomorrow.	•		

Part twelve: (Units 41–44) Connecting the past and the present

		Answer	Study/revise Unit 41	42	43	44
1.	(b)	drunk	•		•	•
	(c)	seen	•			•
	(d)	worn	•			
	(e)	written	•	•		
	(f)	known	•			
	(g)	eaten	•		•	•
	(h)	gone/been	•			•
	(i)	broken	•		•	
	(j)	had	•	•		•
	(k)	got	•			
	(l)	cut			•	
2.	(b)	I broke	•			
	(c)	have you lived		•		
	(d)	have you paid				•
	(e)	Have you been			•	
	(f)	Have you ever eaten	•			
	(g)	We've been married		•		
	(h)	I've already read				•
	(i)	did you eat	•			
	(j)	Have you had		•		
	(k)	Have you written				•
	(l)	Have you dyed			•	
	(m)	has stolen			•	
3.	(b)	I've already done it				•
	(c)	have you been		•		
	(d)	I lived		•		
	(e)	I've never been	•			
	(f)	What have you done			•	
	(g)	haven't bought				•
	(h)	I went	•			
	(i)	I have cleaned			•	
	(j)	I've already posted it				•
4.	(a)	haven't seen	•			
	(b)	Have you been			•	
	(c)	went			•	
	(d)	Have you ever been	•			
	(e)	I haven't been				•
	(f)	Have you booked a hotel				•
	(g)	We've already arranged everything				•
	(h)	have never seen	•			
	(i)	I saw	•			
	(j)	haven't tied			•	
	(k)	have forgotten			•	
	(l)	have been married		•		
	(m)	Have you ever argued	•			
	(n)	have had		•		

APPENDIX

Appendix 5: Key to Further Practice Exercise

Part one: (Units 1-4): Talking about people, places and objects

(Units 1 & 2)

1. (a) I am an engineer.
   (b) My brother is called Raja.
   (c) Is she Chinese?
   (d) Are we in France?
   (e) They are both very intelligent.
   (f) It is a lovely day.

2. (a) Are you a student?
   (b) Is your teacher English?
   (c) Is English easy?
   (d) Is the Eiffel Tower in France?
   (e) Where is your friend?
   (f) What's your name?

(Unit 3)

3. This is my dog. That dog is dangerous.

   Those shoes are too high. These are more comfortable.

   What is this called? It's a rose.

   What is that?

   This is my son.

   John! Those flowers are dead!

   Who are those girls?

   These are my babies.

(Unit 4)

4. (a) This person is English.
   (b) The factory is very noisy.
   (c) The bus is always late!.
   (d) My key is on the table.
   (e) This is my child.
   (f) Where is the man?

5. (a) holidays
   (b) cats
   (c) babies
   (d) daughters
   (e) churches
   (f) women
   (g) classes
   (h) girls
   (i) houses

Part two: (Units 5-7): Talking about routines and habits

(Unit 5)

1. Sheila is a dentist. She likes her work but she lives a long way from her surgery so she usually gets up quite early. She has three children so she helps them get dressed and makes them breakfast. They walk to school, it isn't far. Then she leaves the house at about 7.30. She goes to work by train and then catches a bus. She usually arrives at about 8.30, has a cup of coffee and sees her first patient at 9.00.

2. Manu works in a cinema. She starts work at 3.00 in the afternoon, when the first film is on, and finishes about 11.00 at night. She loves her job because she watches all the new films free! But she goes to bed very late. So, in the morning, she stays in bed until 10.00 or 11.00.

(Unit 6)

3. (a) What does Alfredo do? He's a disc-jockey.
   (b) Does he work in Rome? No, he doesn't.
   (c) What time does he start work? 7.00.
   (d) Does he go to bed late? No, he doesn't.
   (e) Does he think his job is interesting? Yes, he does.
   (f) Does he like getting up early? No, he doesn't.
   (g) When do his friends see Alfredo? At the weekends.
   (h) Do his friends listen to him on the radio? Yes, they do.

4. (a) No, he doesn't work in Madrid.
   (b) No, he doesn't start work at 9.00.
   (c) No, he doesn't go to bed late.
   (d) No, he doesn't hate his job.
   (e) No, he doesn't like getting up early.
   (f) No, his friends don't see Alfredo every day.

APPENDIX

(Unit 7)

5. (a) Alfredo always gets up early.
   (b) Alfredo never sees his friends during the week.
   (c) Sheila is rarely late for work.
   (d) Manu usually enjoys her job.
   (e) Sheila always has a cup of coffee in the morning.
   (f) Sheila's children are often naughty.
   (g) Alfredo is usually tired.
   (h) Manu never gets up early.
   (i) Alfredo's friends often listen to him on the radio.
   (j) Manu always watches new films first.

Part three: (Units 8-12): Referring to people, places and objects

(Units 8-10)

1. Many people know Shakespeare's play *Romeo and Juliet*, but this film "William Shakespeare's Romeo and Juliet" is something new. The Director sets the story in modern day America. Romeo meets Juliet at a party and (a) he falls in love with (b) her immediately. (c) She also loves (d) him. But there's a problem. (e) His family hate (f) hers and (g) her family hate his. Unfortunately (h) their love affair cannot work. Everybody is against (i) them...

2. Hi! How are (a) you? (b) I am very busy at the moment. (c) We are moving house next week and there is a lot to do. Now we have two children, (d) our old house is very small and (e) we need more space. The new house has four bedrooms and (f) it's much nicer. The children are very excited because (g) they will have (h) their own bedrooms. (i) I hope (j) their bedrooms will be tidier now since (k) they have more space.

(Unit 11)

3. (a) A policeman is walking past (b) a house when he hears a shout. 'Rajesh! Don't kill me!' (c) The policeman rushes into (d) the house and he sees (e) a dead body on the floor. There are three people standing near (f) the body—(g) a doctor, (h) a lawyer and (i) an engineer. (j) The policeman arrests (k) the engineer. How does he know who (l) the murderer is? (answer: the doctor and lawyer are *women*)

(Unit 12)

4. (a) Feijoada is something which/that people eat in Brazil.
   (b) A baker is someone who makes bread and cakes.
   (c) A watch is something which/that tells the time.
   (d) A fork is something which/that people use to eat with.
   (e) An air steward is someone who works on an aeroplane.
   (f) A playwright is someone who writes plays.
   (g) Chapati is something which/that people eat in some parts of northern India for dinner.

Part four: (Units 13-17): Amounts

(Unit 13)

1. Estate Agent: 'I've got the perfect house for you, sir!'
   Customer: 'Has it got three bedrooms?'
   Estate Agent: 'Well, in fact, it's got four.'
   Customer: 'Is it expensive? I haven't got much money.'
   Estate Agent: 'No, it's very reasonable. Only Rs. 53,000.'
   Customer: 'Have you got the keys? Can I go and see it?'
   Estate Agent: 'Certainly. I think I've got some free time this afternoon, if you like.'

(Unit 14)

2. (a) some milk
   (b) some paper
   (c) a newspaper
   (d) some rain
   (e) some mushrooms
   (f) some yoghurt
   (g) a tomato
   (h) some bread
   (i) some money
   (j) some toast
   (k) some soap
   (l) a cup of tea
   (m) some coffee
   (n) some cheese
   (o) some chocolate

(Unit 15)

3. (a) Have you got **any** orange juice?
   (b) There aren't **any** potatoes.
   (c) I haven't got **any** money.
   (d) There are **some** eggs in the fridge.
   (e) I'd like to listen to **some** music.
   (f) He usually meets **some** friends at the weekend.
   (g) Why doesn't he have **any** friends?
   (h) Sorry, we don't have **any** milk today.

(Unit 16)

4. (a) How **much** does it cost?
   (b) How **many** times a week do you go swimming?
   (c) How **many** bedrooms has your house got?
   (d) How **much** chocolate do you eat in a week?
   (e) How **much** cake would you like?
   (f) How **many** hours do you work?
   (g) How **many** people do you know?
   (h) How **much** water is there?
   (i) How **many** sandwiches are there?
   (j) How **much** bread is there?

(Unit 17)

5. The weather is **too** hot.
   My flat isn't warm **enough**.
   The hours are **too** long.
   There's **too much** noise!
   I've eaten **too much** chocolate.
   It's **too** wet.
   There **aren't enough** people.
   I haven't eaten **enough**.

Part five: (Units 18-19): Talking about now

(Unit 18)

1. (a) It's raining.
   (b) The children are leaving school.
   (c) They are wearing raincoats.
   (d) They are playing in the rain.
   (e) The sun is shining.
   (f) Two children are carrying bags.

(Unit 19)

2. Yousuf **is** a doctor.
   He **works** in a hospital.
   He **is playing** football.
   He **is wearing** shorts.
   At work he **wears** a white coat.

   Kumar and Sunita **are** teachers.
   They **teach** English.
   They **are having** dinner.
   They often **eat** in restaurants.
   They **like** good food!

   Jagan **is** 26.
   He **is driving** his new car.
   He **is listening** to music.
   He **likes** rock music.
   He **cleans** his car every Saturday.

   Jose **is** Spanish.
   She **lives** in Barcelona.
   She **likes** Barcelona because the sun always **shines**.
   Unfortunately, today it **is raining**.

Part six: (Units 20-22): Prepositions

(Unit 20)

1. (a) It's under the newspaper.
   (b) It's behind the plant.
   (c) It's next to the flowers.
   (d) It's in front of the radio.
   (e) They're on the chair.
   (f) It's in the sink.
   (g) They're near the bread.
   (h) It's opposite the cat.
   (i) It's under the table.
   (j) They're near the table.
   (k) They're in the fridge.
   (l) It's next to the clock.

2. (a) The toy car is on the music system.
   (b) The radio is behind the telephone.
   (c) True
   (d) The bananas are in the saucepan.
   (e) True
   (f) The plant is in front of the book.
   (g) True
   (h) The bread is near the keys.

APPENDIX

(Unit 21)

3. (a) **On** Monday morning **at** 9.00 Louise has got a meeting.
   (b) She's got another meeting **at** 3.00 **on** Tuesday.
   (c) John's birthday is **on** Wednesday and they're having dinner **in** the evening.
   (d) **At** noon **on** 13th April, she's having lunch with the Directors.
   (e) **In** the morning **on** Saturday she's playing tennis.
   (f) **On** Easter Sunday **in** the afternoon she's visiting her grandmother.
   (g) **Next week** is her parents' wedding anniversary.
   (h) She isn't working **at** the weekend.
   (i) On Friday she finishes her job. **In** the future she won't work so hard!

(Unit 22)

4. A: 'Excuse me, how do I get **to** the post office **from** this hotel?'
   B: 'Well, go **out** of the hotel, **across** the road, **over** the bridge, **up** the hill, **through** the park, **down** the hill, **past** the supermarket, **along** the road, **round** the roundabout, **under** the railway bridge and **into** the shopping centre. The post office is on the left'.
   A: 'That sounds complicated. Is there a bus'?
   B: 'Yes, get **on** a number 29 and get **off** next to the swimming pool'.

Part seven:(Units 23-25): Talking about the past I

(Unit 23)

1. (a) Where **was** the hotel? In the Old Town.
   (b) **Was** it nice? Yes, lovely.
   (c) **Was** the weather good? Not bad. It rained a bit.
   (d) **Were** the museums good? Yes, very interesting.
   (e) What **was** the food like? Delicious. I ate so much!
   (f) **Were** you on your own? No, I went with David.

2. (a) The weather **wasn't** very good.
   (b) The Old Town **wasn't** very crowded.
   (c) The museums **weren't** expensive.
   (d) I **wasn't** very tired at the end of the day.
   (e) Vinay **wasn't** very interested in the museums.
   (f) We **weren't** in Prague for very long—just a week.
   (g) The other guests in the hotel **weren't** very friendly.

(Unit 24)

3. (a) Seema **made** her own wedding dress.
   (b) I **flew** to Paris because it's quicker than the train.
   (c) She **sang** really well
   (d) Raja **threw** a stone and **broke** the window!
   (e) I **wrote** to her about a week ago.
   (f) Last night I **went** to a party and **lost** my umbrella. I think someone **stole** it.
   (g) He **drank** six cups of coffee and didn't sleep all night!
   (h) I **built** this house myself. It **took** me six years.
   (i) She **paid** the bill and **left**.

4. (a) I really **enjoyed** the film.
   (b) He **carried** the heaviest bag.
   (c) The car **stopped** at the traffic lights.
   (d) He **studied** really hard to pass his exam.
   (e) I **tried** to walk but it was too far.
   (f) They **planned** to go to Buenos Aires but in the end they couldn't.

(Unit 25)

5. (a) **Why did you go there?**
   (b) **Where did you teach?**
   (c) **Did you teach children?**
   (d) **Did you enjoy it there?**
   (e) **Did you learn Czech?**
   (f) **Did you make Czech friends?**
   (g) **What did you do in your spare time?**

6. (a) **Yes, he did.**
   (b) **No, he didn't.**
   (c) **Yes, he did.**
   (d) **No, he didn't.**
   (e) **Yes, he did.**
   (f) **No, he didn't.**
   (g) **Yes, he did.**

APPENDIX

Part eight: (Units 26-31): Adding meaning

(Unit 26)

1. (a) Would you like some coffee? No, thanks.
   (b) Would you like to sit down?
   (c) I think I'd like a cup of tea—I'm thirsty.
   (d) He likes listening to very loud music. I hate it!
   (e) It's raining. Would you like to borrow my umbrella?
   (f) I don't like swimming much. It's usually too cold in England.
   (g) My parents would like to meet you. Shall I introduce you?

2. (a) A: 'Would you like to go (go) to the cinema next week? There's a new thriller on.'
   B: 'Well, I like going to the cinema but I hate thrillers! I like seeing comedies better.'
   (b) A: 'Do you like eating out in restaurants?'
   B: 'Yes, I love it! I really like eating Indian food.'
   A: 'Would you like to go out for an Indian meal tonight?'
   B: 'Yes, please!'
   (c) A: 'I'd like you to meet my friends. Why don't we all go out for dinner next week?'
   B: 'Oh, I'm really shy. I don't like meeting new people.'

(Unit 27)

3. (a) Can I borrow some gloves please?
   (b) Can/May I borrow a pen?
   (c) Could/Can you close the door?
   (d) Can I pay by cheque?
   (e) Could/Can you lend me Re 1?
   (f) Can/May I turn on the television?
   (g) Can/Could you telephone me later?

4. (a) A: 'May/Can I use the phone?'
   (b) B: 'Well, could/can you give me a lift?'
   (c) B: 'Wait...could/can you lend me a pen?'
   (d) A: 'Can/May I read that magazine when you've finished with it?'
   (e) A: 'Can/Could you tell me the time please?'
   (f) A: 'Can/May we sit here?'

(Unit 28)

5. (a) She can play the guitar.
   (b) She can drive.
   (c) She can play chess.
   (d) She can use a computer.
   (e) She can swim.
   (f) She can speak French.

6. (a) She could play the guitar.
   (b) She couldn't drive.
   (c) She could/couldn't play chess. (What do *you* think?)
   (d) She could/couldn't use a computer. (What do *you* think?)
   (e) She could/couldn't swim. (What do *you* think?)
   (f) She could/couldn't speak French. (What do *you* think?)

(Unit 29)

7. (a) In a cinema you have to buy a ticket.
   (b) In a library you have to be quiet.
   (c) At the traffic lights you have to wait until the light turns green.
   (d) In an expensive restaurant you have to wear a tie. (if you're a man!)
   (e) In many swimming pools you have to wear a hat.
   (f) In the bank you often have to wait in a queue.

8. When Suresh was at school
   (a) He had to do homework. (+)
   (c) He didn't have to get up very early. (-)
   (e) He didn't have to work on Saturdays. (-)
   (g) He had to study French. (+)
   (i) He had to wear a uniform. (+)

   Now he's working in a supermarket
   (b) He doesn't have to do homework. (-)
   (d) He has to get up at 6.00. (+)
   (f) He has to work on Saturday mornings. (+)
   (h) He doesn't have to study French. (-)
   (j) He *still* has to wear a uniform! (+)

(Unit 30)

9. (a) You should take out insurance.
   (b) You should write your address on your luggage.
   (c) You shouldn't take very heavy luggage.
   (d) You should buy a guidebook.
   (e) You shouldn't carry too much cash.
   (f) You should learn to speak a little of the language.

APPENDIX

10. You (a) **shouldn't listen** to your 'friends'. They are being very cruel. But you (b) **should try** to take more exercise. You (c) **should walk** to school rather than take the bus and you (d) **should eat** more fruit and less chocolate.

I think you (e) **should tell** your friend that she (f) **should stop** smoking. Obviously it is making her ill. Tell her that if she wants to be healthy and able to run fast she (g) **shouldn't smoke** at all.

Your parents (h) **shouldn't make** you eat meat it you want to be vegetarian but you (i) **shouldn't expect** them to cook two meals every night. You (j) **should cook** your own dinner.

(Unit 31)

11. (a) **She might/may be on holiday.**
(b) **He mightn't/may not like me.**
(c) **He might/may pass the exam.**
(d) **They might/may live in Sri Lanka.**
(e) **I might/may go out tonight.**
(f) **I might/may stay at home.**
(g) **He might be a doctor.**
(h) **They might/may speak Bengali.**
(i) **She mightn't/may not speak English.**
(j) **They mightn't/may not live here.**
(k) **We might/may be lost.**

Part nine: (Units 32-33): Talking about the past II

(Unit 32)

1. **At 9am Elaine was having breakfast and John was driving to work.**
At 10am Elaine was visiting an exhibition and John was writing letters.
At 12.30pm Elaine was having lunch and John was having a meeting with a Director.
At 3pm Elaine was meeting clients and John was doing the accounts.
At 6pm Elaine was having dinner with the Director of the Dublin office and John was driving home.

(Unit 33)

2. (a) **It was raining when she left the hotel.**
(b) **She was driving to the airport when the taxi broke down.**
(c) **She was standing in the check-in queue when someone stole her handbag.**
(d) **She was talking to the police when the plane left without her.**
(e) **She was sitting on the plane when she spilt her drink.**
(f) **She was waiting for her luggage when someone told her it was lost.**
(g) **She was really feeling tired and annoyed when she got home.**

3. 'The journey home was terrible. First it (rain) **was raining** when I left the hotel, so I got wet. Then the taxi **broke down** on the way to the airport. Then, while I was waiting in the check-in queue someone **stole** my handbag so I had to go to the police. And then I **missed** my plane because I was talking to the police for so long! I was really angry. Then, I finally got on another plane. I **was beginning** to relax a bit when I spilt my orange juice everywhere! We got to London at last and I **was waiting** for my luggage when a man came and told me it was lost! 'It might be in Rome.' he said. So you can understand why I **was feeling** unhappy and tired when I got home!'

Part ten:(Units 34-37): Describing

(Units 35 and 36)

1. (a) **The Amazon is longer than the Thames.**
The Nile is the longest.
(b) **A motorbike is faster than a bicycle.**
A car is the fastest.
(c) **Gold is more precious than silver.**
Platinum is the most precious.
(d) **An orange is bigger than a grape.**
A grapefruit is the biggest.
(e) **England is hotter than Norway.**
Thailand is the hottest.
(f) **Fruit-juice is healthier than coca-cola.**
Water is the healthiest.
(g) **A magazine is more expensive than a newspaper.**
A book is the most expensive.

APPENDIX

2. (a) What are **the newest** states in India? **Jharkhand, Uttaranchal, Chhattisgarh (4)**
   (b) Which is **the** second **biggest** city in Inida? **New Delhi (3)**
   (c) Which restaurant in London is owned by three of **the most famous** American film stars? **Planet Hollywood (5)**
   (d) What is **the youngest** age you can marry in India? **18 for girls and 21 for boys (6)**
   (e) What is India's **most popular** tourist attraction? **Taj Mahal (2)**
   (f) What is India's **largest** Residence? **Rashtrapati Bhavan (1)**
   (g) Which is India's **highest** dam? **Bhakhra Dam (7)**

(Units 34 and 37)

3. large **adjective**, poor **adjective**, patiently **adverb**, magic **adjective**, immediately **adverb**, new **adjective**, slowly **adverb**, angry **adjective**, comfortable **adjective**, angrily **adverb**

4. Once upon a time there was a very **poor** fisherman and his wife. One day the fisherman caught a fish which spoke to him. 'Let me go, fisherman.' it said. 'I am a **magic** fish.' So the fisherman let him go. He returned home to his wife but when he told her the story she was very **angry**. 'Why didn't you ask him to give us a **large** house instead of this small hut we live in?' she asked, 'Go back and ask him for a house.' So the fisherman went back to the lake, called the fish and told him what his wife had said. 'Go home' said the fish, 'she has it already'. When the fisherman got home his wife was in a lovely **new** house.

But two weeks later his wife said, 'This house is very small and not very **comfortable.** Go and ask the fish for a castle.' The fisherman didn't want to but he went back to the fish and asked him for a castle. 'Go home,' said the fish, **patiently** 'she has it already.'

When the fisherman got home his wife was very happy with her new castle but the next day she said, 'Now I live in a castle I want to be Queen. Go and ask the fish.' The fisherman went to ask the fish. 'Go home', said the fish, 'she is Queen already.'

But when the fisherman got home his wife was watching the sun **slowly** going down. 'Why can't I do that?' she asked. 'Go back to the fish **immediately** and tell him I want to be Master of the Universe!' The fisherman went back to the fish and asked him but the fish said **angrily**, 'Go home. Your wife is back in her small hut.'

Part eleven: (Units 38-40): Talking about the future

(Unit 38)

1. A: 'When (meet) **are** you **meeting** Mr Joshi?'
   B: 'At lunchtime. We **are having** lunch in Quaglino's'
   A: 'Lucky you! **Are** you **meeting** him at the restaurant?'
   B: 'No, he'**s coming** here. He **is giving** me a lift.'
   C: 'What time **does** the train **leave**?'
   D: 'Twelve o'clock. So hurry up!'
   C: 'Where **are** we **meeting** the others?'
   D : 'On the platform.'
   E: 'When **are** you **going** back to University?
   F: 'Well, term **starts** on October 3rd but I'**m going** back a few days early.'
   E: 'Why?'
   F: '**I'm moving** in to my new flat on September 30th.'

(Unit 39)

2. (a) **She's going to type some letters.**
   (b) **She's going to pay the teachers.**
   (c) **She's going to telephone the Director.**
   (d) **She's going to check the registers.**
   (e) **She's going to check how many students there are in each class.**

3. Teacher 1: 'Ola? **Are** we **going to** get paid today?'
   Ola: 'Yes, I'**m going to** pay you all this afternoon, don't worry.'

   Teacher 2: 'Ola? How many students are there in class B501?'
   Ola: 'Can I tell you later? I'**m going to** check how many students there are this afternoon. OK'?

   Teacher 3: 'Ola? Those plants look almost dead!'
   Ola: 'Oh! OK. I'**ll** give them some water.'

   Teacher 4: 'Ola? Is the Director coming here today?'
   Ola: 'No, but I'**m going to** ring him later. Do you want me to pass on a message?'

   Teacher 5: 'Ola! The phone's ringing. Shall I answer it?'
   Ola: 'No, it's OK. I'**ll** answer it.'

   Ola: 'Have you completed your registers properly?'
   Teacher 6: 'Er...'
   Ola: 'Well, I'**m going to** check them this afternoon.'

(Unit 40)

4. (a) They're going to dance.
   (b) They're going to rob a bank.
   (c) She's going to answer the phone.
   (d) It's going to rain.
   (e) He's going to fall in.
   (f) She's going to miss the bus.

5. Gypsy: 'You (have) **will have** a long and happy life.'
   Client: 'When **will** I **get married**?'
   Gypsy: 'Oh, you **won't marry** early. You **will meet** your husband when you are about thirty.'
   Client: 'What **will** his job **be**?'
   Gypsy: 'He **will be** a businessman.'
   Client: '**Will** we **have** any children?'
   Gypsy: 'Yes, you **will have** six children.'
   Client: 'Six?!'

APPENDIX

Part twelve: (Units 41-44): Connecting the past and the present

(Unit 41)

1. (a) Shankar has climbed Mount Everest.
   (b) Sushma has never been on television.
   (c) Jaya and Ravi have never climbed Mount Everest.
   (d) Shankar has never written a book.
   (e) Sushma has met the British Queen.
   (f) Jaya and Ravi have been on television.
   (g) Shankar has had an accident.
   (h) Sushma has written a book.
   (i) Jaya and Ravi have never met the British Queen.

2. (a) Has Shankar ever met the British Queen? No, he hasn't.
   (b) Has Sushma ever been on television? No, she hasn't.
   (c) Have Jaya and Ravi ever written a book? No, they haven't.
   (d) Has Sushma ever had an accident? No, she hasn't.
   (e) Has Shankar ever been on television? Yes, he has.
   (f) Have Jaya and Ravi ever had an accident? Yes, they have.

(Unit 42)

3. (a) He's been married for ten years.
   He's been married since 1987.
   (b) He's lived in Ecuador for twelve years.
   He's lived in Ecuador since 1985.
   (c) They've been teachers since 1989.
   They've been teachers for eight years.
   (d) I've had a computer for a year.
   I've had a computer since 1996.
   (e) She has played the piano for eleven years.
   She has played the piano since she was six.
   (f) I've spoken Japanese for three years.
   I've spoken Japanese since 1994.
   (g) It has been sunny for a week.
   It has been sunny since last week.
   (h) The shop has been open for two years.
   The shop has been open since 1995.
   (i) We have been at University for three years.
   We have been at University since 1994.

4. (a) How long has he been married?
   (b) How long has he lived in Ecuador?
   (c) How long have they been teachers?
   (d) How long have I/you had a computer?
   (e) How long has she played the piano?
   (f) How long have you spoken Japanese?
   (g) How long has it been sunny?
   (h) How long has the shop been open?
   (i) How long have we/they been at University?

(Unit 43)

5. (a) He's shaved his beard.
   (b) He's grown his hair.
   (c) He's put on weight.
   (d) He's got older.
   (e) He's started wearing a tie.
   (f) He's bought some new clothes.
   (g) He's stopped wearing an earring.
   (h) He's got married.
   (i) He's become smarter.

6. (a) Has he cut his hair? — No, he hasn't.
   (b) Has he grown a moustache? — No, he hasn't.
   (c) Has he put on weight? — Yes, he has.
   (d) Has he started wearing a tie? — Yes, he has.
   (e) Has he lost weight? — No, he hasn't.
   (f) Has he got married? — Yes, he has.
   (g) Has he shaved his beard? — Yes, he has.

(Unit 44)

7. (a) He's already posted the letters.
   (b) He's already paid in the cheque.
   (c) He's already taken out some cash.
   (d) He's already bought some bread and milk.
   (e) He hasn't got any petrol for the car yet.
   (f) He hasn't taken the dog to the vet yet.
   (g) He hasn't paid the electricity bill yet.
   (h) He hasn't bought any aspirin yet.

8. (a) Has Raj posted the letters yet? — Yes, he has.
   (b) Has Raj paid in the cheque yet? — Yes, he has.
   (c) Has Raj taken out some cash yet? — Yes, he has.
   (d) Has Raj bought some bread and milk yet? — Yes, he has.
   (e) Has Raj got some petrol for the car yet? — No, he hasn't.
   (f) Has Raj taken the dog to the vet yet? — No, he hasn't.
   (g) Has Raj paid the electricity bill yet? — No, he hasn't.
   (h) Has Raj bought some aspirin yet? — No, he hasn't.

Index